IMAGES
of America

WEATHERFORD
THE EARLY YEARS

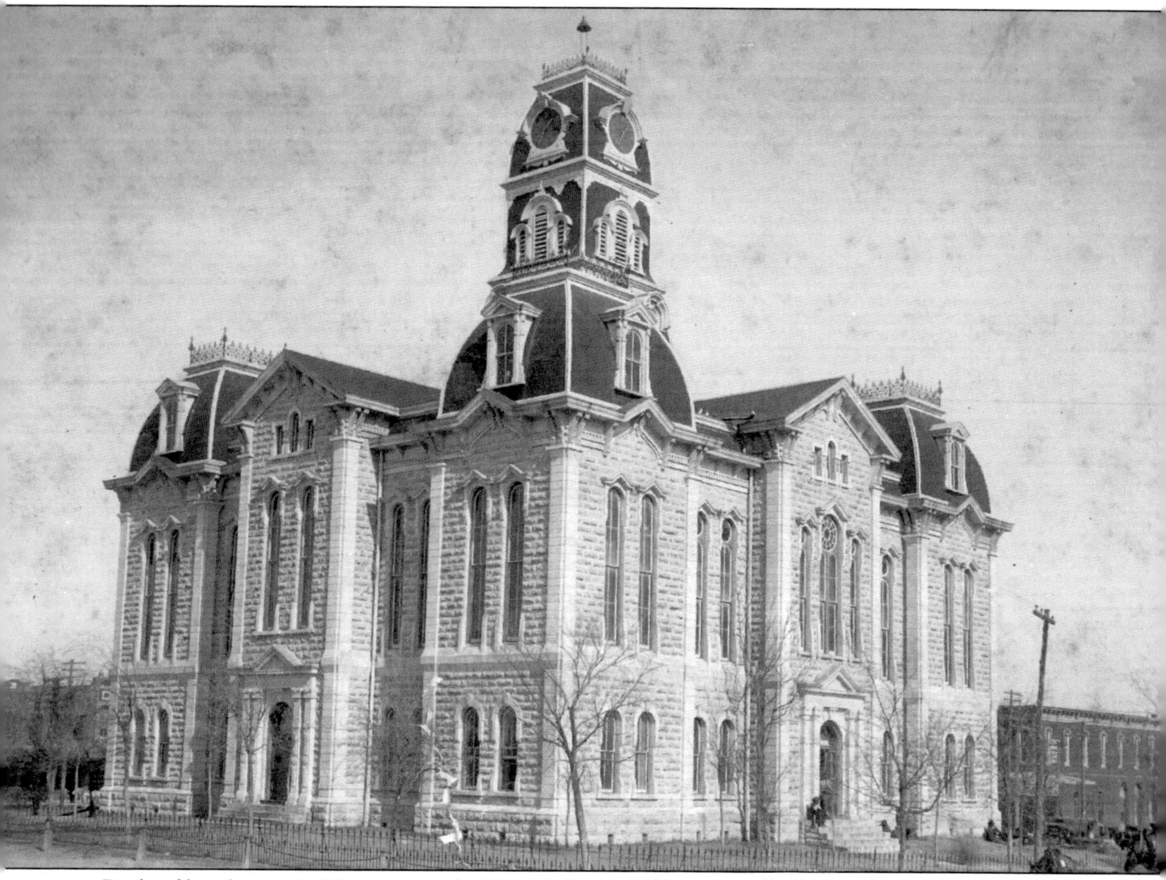

Built of local quarried limestone, the French Second Empire–style Parker County Courthouse is the focal point of the downtown square. Designed by the Waco architectural firm Dodson and Dudley, the courthouse was completed in 1886 at a cost of $55,555.55. It is shown here after the installation of the Seth Thomas clockworks in 1897. An extensive restoration project completed in 2004 returned the second floor courtroom to its original size—one of the largest in Texas. The Parker County Courthouse is not just the seat of county governance; it is the heart of Weatherford. (BSM.)

ON THE COVER: Parker County watermelons garnered national acclaim after winning first prize at the 1904 St. Louis World's Fair. The second-annual Tom Watson Watermelon Slicing was held on August 1, 1921, to celebrate Parker County's growing watermelon produce industry. The crowd gathered on the grounds of Weatherford High School, across Palo Pinto Street from the newly opened Hotel Parker, and consumed over 600 of the famous long Tom Watson–variety melons. (UTA, Texas Photograph Collection.)

IMAGES
of America

WEATHERFORD
THE EARLY YEARS

Jonelle Ryan Bartoli and
Brenda S. McClurkin

ARCADIA
PUBLISHING

Copyright © 2012 by Jonelle Ryan Bartoli and Brenda S. McClurkin
ISBN 978-0-7385-8549-9

Published by Arcadia Publishing
Charleston, South Carolina

Printed in the United States of America

Library of Congress Control Number: 2012934222

For all general information, please contact Arcadia Publishing:
Telephone 843-853-2070
Fax 843-853-0044
E-mail sales@arcadiapublishing.com
For customer service and orders:
Toll-Free 1-888-313-2665

Visit us on the Internet at www.arcadiapublishing.com

We dedicate this book to the guardians of Weatherford and Parker County history—past, present, and future.

Contents

Acknowledgments

The writing of *Weatherford: The Early Years* was a journey not undertaken alone. We gratefully acknowledge the following individuals for their invaluable assistance and support along the way: John Anderson, Mary Ellen Duke Astudillo, Evelyn Barker, Lin Bearden, Jean Bennett, Paula Bonner, Tara Carlisle, Margaret Daniel, Bill Fant, Dale Fleeger, Tammy Gazzola, Aryn Glazier, Ann Halligan, Cindy Harriman, Ann Hodges, Barney B. Holland Jr., Peggy Hutton, Tom Kellam, Louise Klasing, Vicki Knuth, Sue Lay, Martha Lott, Tom Madden, Evon Markum, Anne Peterson, Kathleen Poznick, Zan Prince, Ruth Resurrección, Calvin Scott, Delissa Slimp, Cathy Spitzenberger, Warren Stricker, Martha Tandy, Donna Thurston, Jerre Tracy, Jon Vandagriff, Tom Wancho, Bill Warren, Lisa Watson, John Westhoff, Lea Worcester, Mark Worthington, and Marian Wyler.

Images incorporated into this book have been provided courtesy of Mary Ellen Duke Astudillo (MEDA); Texas Collection, Baylor University, Waco, Texas (BU); Borden and Westhoff, LLP (BW); Christopher Cornwall (CC); Couts-Moseley family collection (CMFC); Doss Heritage and Culture Center, Weatherford, Texas (DHCC); Bill Fant (BF); First National Bank, Weatherford, Texas (FNB); Kathy Fowler (KF); Historic Fort Worth, Inc. (HFW); Library of Congress (LC); Brenda S. McClurkin (BSM); Jim Mullin (JM); family of D.O. Norton (DON); Panhandle Plains Historical Museum, Canyon, Texas (PPHM); Texas Pythian Home, Weatherford, Texas (TPH); Special Collections, University of Texas at Arlington Library, Arlington, Texas (UTA); Dolph Briscoe Center for American History, University of Texas at Austin (UT); Vandagriff Collection (VC); Weatherford College, Weatherford, Texas (WC); Weatherford Public Library, Weatherford, Texas (WPL); Mark Worthington family (MW); and Beinecke Rare Books and Manuscripts Library, Yale University (YU).

Due to the book's chronological format, time frames were assigned to undated photographs based on clothing, hairstyles, automobiles, buildings, or other content. Preference was given to previously unpublished or rarely published images that would provide fresh insight into Weatherford's past. Although limited space required many subjects to be set aside, their importance to the story of Weatherford is by no means discounted.

Special thanks goes to Winnie Rodgers, Simone Williams, and Stacia Bannerman, acquisitions editors at Arcadia Publishing, for their continued guidance and encouragement. We are also most indebted to our husbands, Larry Bartoli and Howard McClurkin, for their unconditional support, understanding, and compassion.

Introduction

From humble frontier beginnings, Weatherford has matured into a modern city with a hometown feel and strong identity with its historical roots. The story of Weatherford is a story of its people, a cast of characters from all walks of life who continually strive to make Weatherford an extraordinary place to live.

In 1854, pioneers began to immigrate to the area between the Brazos and Trinity Rivers, seeking lush prairie grasses, rich soil, abundant timber, and building stone. Parker County was created in December 1855, and the following April, voters selected the current site of Weatherford as the county seat. The town was laid out, reserving 500 square feet for the courthouse. The first courthouse, constructed of rough-hewn lumber on the north side of the square, was ready for the November 1856 district court session. It was replaced in 1858 with a two-story brick structure built on the current courthouse site.

The country was unsettled, and the times were uncertain. The withdrawal of federal troops from frontier posts during the Civil War coupled with the enlistment of an estimated 800 Parker County men for Confederate service left the area vulnerable to Indian raids. Situated on the edge of the frontier, Weatherford was well positioned to be a point of supply for those venturing farther west. It was also a place of refuge from marauding Indians.

By 1874, the Indian threat had subsided. Three years later, Gov. Richard Hubbard declared that Parker County was no longer a frontier area. Weatherford continued to grow and thrive. Fire destroyed the second courthouse in May 1874, but by 1878, construction of the third courthouse, a two-story stone edifice, was underway. Agents for the Texas & Pacific Railway visited Weatherford in 1876 and selected a site for their depot. Although the first passenger train did not arrive until 1880, it was the harbinger of change that would transform the frontier town to a commercial center.

Two additional railroads soon followed: the Gulf, Colorado & Santa Fe in 1887 and the Weatherford, Mineral Wells & Northwestern in 1889. Rail transportation was an economic boon to Weatherford. Not only were distant markets opened to Parker County agricultural products and livestock, travel times were shortened and a wider range of goods became available, including building materials that would transform the look and feel of the growing town. By the end of the decade, three national banks had been chartered in Weatherford: Citizens National Bank, First National Bank, and Merchants & Farmers National Bank, all of which provided needed capital for growth. The third county courthouse succumbed to fire in 1884. From its rubble arose the French Second Empire courthouse, which has observed all of the goings-on around the public square since 1886. City services were augmented with the construction of the Water, Light, and Ice Plant and the formation of Volunteer Fire Company A. The public Central High School was completed on Palo Pinto Street in 1885. In 1889, David Switzer arrived from Granbury to become the president of the newly formed Weatherford College.

Citizens had great expectations as they entered the last decade of the 19th century. Spires of the Methodist Episcopal Church and First Presbyterian Church rose on South Main Street. Switzer added "Old Main" to the front of the Masonic Institute building in 1894. Cisterns and hydrants were built to help douse fires. Telephone service previously only available in the central business district was extended to residential neighborhoods. Entertainment continued at the Haynes Opera House on the square, and free mail service began in 1899.

As the new century dawned, Weatherford received state and national honors. Local congressman S.W.T. Lanham was elected Texas governor in 1902 and served two consecutive terms. He was the last Confederate soldier to be governor of Texas. Twelve watermelons weighing up to 106 pounds each won first prize at the St. Louis World's Fair in 1904. In 1905, Weatherford bested eight other locales to become the site of the Knights of Pythias Widows and Orphans Home. With the construction of more new places of worship—Grace Presbyterian, First Baptist, and St. Stephen's Catholic churches—Weatherford became known as the "City of Churches." Real estate developers called the city the "Athens of Texas." The appearance of automobiles necessitated street improvements, so bridges were widened on North Main, Bridge, and Elm Streets, while North and South Main Streets were oiled to settle the dust.

Civic pride made Weatherford citizens feel that their reputation as the "City Beautiful" was well deserved. In 1910, sidewalks 14 feet wide were built approaching all four courthouse doors, and two sanitary drinking fountains replaced the water trough on the courthouse lawn. The new Santa Fe railroad depot was completed on Fort Worth Street, and a new combination city hall and firehouse was underway on Palo Pinto Street. The Georgian Revival federal post office opened in 1914. Of economic impact, the construction of the "Kuteman Cut-off" reduced the drive to Fort Worth by approximately six miles, oil was struck in neighboring Ranger in 1918, and peanut farming became profitable around 1915, the same year the boll weevil wiped out cotton production.

By 1917, war news permeated life in Parker County, which sent its quota of 500 young men into World War I military service. The county also contributed two railcars of peach pits for use in gas mask filters. On November 11, 1918, a large crowd gathered on the courthouse lawn to celebrate Armistice Day, even though the county was in the midst of two influenza epidemics. Approximately 800 influenza cases were reported in December alone. The public observed quarantine restrictions and disinfectant campaigns to combat the spread of the contagion.

As soldiers returned home, a spirit of renewed hope enveloped the community. Thurber bricks were used to pave the Weatherford-to-Mineral Wells portion of a cross-country highway in 1920. By 1921, Weatherford had a new high school. Fort Worth radio station WBAP began broadcasting in February 1923. It was the first station received in Weatherford and often featured the Pythian Home Girl's Mandolin Orchestra. Weatherford theatergoers had a choice of three venues: the Texan on North Main and the Princess and the Palace, which were adjacent to each other on the north side of the square. Weatherford was a destination point for automobile travelers by 1929, the first year the Weatherford Chamber of Commerce stocked road maps.

Depression-era New Deal programs helped Weatherford navigate the 1930s. Farmers removed 5,663 acres from crop production. Civil Works Administration funds paved North and South Main Streets and built a sewage disposal plant. Construction of curbs and gutters and three elementary schools were financed by the Works Progress Administration. Forty women worked in a WPA program that produced 2,000 garments per month. During this decade, a new city hall building was dedicated in 1934, signs proclaiming Weatherford to be the "Texas Fruit and Melon Center" were erected on the courthouse lawn in 1937, and the first Peach Pilgrimage, forerunner of today's Peach Festival, was staged in 1939.

Weatherford continues to maintain a strong sense of community pride in its historical past as it looks forward to the future. Enjoy your journey, decade by decade, through Weatherford's early years.

One

1856–1879
A Frontier Town

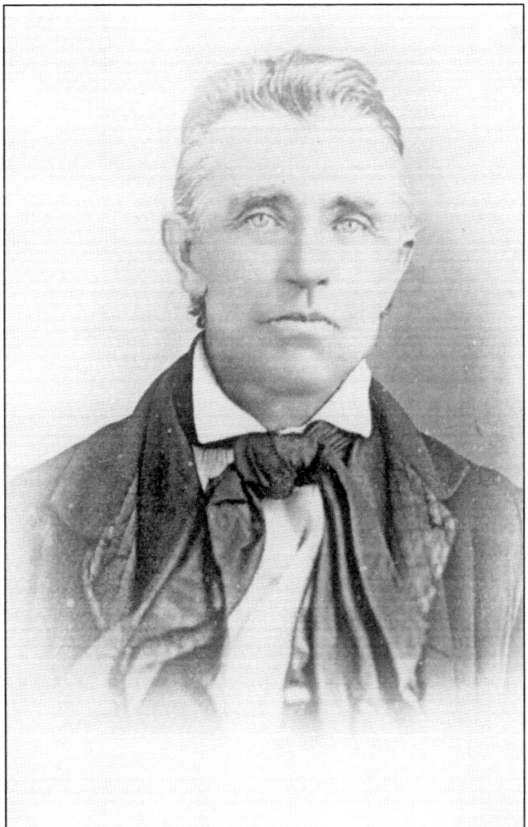

Parker County was created by the Texas Legislature on December 12, 1855. Tarrant County representative Isaac Parker and his counterpart in the senate, Jefferson Weatherford of Dallas, played prominent roles in establishing the jurisdictions bearing their names. Isaac Parker moved his family to a site eight miles east of Weatherford in 1872. There, he lived to 91 years of age, sharing the stories of his eventful life. (DHCC.)

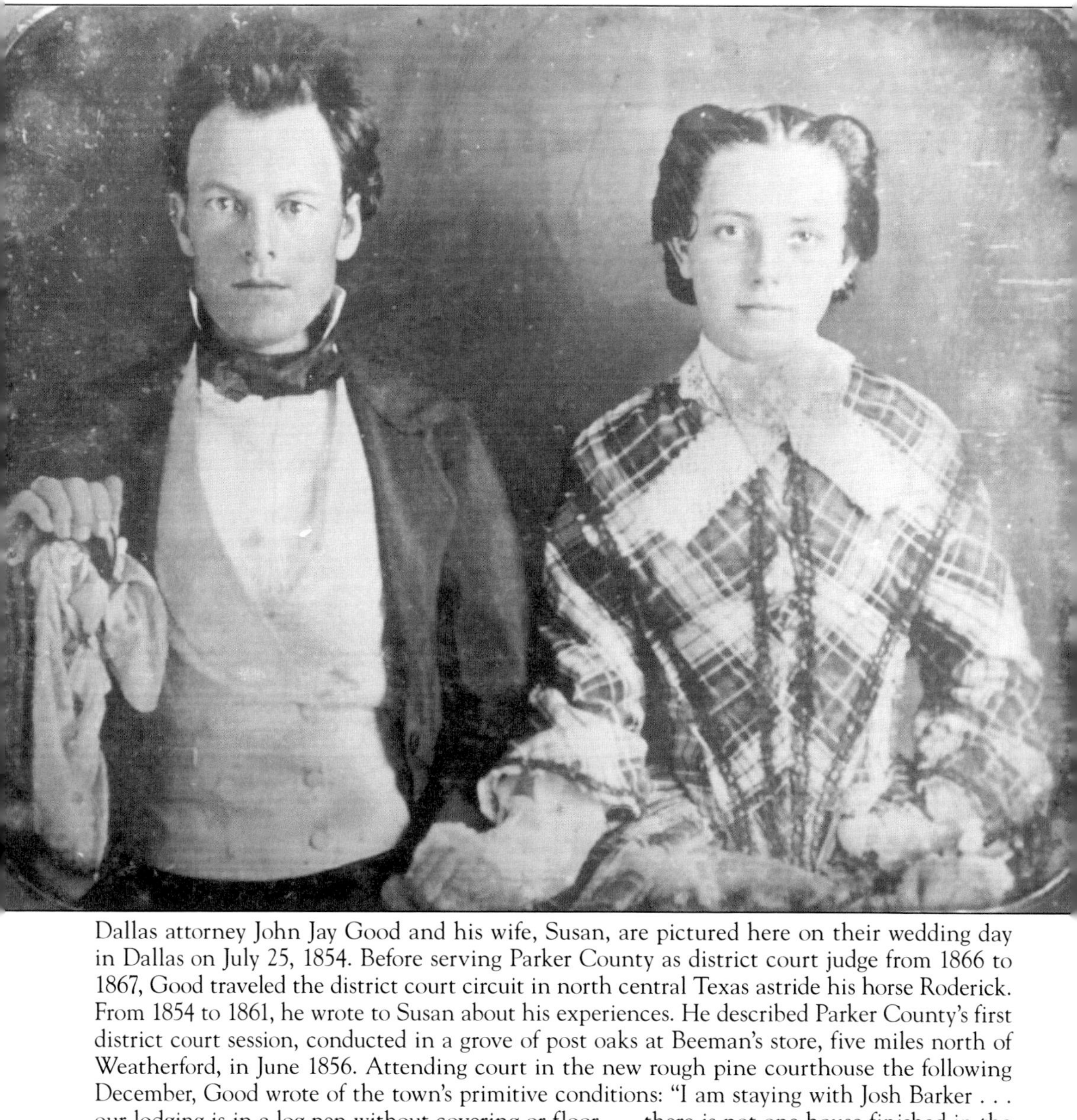

Dallas attorney John Jay Good and his wife, Susan, are pictured here on their wedding day in Dallas on July 25, 1854. Before serving Parker County as district court judge from 1866 to 1867, Good traveled the district court circuit in north central Texas astride his horse Roderick. From 1854 to 1861, he wrote to Susan about his experiences. He described Parker County's first district court session, conducted in a grove of post oaks at Beeman's store, five miles north of Weatherford, in June 1856. Attending court in the new rough pine courthouse the following December, Good wrote of the town's primitive conditions: "I am staying with Josh Barker . . . our lodging is in a log pen without covering or floor . . . there is not one house finished in the place and the accommodations look and feel like one was out of doors . . . we have a large fire out in front of the house around which we all huddle, tell anecdotes, and keep warm . . . I have not seen a handsome woman or baby since leaving home. This county is not famed for either." (UTA, John J. Good Family Papers.)

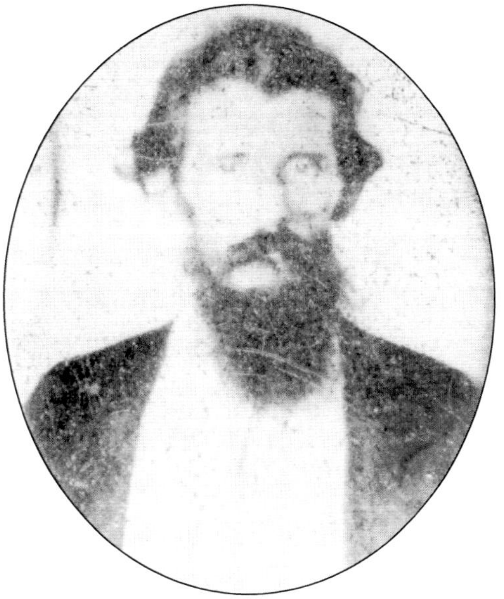

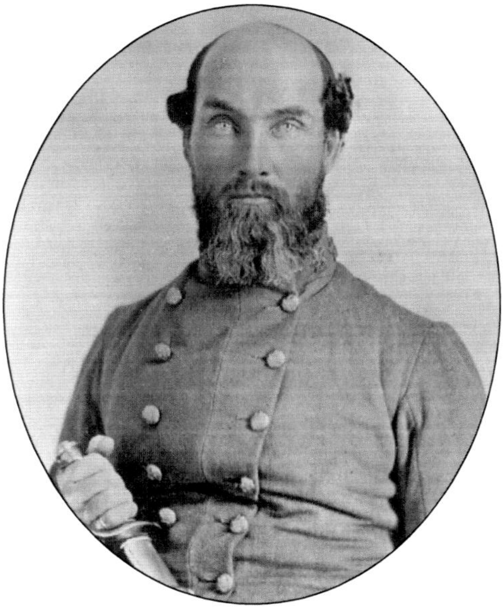

R.A. Vanhorn brought a printing press to Weatherford in early 1858. In conjunction with attorneys David O. Norton (above left) and Charles L. Jordan, he published the first edition of the *Frontier News* (shown in facsimile) on June 26, 1858. The paper continued under varying ownerships until 1862. Norton surveyed and auctioned town lots in 1856, was city alderman in 1858, was elected city recorder in 1863, and succeeded Good as district court judge in 1867. John R. Baylor (above right) and H.A. Hamner started the short-lived *White Man* newspaper in Weatherford in 1860. Hostile to Indians, the *White Man* inspired great excitement in the general public. Baylor, an attorney, Indian fighter, and rancher, was a colonel in the Confederate army and was elected to the Confederate Congress from Parker County in 1863. (Above left, DON; above right, BU; below, UTA.)

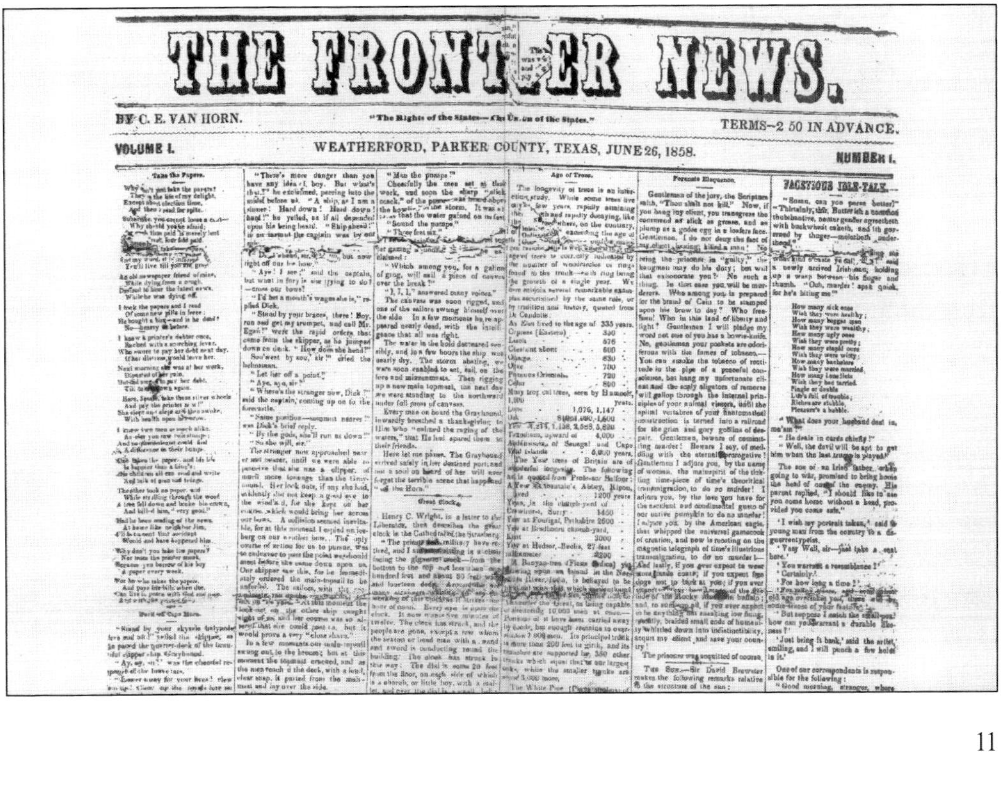
THE FRONTIER NEWS.

BY C. E. VAN HORN. "The Rights of the States—the Union of the States." TERMS—2 50 IN ADVANCE.

VOLUME I. WEATHERFORD, PARKER COUNTY, TEXAS, JUNE 26, 1858. NUMBER 1.

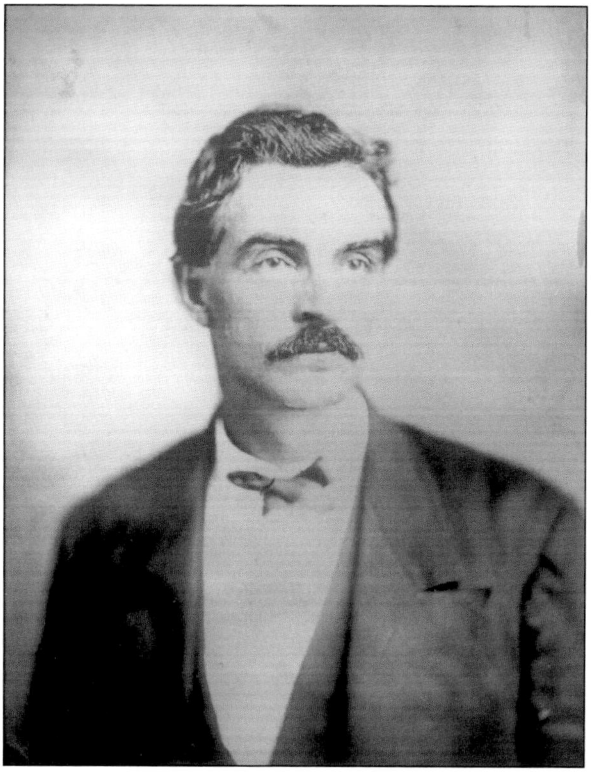

Dr. Stephen Dorris Conger, a physician, was elected mayor of Weatherford on January 20, 1863, filling the unexpired term of F.A. Leach, who resigned the post in 1862 to enter Confederate service. Conger, along with fellow candidates for the other vacant positions of recorder, treasurer, constable, and three aldermen, received the unanimous vote of all 12 electors. (HFW.)

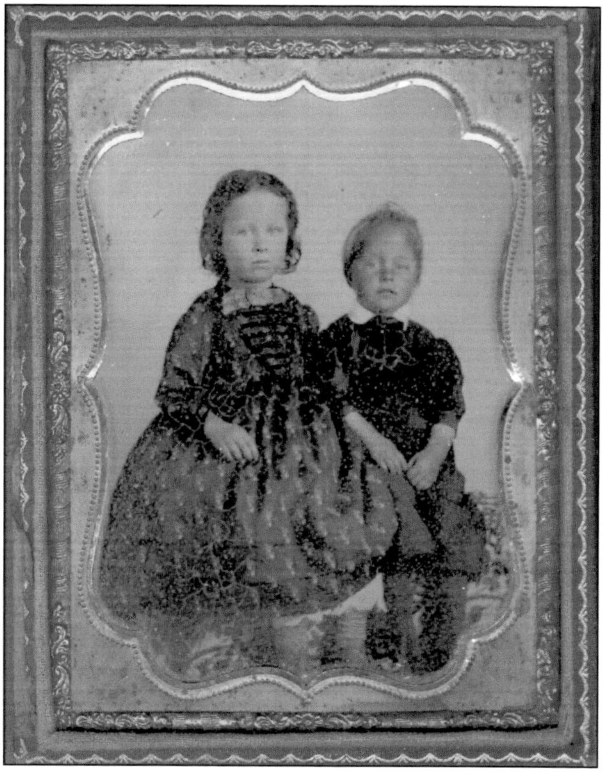

Sarah (left) and Thomas Conger, the eldest children of Dr. Stephen D. and Mary Rhodes Conger, are pictured in this c. 1862 ambrotype around the time their father was elected mayor of Weatherford. Sarah married William H. Eddleman in January 1877, and the couple had one daughter, Carrie. Sarah Conger Eddleman was a Pythian Sister and served as temporary chairman of the Twentieth Century Club during its organization in 1900. (HFW.)

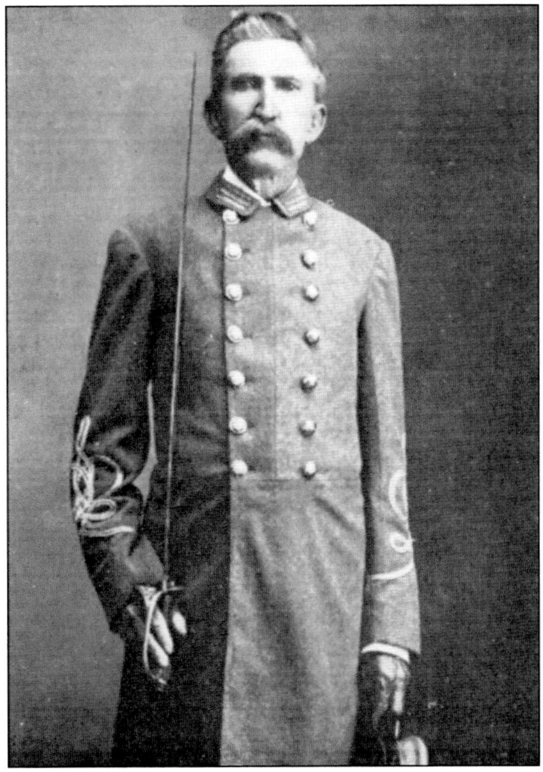

An estimated 800 men from Parker County joined the Confederate army, many in the 19th Texas Cavalry, Parson's Brigade. Robert W. Bonner enlisted in the 12th Texas Cavalry, Parson's Brigade in his native Navarro County and carried this Confederate flag in many battles. Bonner and his family moved to Weatherford in 1882. The following year, Bonner partnered with David C. Haynes in a grocery business on the ground floor of the Haynes Opera House. In 1908, Bonner formed a group of Confederate veterans called the Parker County Grays. He was elected adjutant general of the 4th Brigade, United Confederate Veterans (Texas), a position he held for over 20 years. This battle-scarred flag was displayed at every brigade reunion from 1880 until 1923, when it was presented to Bonner by the United Confederate Veterans. (Both, JRB.)

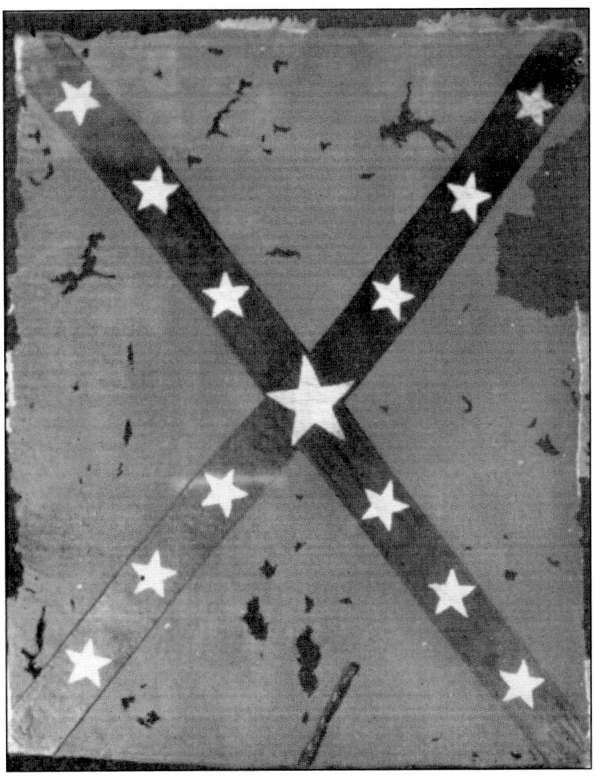

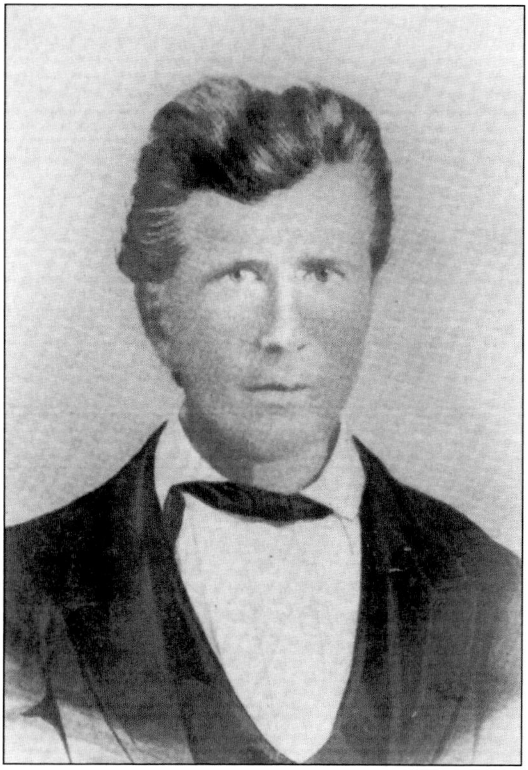

Oliver Loving supported his wife, Susan, and nine children by driving cattle over new and established trails from Texas to Wyoming. "The Dean of Texas Trail Drivers" was wounded by Indians in New Mexico during an 1867 cattle drive. On his deathbed, he asked partner Charles Goodnight to continue their partnership until his debts were paid, spare Susan unnecessary worry, and return his body to Weatherford for burial. (WPL.)

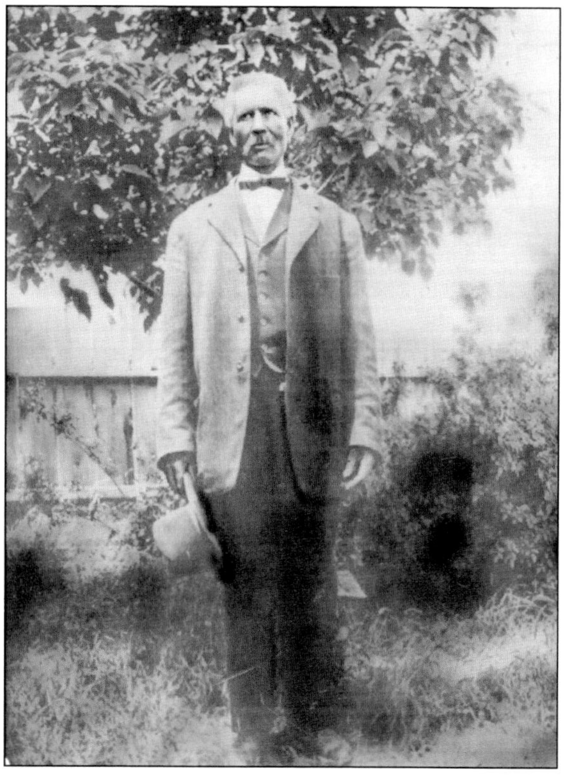

Bose Ikard left the employ of former master Dr. Milton Ikard in 1866 to drive cattle over trails created by Goodnight and Loving across New Mexico, Colorado, and Wyoming. Bose carried gold from the sale of cattle in special pouches concealed under his saddle. Goodnight, Loving, and Ikard inspired characters developed by Larry McMurtry in the *Lonesome Dove* saga. Loving and Ikard are buried in Old City Greenwood Cemetery. (DHCC.)

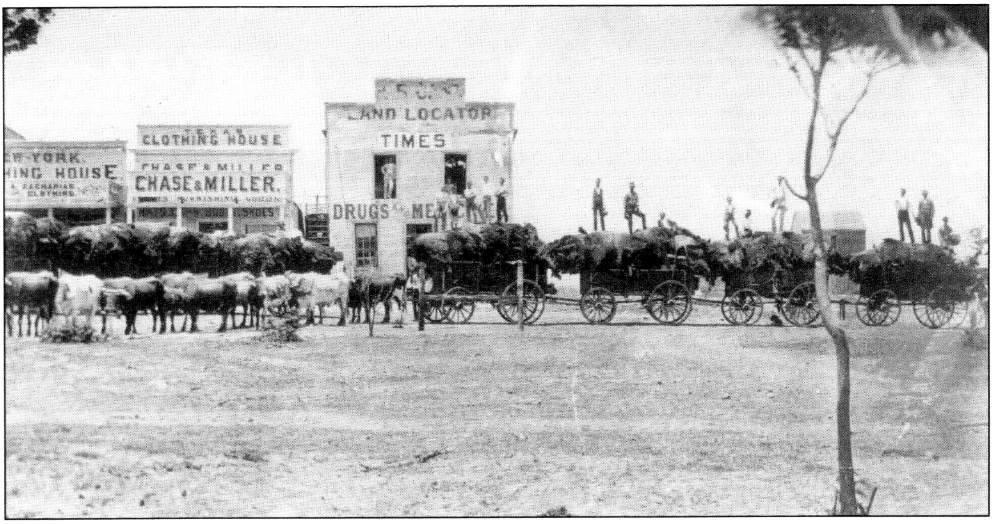

Oxen-drawn wagons laden with buffalo hides are pictured on the west side of the courthouse square in what is said to be the earliest photograph of Weatherford from around 1874. The two-story building behind the wagons housed A.B. Gant, land locator and druggist, and the office of the *Weatherford Times* newspaper. Chase and Miller and the New York Store were clothiers that occupied two smaller buildings to the south. (UTA, Fort Worth *Star-Telegram* Collection.)

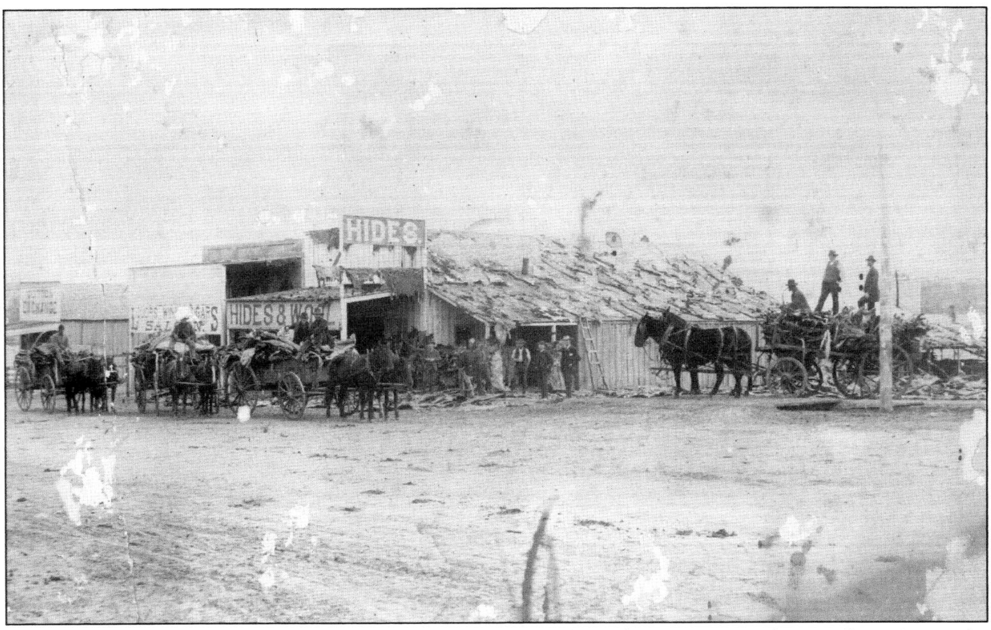

Thousands of buffalo hides came through Weatherford on the way to market in the 1870s. *The History of Parker County* cites a *Galveston News* story reporting that during the height of the season from April to July 1876, 100 wagonloads of hides were driven through Weatherford daily. Buffalo hides can be seen drying on the roof of this undated photograph of the Crowdus Bros. hide company on North Main Street. (UTA, Fort Worth *Star-Telegram* Collection.)

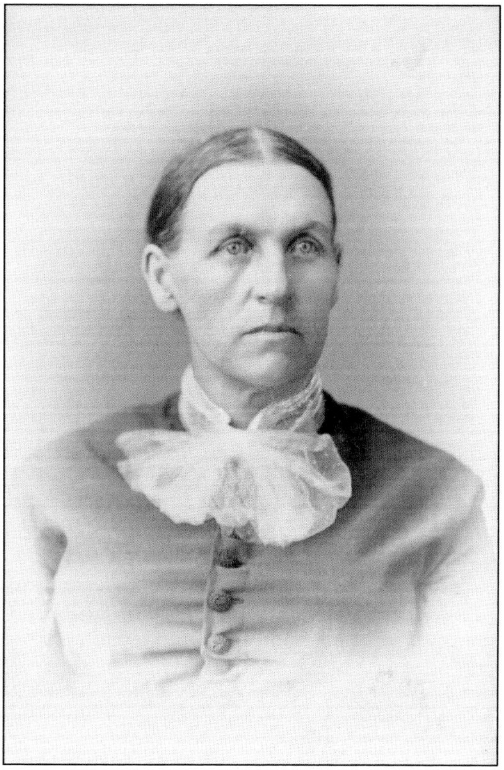

In 1866, Martha Hardin Couts warned her husband that if he attempted to drive cattle across the Colorado mountains to California, his frostbitten ears and feet would fall off. James Robertson Couts returned to Weatherford with ears and feet intact, plus $50,000 in gold, with which he established Couts and Fain Bank, the first bank west of Dallas. Couts Memorial Methodist Church was named in Martha's memory in 1894. (Both, DHCC, Citizens National Bank Records.)

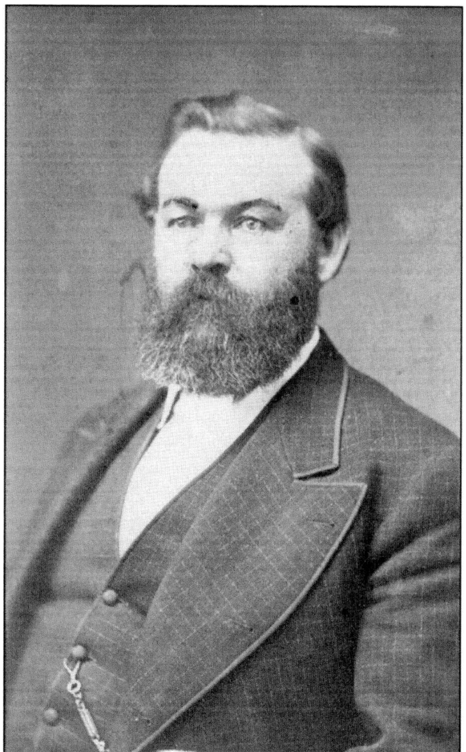

The 1858 courthouse was lost to fire on May 13, 1874. In 1877, plans were briefly made to construct the new courthouse on the northwest corner of the square, dividing the public square into four building lots. The cornerstone of this third Parker County courthouse was laid on June 24, 1878. Built from H.W. Wilson's plans for $21,000, it too was destroyed by fire on March 1, 1884. (UTA, Mary Kemp Collection.)

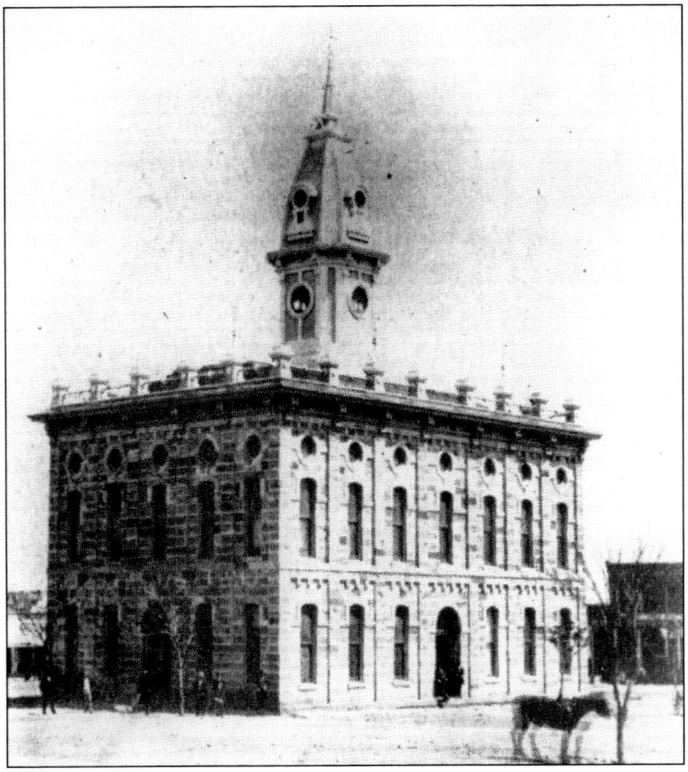

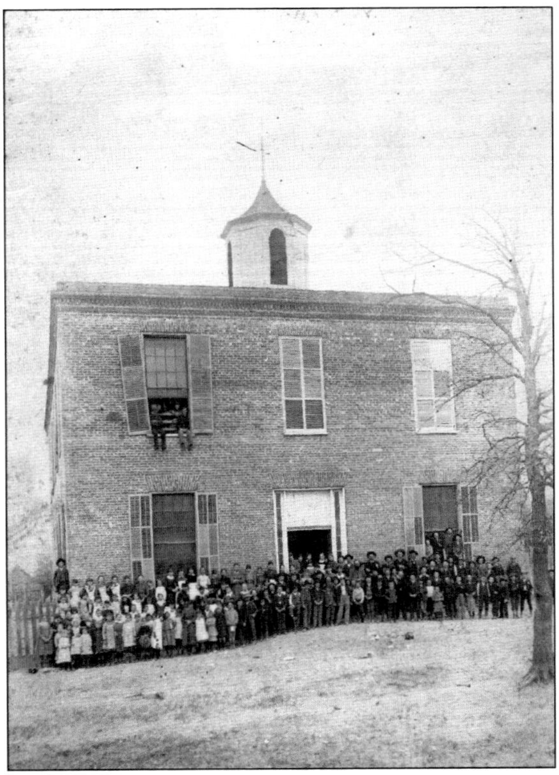

Phoenix Masonic Lodge No. 275 commenced construction of a two-story brick building for school and lodge purposes in 1869. The Weatherford High School Association leased the unfinished edifice in January 1875 and completed its construction. The Masonic Institute was dedicated on October 9, 1875, and is pictured here in 1879. The inaugural class of six high school students graduated on June 15, 1876. The lodge sold the building in 1885 to M.C. Brown, who leased it to Methodist Episcopal Church, South congregation. Trustees expanded the curriculum to include college-level coursework and changed the school's name to Cleveland College in hopes that Pres. Grover Cleveland might offer financial support. When Brown was unable to make his payments, the lodge sold the Masonic Institute to the Weatherford District of the Methodist Episcopal Church, South in June 1889. (WC.)

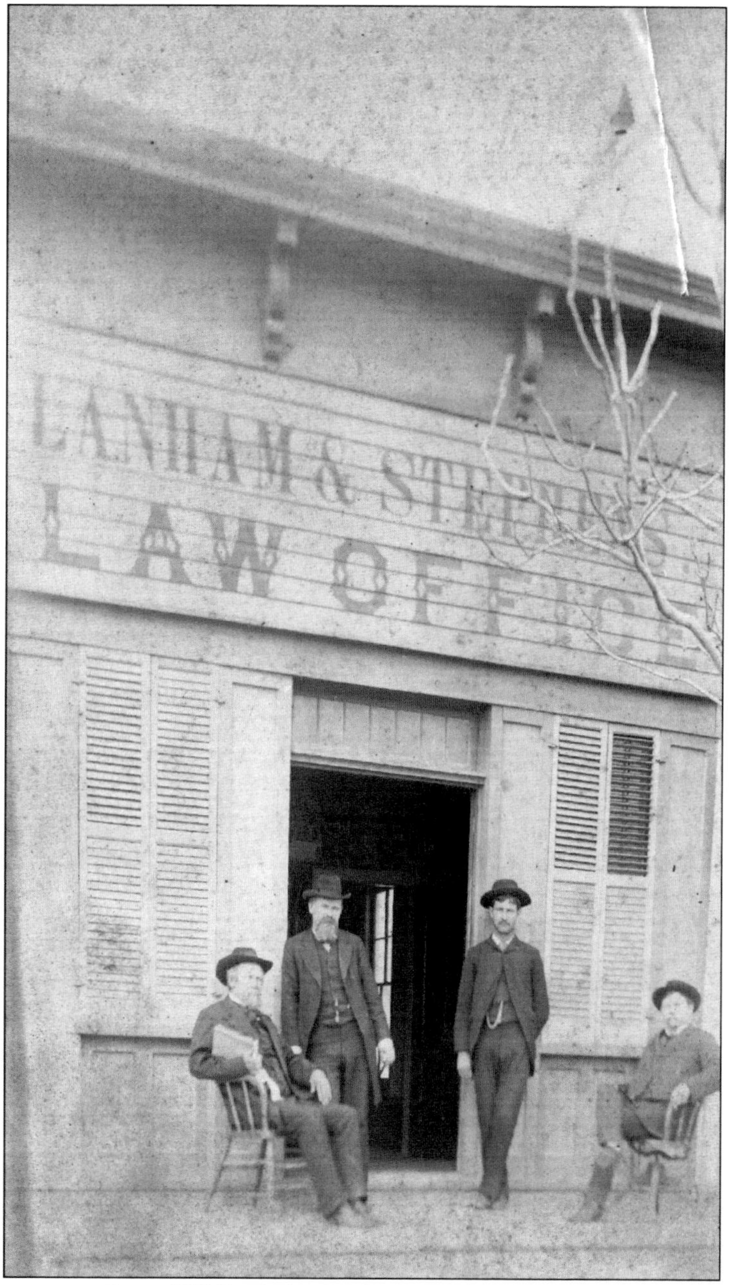

South Carolina native Samuel Willis Tucker Lanham rose from private to second sergeant during his Confederate service in the 3rd South Carolina Regiment. He and his wife, the former Sarah Meng, migrated to Weatherford in 1868, where he taught school with Mollie Dyer, later the wife of Charles Goodnight. Admitted to the bar in 1869, Lanham was elected county district attorney in 1870. His most noted prosecution was the 1871 conviction of Kiowa Indian chiefs Satanta and Big Tree for murdering seven teamsters under the employ of Henry Warren. Lanham and I.W. Stephens acquired property on the southwest corner of the square in 1877. This frame building is thought to be the predecessor to the two-story brick structure at 118 Houston Avenue. Lanham is standing in the doorway, second from the left. (UT, S.W.T. Lanham Papers.)

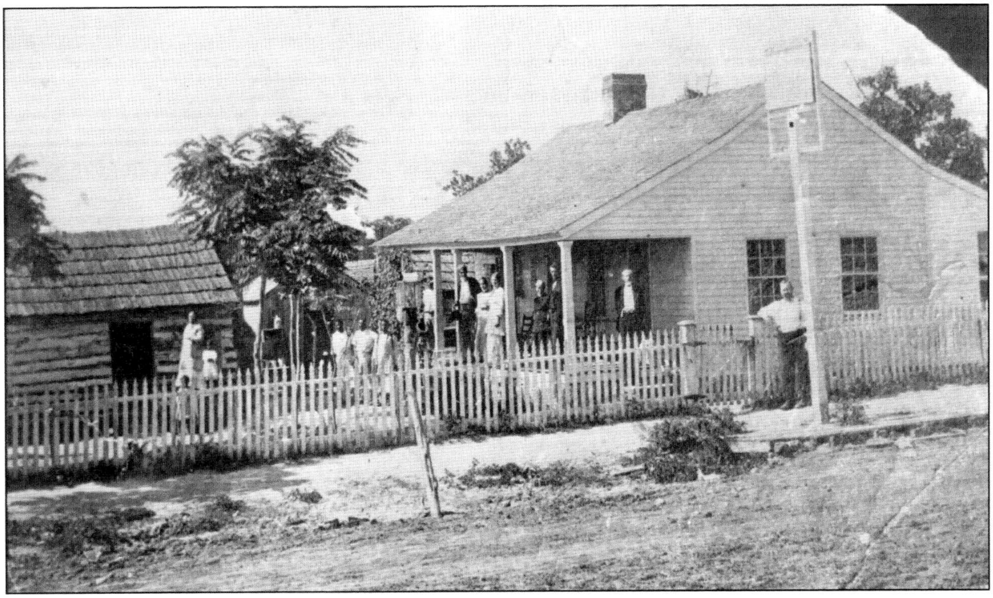

Frontier travelers depended upon the hospitality provided at the Sikes House. Traveling drummers praised the abundant tables laid by Mammy Sikes at mealtimes. Thespians engaged at the Haynes Opera House enjoyed the old-fashioned plantation dances held in the broom-swept yard. Sikes was an intelligent, single-minded woman who milked her own cows and proudly drew the purest water from her well. The inn later became the Montfort Hotel. (UTA, Fort Worth *Star-Telegram* Collection.)

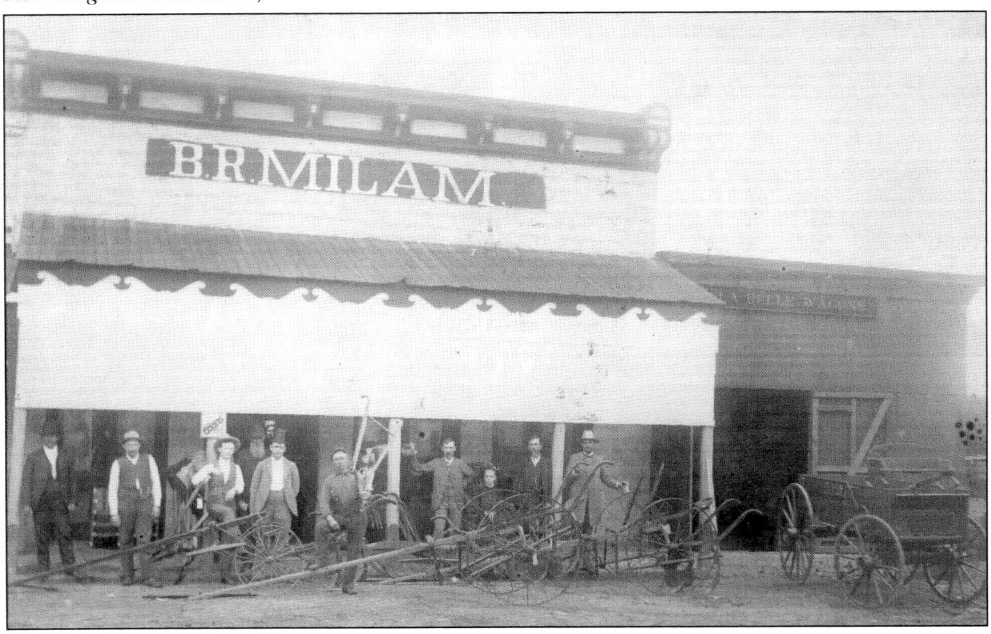

Merchant Benjamin Rush Milam, nephew and namesake of the fallen Texas Revolution hero, was a vendor of dry goods, notions, boots, shoes, and gentlemen's furnishings. In an 1877 newspaper ad, he publicized his large stock of Avery steel and cast-iron plows and his agency for Studebaker wagons. His farm plows are featured in this undated photograph, although at the time, Milam was an agent for LaBelle wagons. (UTA, Texas Photograph Collection.)

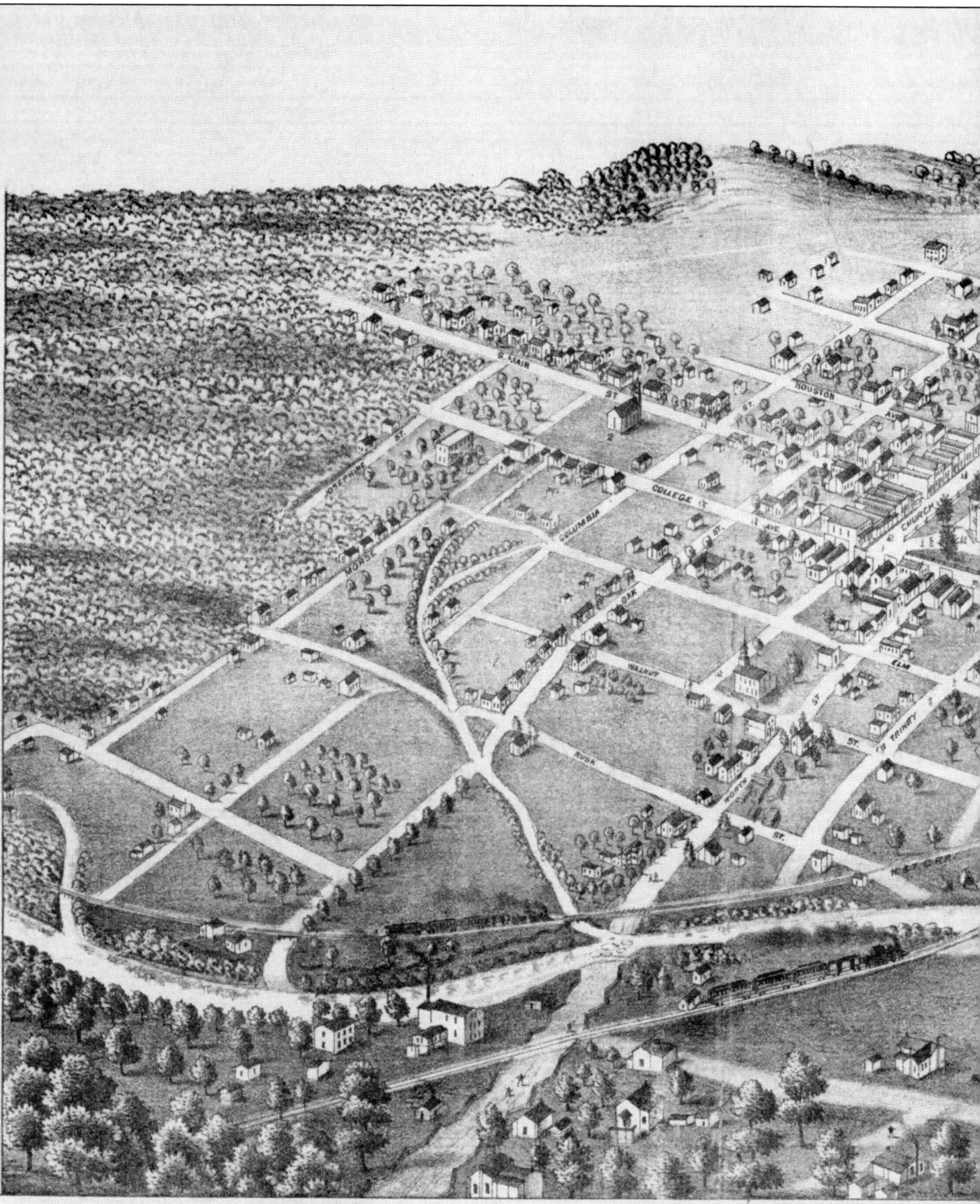
S. MAIN ST.
HOUSTON AV.
JOSEPHINE ST.
COLLEGE ST.
COLUMBIA ST.
CHURCH
MORSE ST.
OAK
WALNUT ST.
ELM
RUSK ST.
NORTH ST.
TRINITY
1 METHODIST CHURCH
2 1st PRESBYTERIAN "
3 EPISCOPAL "
4 BAPTIST "
5 CHRISTIAN "
6 HIGH SCOOOL
BIRDS EYE VIEW
WEATHERFO
PARKER CO. TEXAS
1877

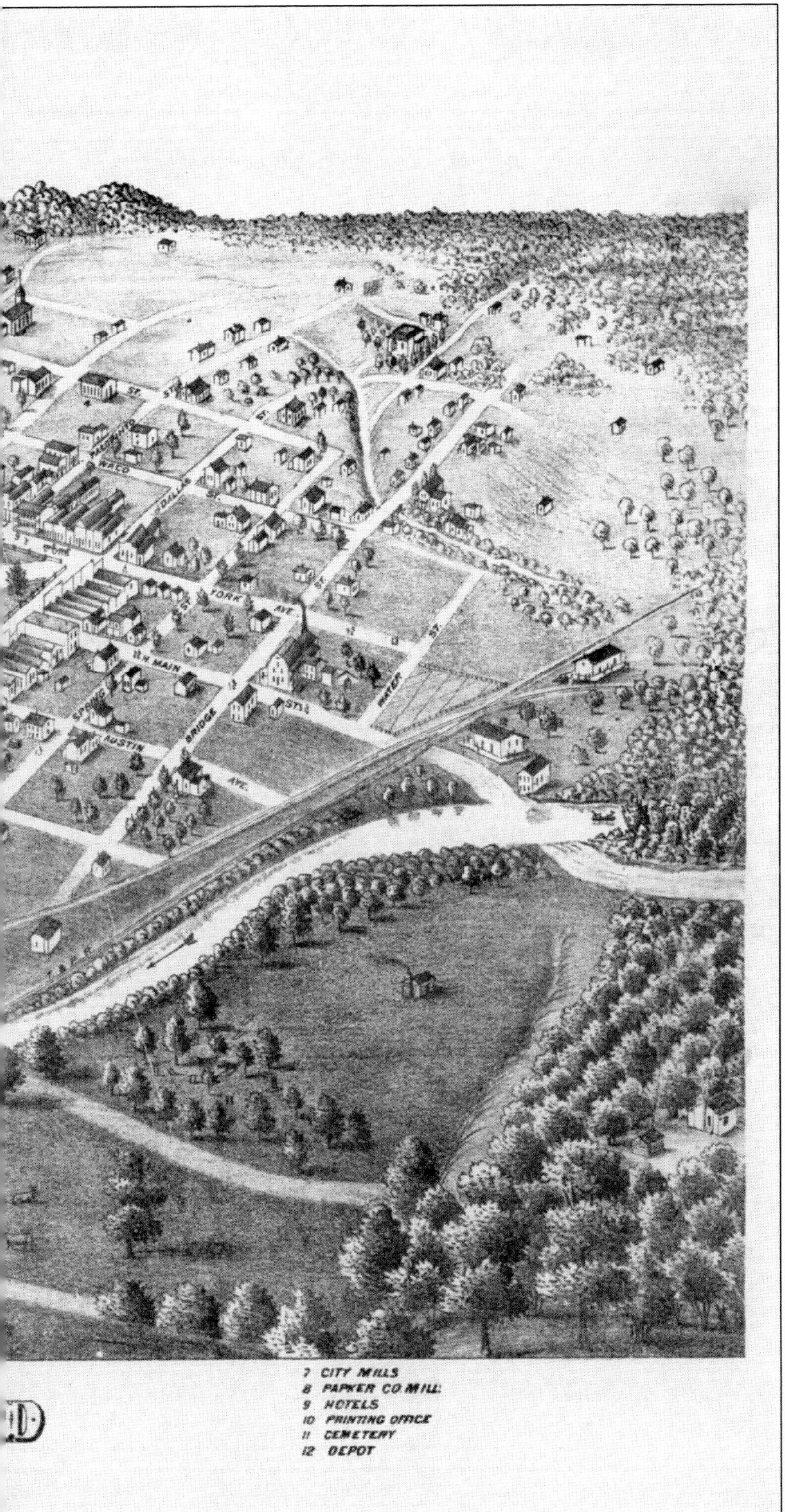

The artist of this 1877 bird's-eye-view map of Weatherford is thought to be D.D. Morse, creator of similar maps of Fort Worth, McKinney, and Waxahachie. The town is viewed from the east looking west, and significant buildings are identified at the base of the map. Artistic license was taken in depicting the Houston & Texas Central and Texas & Pacific railroads running along Town Creek. Although both were anticipated in 1877, the Texas & Pacific Railway was the first railroad to arrive in 1880. The Houston & Texas Central Railway was never extended to Weatherford, although the Santa Fe Railroad later roughly adopted its depicted alignment. Liberties may have also been taken with the representation of the courthouse. No illustration of the 1858 courthouse is extant. The courthouse pictured here bears no resemblance to the third structure completed in 1878. (WPL.)

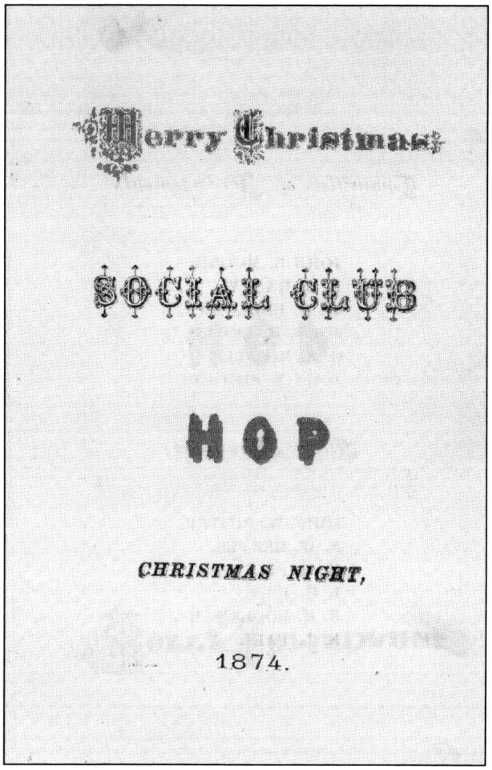

The first-annual hop of the Social Club of Weatherford, held at Leach and Milam's Hall on Christmas night 1874, was the social event of the season. The committees of invitation and arrangements were all businessmen, including banker Henry Warren, attorneys Benjamin G. Lanham and George A. McCall, and merchants William H. Eddleman and Lewis H. Ross. (BSM.)

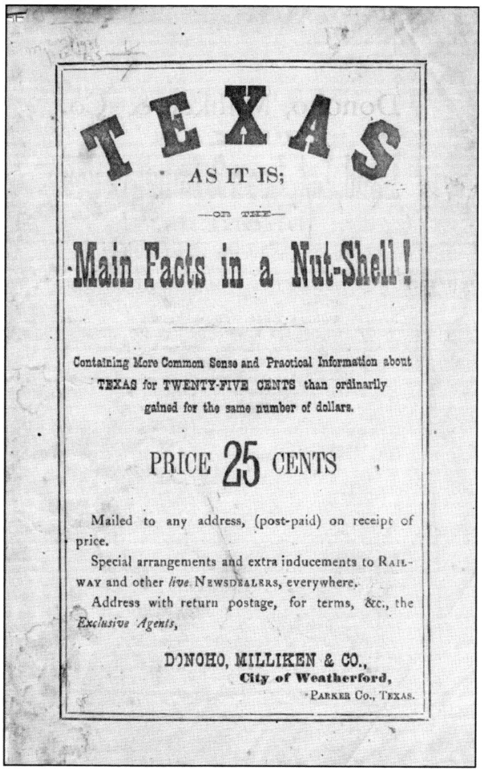

Real estate agents Donoho, Milliken & Co. proclaimed Weatherford to be "the coming city" in their self-published pamphlet *Texas as It Is, Main Facts in a Nut-Shell!* Printed in 1876–1877 to encourage emigration to Parker County, the booklet included a Texas map showing all roads leading to Weatherford. A city map highlighted the north-side Palace Park residential addition. It also solicited subscriptions to build a "centennial public school building." (YU.)

Two

1880–1889

ALL ABOARD

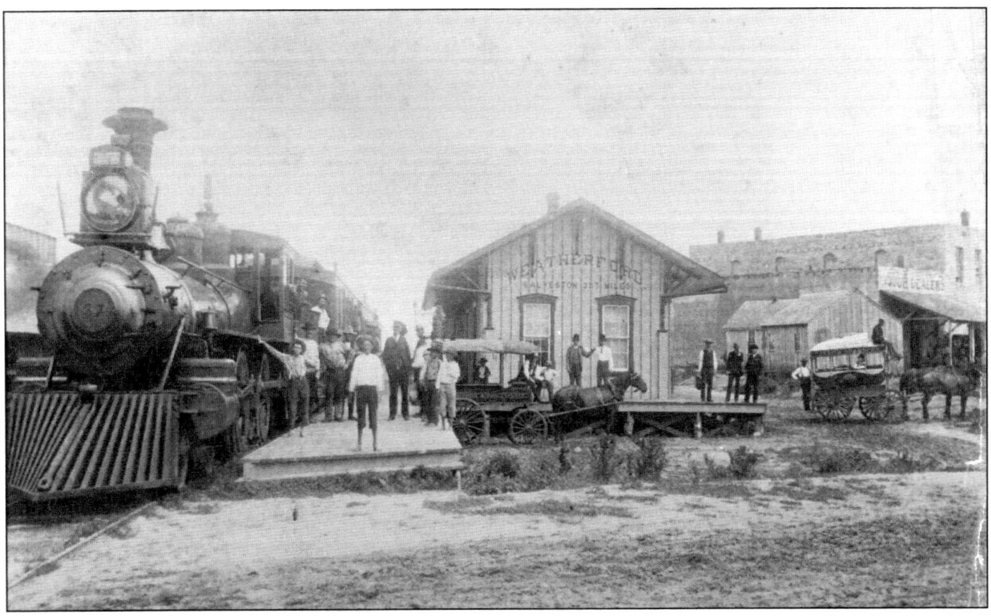

The Gulf, Colorado & Santa Fe Railway began operations in Weatherford in 1887. The Weatherford, Mineral Wells & Northwestern Railway followed in 1892. Rail service boosted Weatherford's prosperity, opening distant markets to local agricultural products and manufactured goods. Weatherford began an architectural transformation as cast-iron storefronts, windows, and other building accoutrements became available. The first Santa Fe depot was located at the end of York Avenue. (VC.)

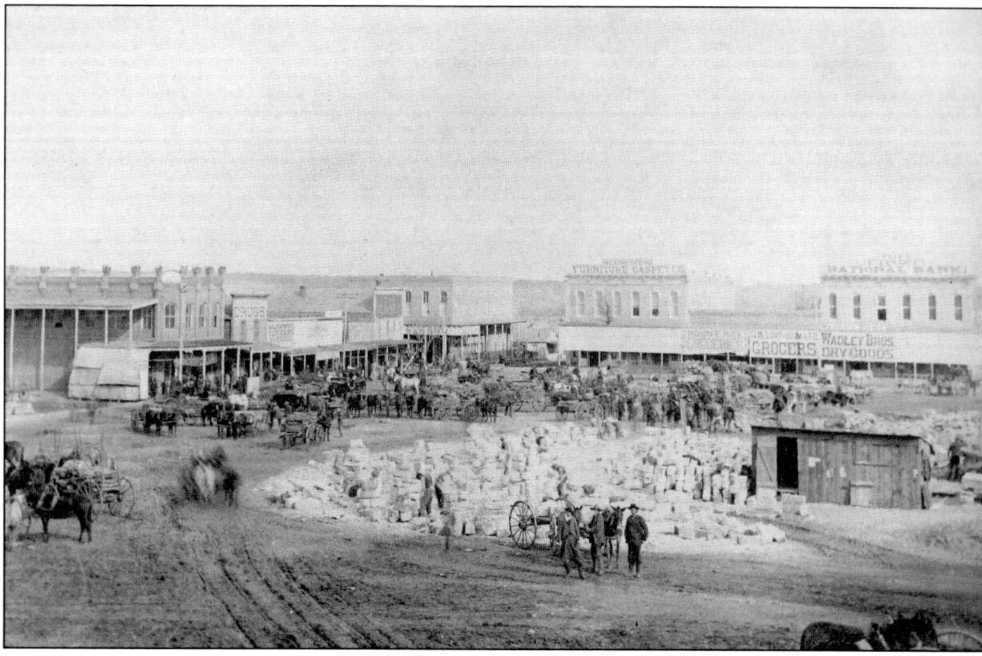

On June 9, 1884, James H. Milliken and Company was awarded the $55,555.55 contract to construct Parker County's fourth courthouse. This vista of the northeast quadrant of the public square shows the completed demolition of the burned ruins of the 1878 courthouse and stone stockpiled for the new building. While the new courthouse was being constructed, court activities were conducted from the Ross building on the northeast corner of the square. (DHCC, James Doss Collection.)

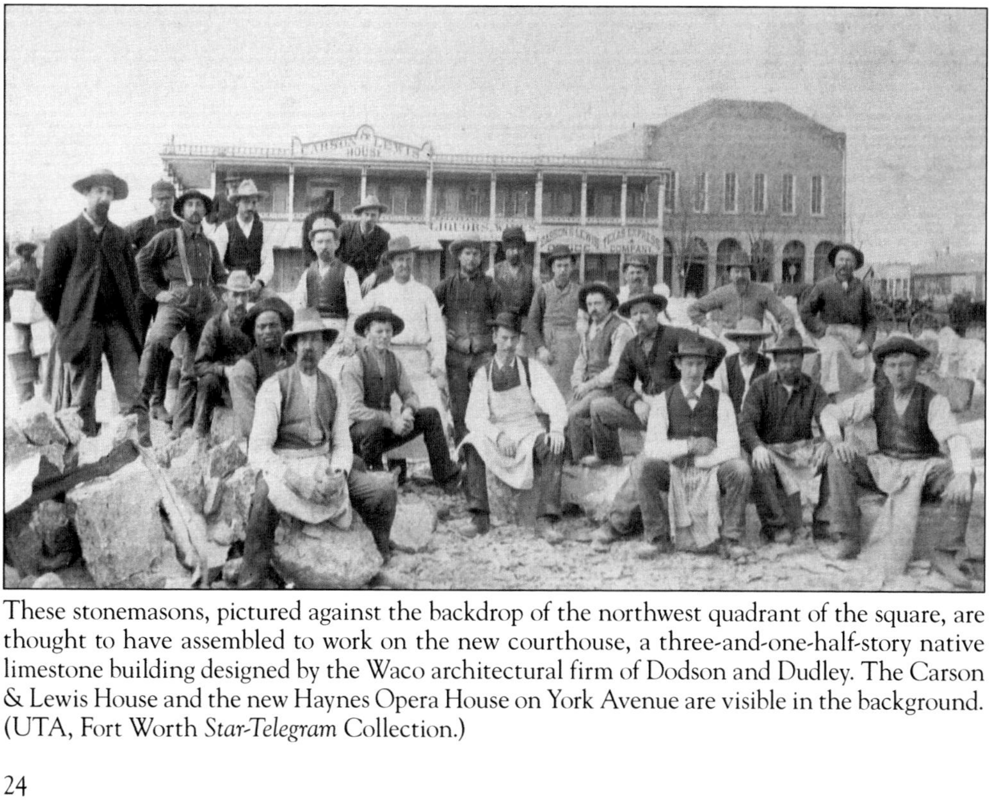

These stonemasons, pictured against the backdrop of the northwest quadrant of the square, are thought to have assembled to work on the new courthouse, a three-and-one-half-story native limestone building designed by the Waco architectural firm of Dodson and Dudley. The Carson & Lewis House and the new Haynes Opera House on York Avenue are visible in the background. (UTA, Fort Worth *Star-Telegram* Collection.)

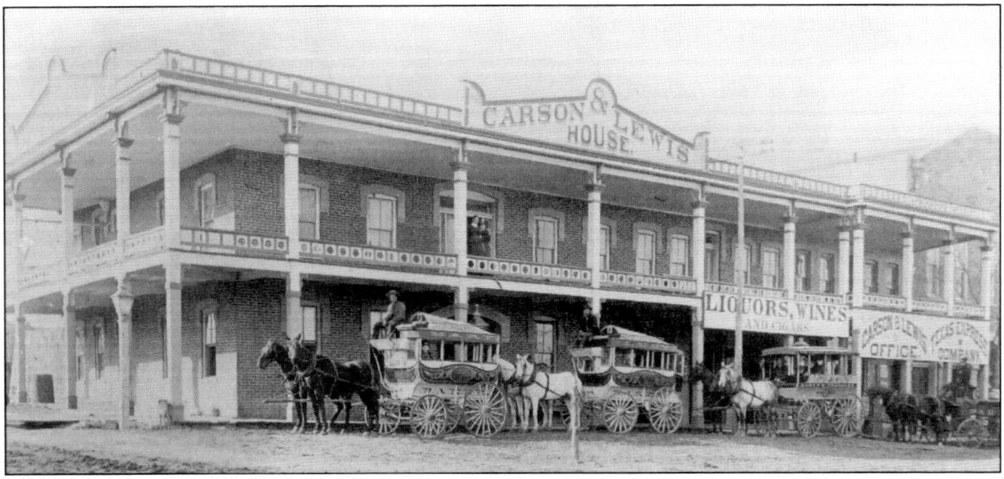

Brothers-in-law Joe Carson and Tom Lewis partnered in many business ventures, including a cotton gin, hog farm, flour mill, and coffin manufactory. The Carson & Lewis House, a two-story brick hotel with veranda, was perhaps their most outstanding commercial accomplishment. It dominated the west side of the downtown square from 1860 until 1910, when it is said to have been destroyed by fire. The Kuteman Block, a three-story office building, replaced the hotel by 1911. (UTA, Fort Worth *Star-Telegram* Collection; WPL.)

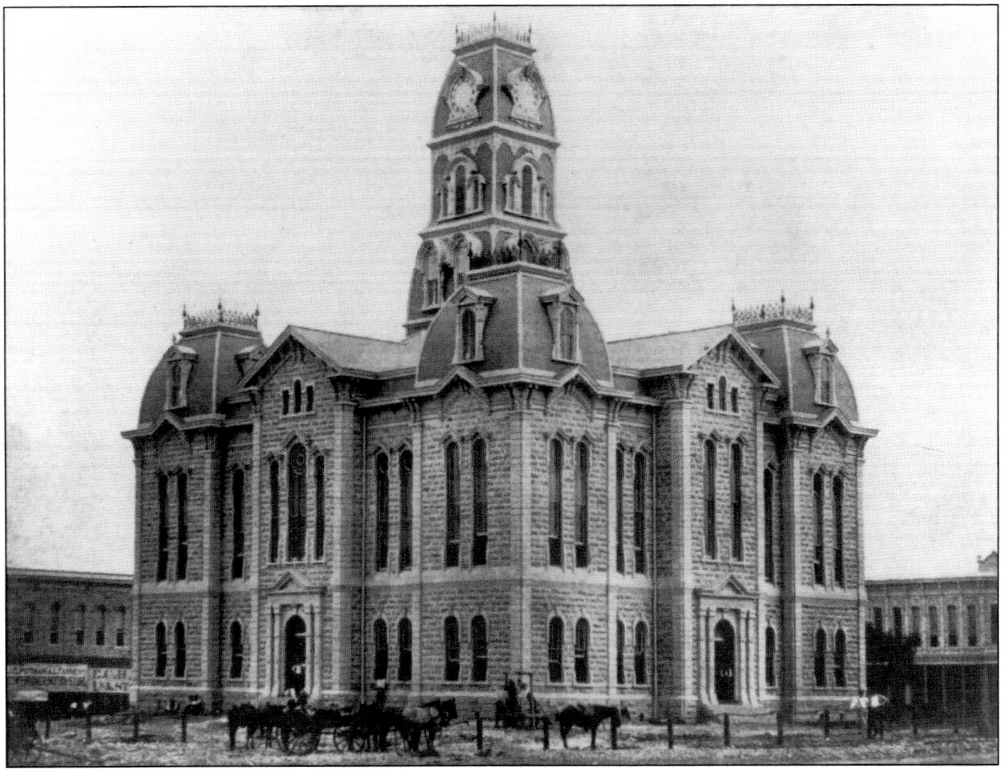

This view of the Parker County Courthouse appears to have been taken shortly after its completion in 1886. A close look at the central tower reveals that the clock face on each side has no hands. In 1897, county commissioners invested $975 to purchase and install a Seth Thomas clockworks in the tower, making clocks on all four sides operational. (FNB.)

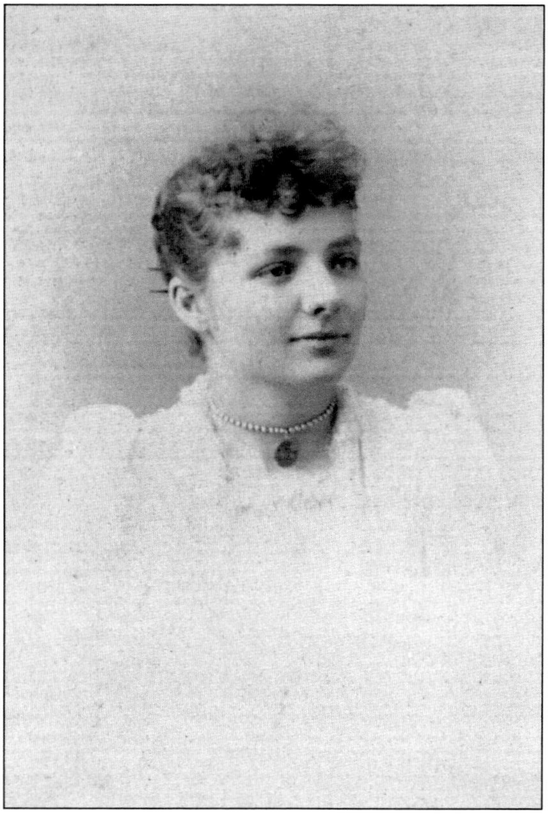

Mollie Montfort Steele, a young divorced mother and music teacher, moved from Kentucky to Weatherford in the late 1880s with the written endorsements of the parents of her former students in hand. Her father, James F. Montfort, also moved to Weatherford and took over the Sikes House, changing the name to the Montfort Hotel. He later became proprietor of the Carson & Lewis House. (UTA, Montfort, Sawtelle, and Gilbert Family Papers.)

The Weatherford Opera House Company added a second floor to the David C. Haynes grocery in 1883. Shares of capital stock were offered to the public for $25 per share. Located adjacent to the Carson & Lewis House, the Haynes Opera House hosted melodramas, minstrel shows, commencements, and a variety of cultural events for over 30 years. The building was destroyed by fire in 1914. (BSM.)

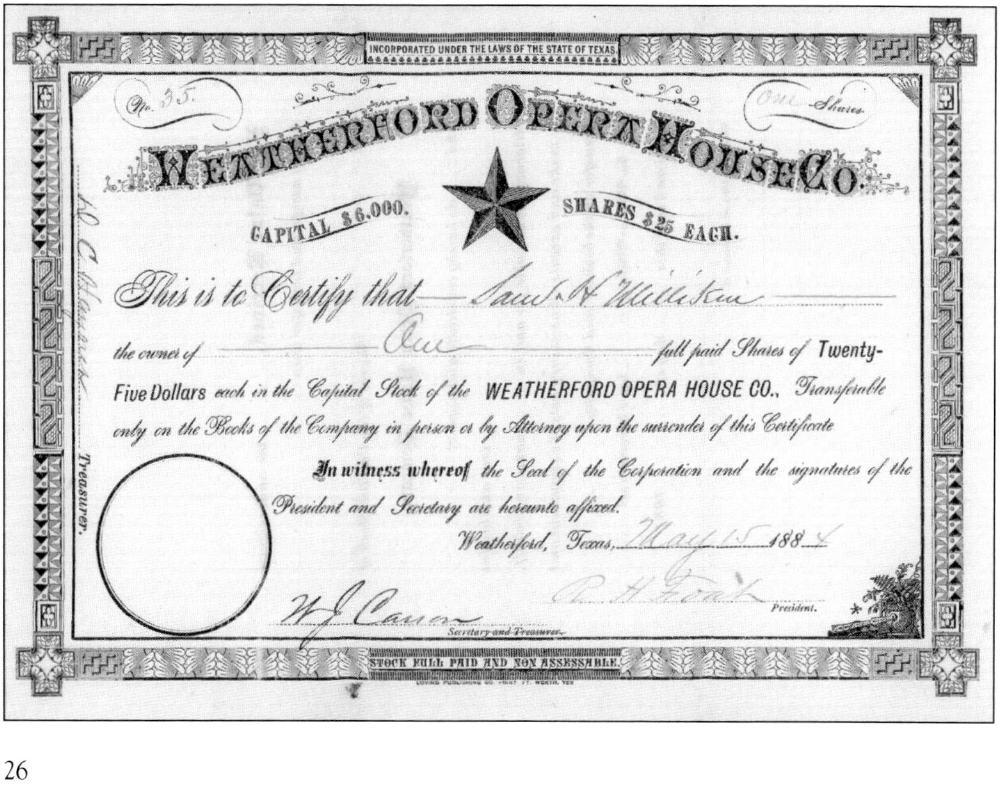

INCORPORATED UNDER THE LAWS OF THE STATE OF TEXAS.

No. 35. One Shares.

WEATHERFORD OPERA HOUSE CO.

CAPITAL $6,000. SHARES $25 EACH.

This is to Certify that Saml. H. Milliken the owner of One full paid Shares of Twenty-Five Dollars each in the Capital Stock of the WEATHERFORD OPERA HOUSE CO., Transferable only on the Books of the Company in person or by Attorney upon the surrender of this Certificate

In witness whereof the Seal of the Corporation and the signatures of the President and Secretary are hereunto affixed.

Weatherford, Texas, May 15 1884

W. J. Carson Secretary and Treasurer.

R. H. Foat President.

Treasurer.

STOCK FULL PAID AND NON ASSESSABLE.

Mollie Steele quickly garnered a growing clientele of piano and voice students and frequently directed programs and operettas at the Haynes Opera House. Steele married respected merchant Edward Porter Sawtelle, who also enjoyed the arts and often performed in her musical programs. Her portrait on the opposite page and this Haynes Opera House program for *Three Bears and Golden Hair*, under her direction, probably date from the late 1880s to early 1890s. (KF; UTA, Montfort, Sawtelle, and Gilbert Family Papers.)

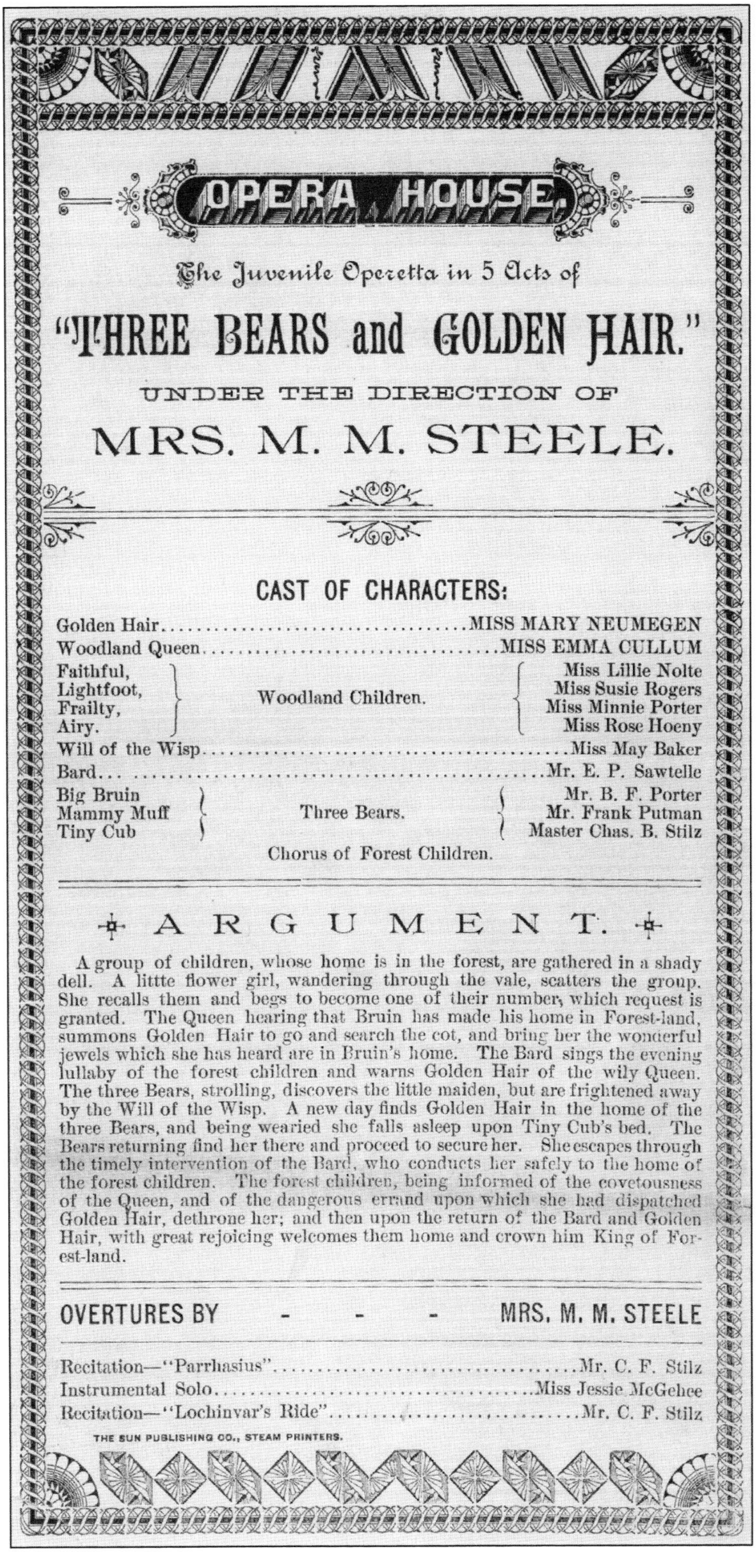

OPERA HOUSE.

The Juvenile Operetta in 5 Acts of

"THREE BEARS and GOLDEN HAIR."

UNDER THE DIRECTION OF

MRS. M. M. STEELE.

CAST OF CHARACTERS:

Golden Hair		MISS MARY NEUMEGEN
Woodland Queen		MISS EMMA CULLUM
Faithful,	Woodland Children.	Miss Lillie Nolte
Lightfoot,		Miss Susie Rogers
Frailty,		Miss Minnie Porter
Airy.		Miss Rose Hoeny
Will of the Wisp		Miss May Baker
Bard		Mr. E. P. Sawtelle
Big Bruin	Three Bears.	Mr. B. F. Porter
Mammy Muff		Mr. Frank Putman
Tiny Cub		Master Chas. B. Stilz

Chorus of Forest Children.

ARGUMENT.

A group of children, whose home is in the forest, are gathered in a shady dell. A littte flower girl, wandering through the vale, scatters the group. She recalls them and begs to become one of their number, which request is granted. The Queen hearing that Bruin has made his home in Forest-land, summons Golden Hair to go and search the cot, and bring her the wonderful jewels which she has heard are in Bruin's home. The Bard sings the evening lullaby of the forest children and warns Golden Hair of the wily Queen. The three Bears, strolling, discovers the little maiden, but are frightened away by the Will of the Wisp. A new day finds Golden Hair in the home of the three Bears, and being wearied she falls asleep upon Tiny Cub's bed. The Bears returning find her there and proceed to secure her. She escapes through the timely intervention of the Bard, who conducts her safely to the home of the forest children. The forest children, being informed of the covetousness of the Queen, and of the dangerous errand upon which she had dispatched Golden Hair, dethrone her; and then upon the return of the Bard and Golden Hair, with great rejoicing welcomes them home and crown him King of Forest-land.

OVERTURES BY - - - MRS. M. M. STEELE

Recitation—"Parrhasius" .... Mr. C. F. Stilz
Instrumental Solo .... Miss Jessie McGehee
Recitation—"Lochinvar's Ride" .... Mr. C. F. Stilz

THE SUN PUBLISHING CO., STEAM PRINTERS.

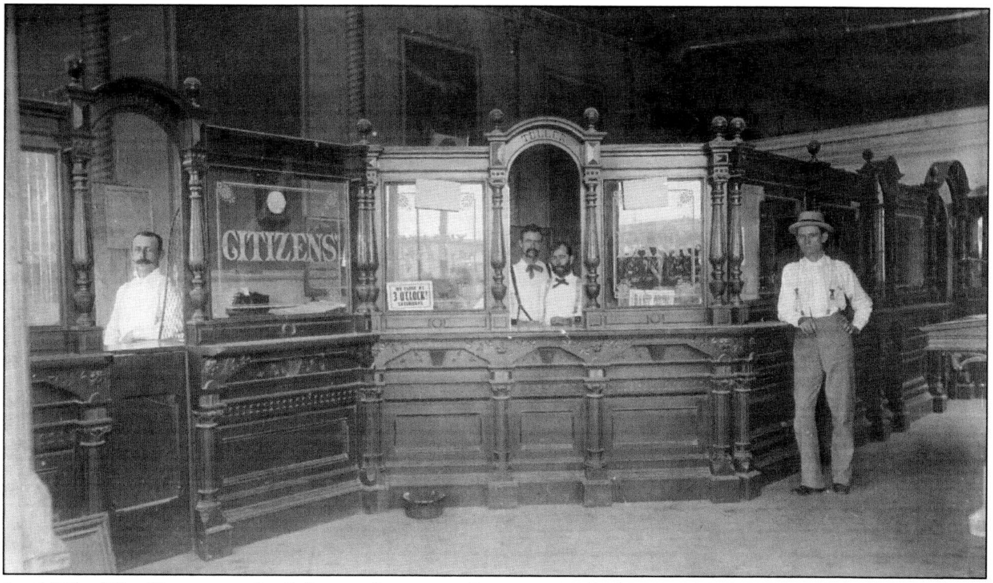

In 1882, J.R. Couts applied for and received a national charter for his bank, granted under the name Citizens National Bank. He acquired the west corner of North Main Street and the courthouse square and constructed an impressive two-story stone building occupied by the bank in 1885. A rare glimpse of the bank interior reveals a stained-wood teller booth featuring etched glass windows. The bank maintained hours on Saturdays until 3:00 p.m. Citizens' successor, First Financial Bank, still operates from this location. (UTA, Fort Worth *Star-Telegram* Collection.)

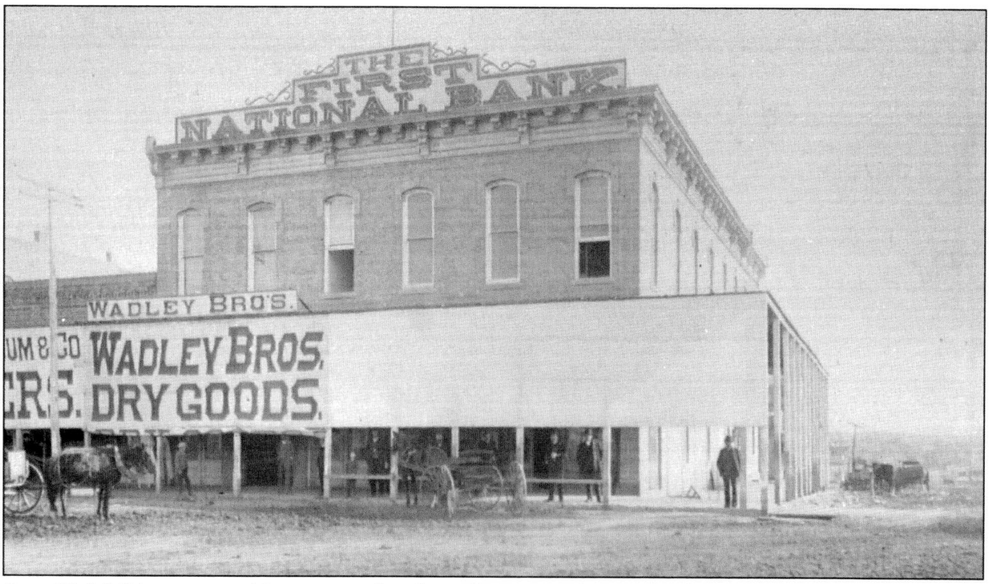

Sam H. Milliken merged his private banking firm into the newly chartered First National Bank when it opened on July 1, 1880. This two-story brick building was erected to accommodate the new bank, promising "the most perfect security against fire and burglars." Now the oldest chartered bank in Texas, First National Bank remained at its original location at the corner of Fort Worth Street and the square until 1964. (UTA, Fort Worth *Star-Telegram* Collection.)

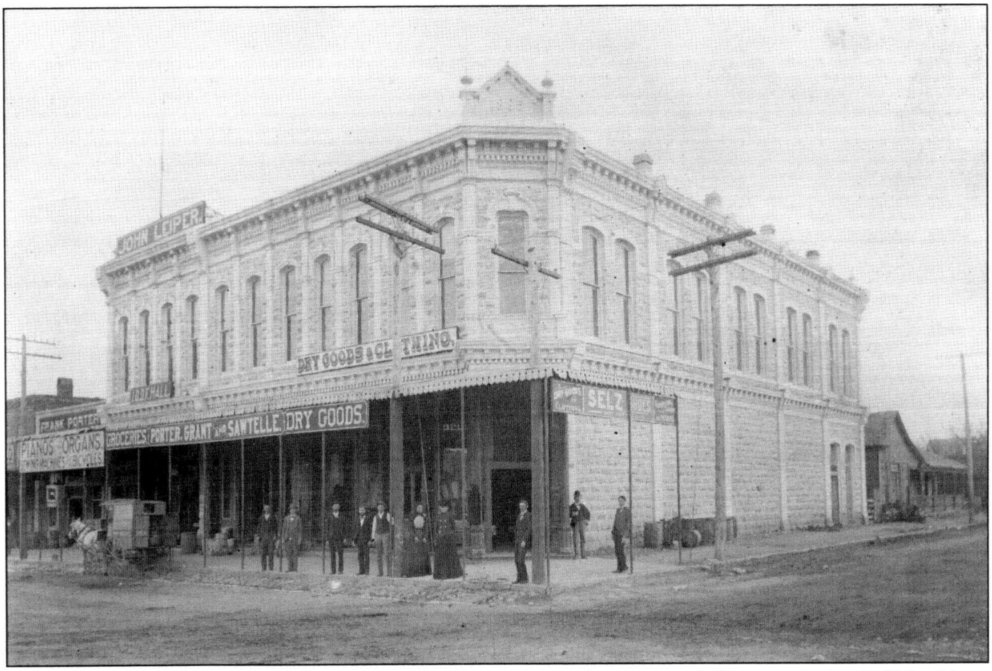

The dry goods firm of Porter Bros. and Kidwell constructed what is now known as the Hill Building at the southeast corner of South Main Street and the courthouse square in 1885. Shown here in the late 1890s, the building was occupied by popular dry goods merchants Porter, Grant, and Sawtelle until 1911. A fire on January 10, 1912, caused significant damage to the structure, which is visible today in the blonde brick reconstruction of its west facade. (WPL.)

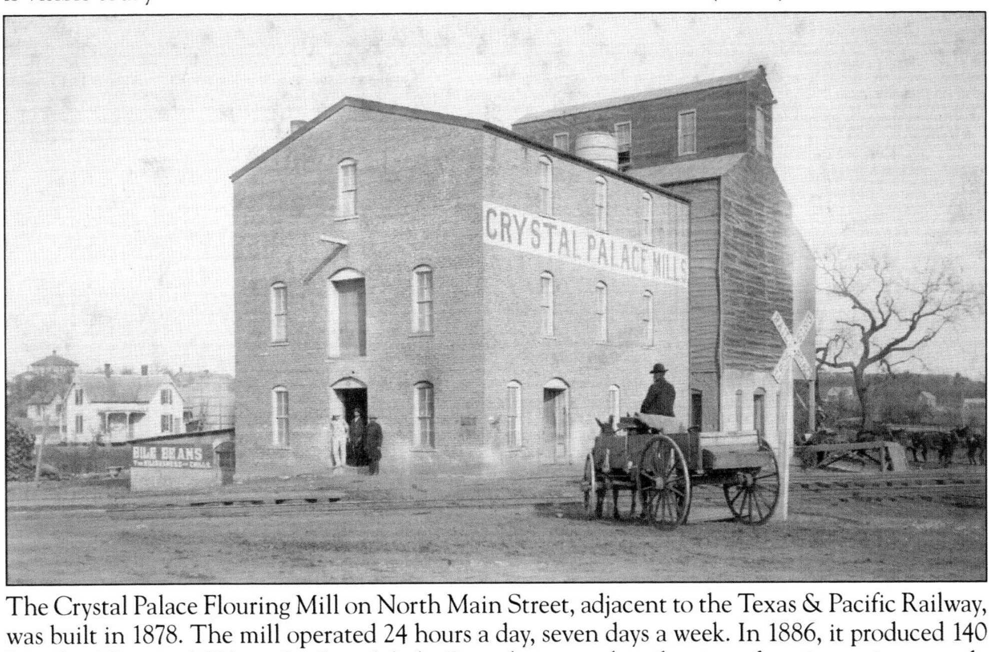

The Crystal Palace Flouring Mill on North Main Street, adjacent to the Texas & Pacific Railway, was built in 1878. The mill operated 24 hours a day, seven days a week. In 1886, it produced 140 barrels of flour and 50 barrels of meal daily. Over the years, the vibration of passing trains severely damaged its brick walls. The building was abandoned after the mill closed in 1928. (WPL; UTA, Fort Worth *Star-Telegram* Collection.)

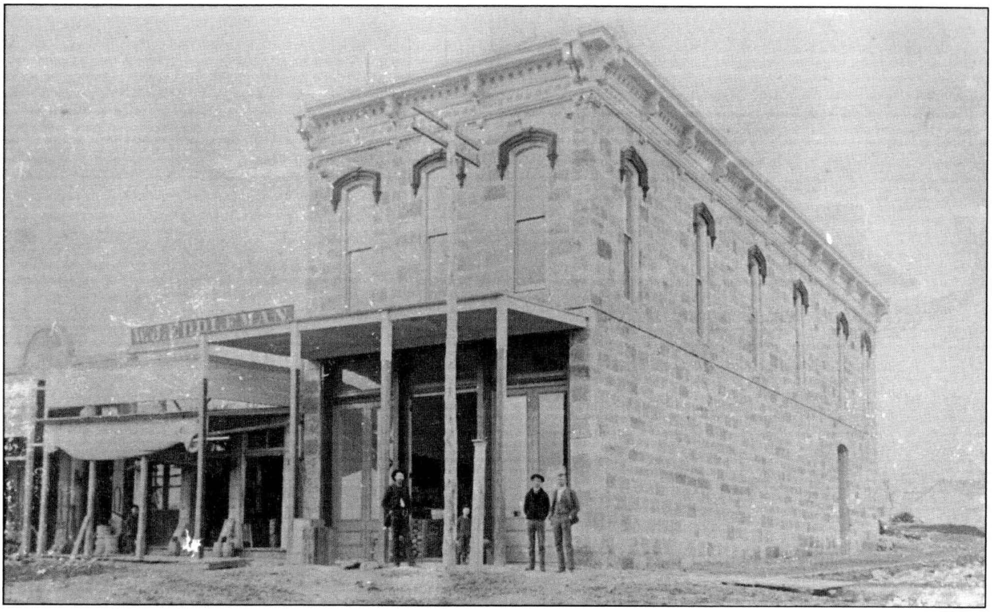

Wiley J. Eddleman constructed this two-story stone building in 1884 for his dry goods business. It was located at 102 Houston Avenue, the former site of A.B. Gant Land Locators. Merchants & Farmers National Bank, founded by Wiley's brother William H. Eddleman, commenced operation here in 1889. A simpler three-story stone structure was erected in 1902 following a fire. Its third story was removed by 1931. (VC.)

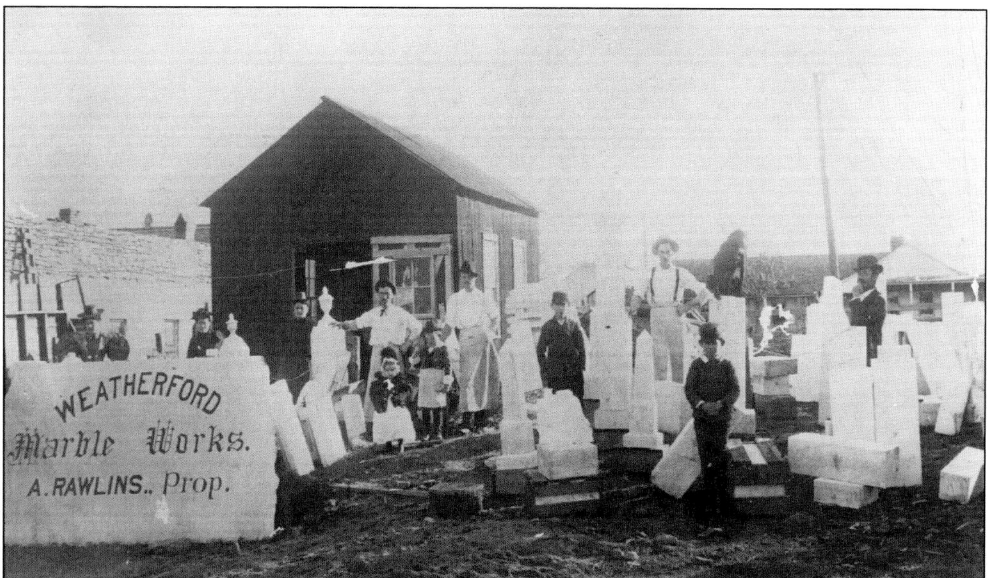

English-born stonecutter Alex Rawlins opened Weatherford Marble Works on the south side of the square in 1884. The business relocated to Palo Pinto Street in 1887. Granite cemetery monuments were manufactured by hand until power machinery was installed in 1918. When his two sons joined him in 1915 and 1920, the business name was changed to Alex Rawlins and Sons. Still family owned, Rawlins celebrated its 125th anniversary in 2009. (VC.)

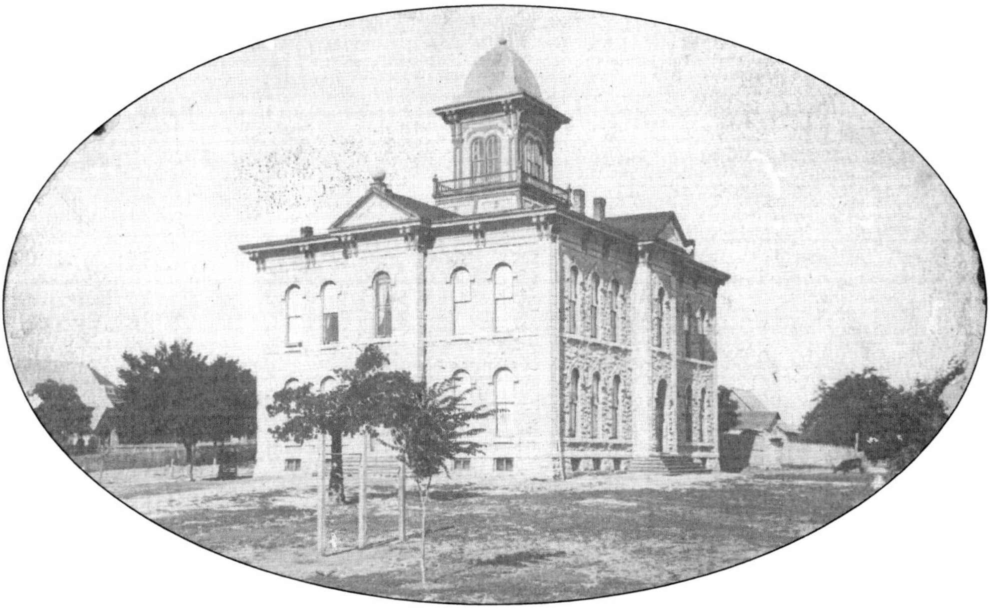

Weatherford began its system of public education in the 1880s with 250 students, but with no schoolhouse or furniture. This building, the Central High School, constructed on Palo Pinto and Alamo Streets, was completed in 1885. By 1888, the system had grown to serve 600 students taught by 10 teachers. In addition to the Central High School, there were three ward schools, including one attended by African American children. (WC.)

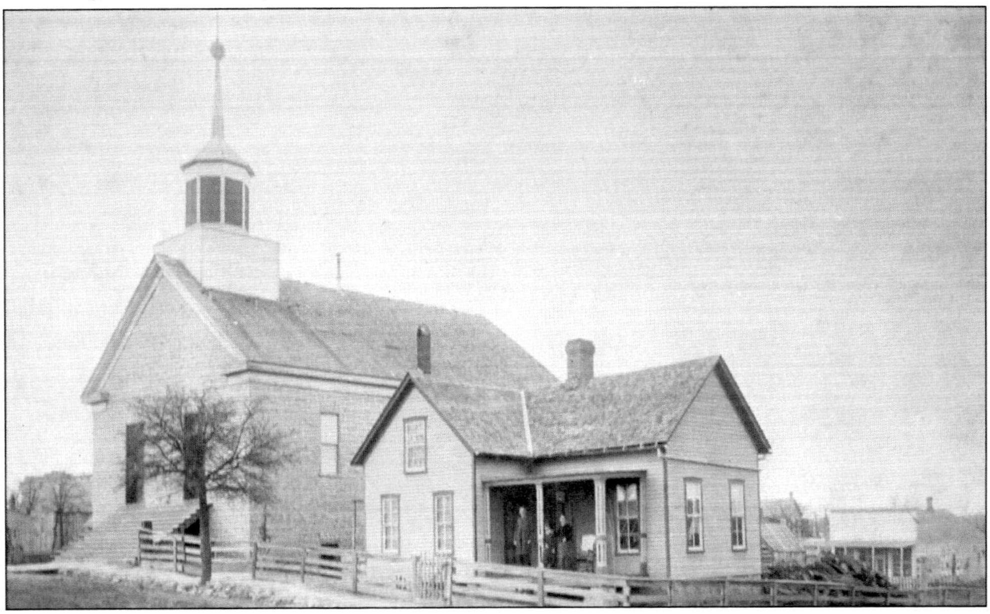

Rev. Pleasant Tackett organized the 11-member Weatherford Methodist Episcopal Church, South congregation in April 1857. Construction of this stone church on East Church and Walnut Streets began in 1867 and finished around 1874. The first floor was used for Sunday school, lectures, and prayer and social meetings. The south stairway led to the second floor "audience chamber." The building was destroyed during a storm on June 6, 1886. (UTA, Fort Worth *Star-Telegram* Collection.)

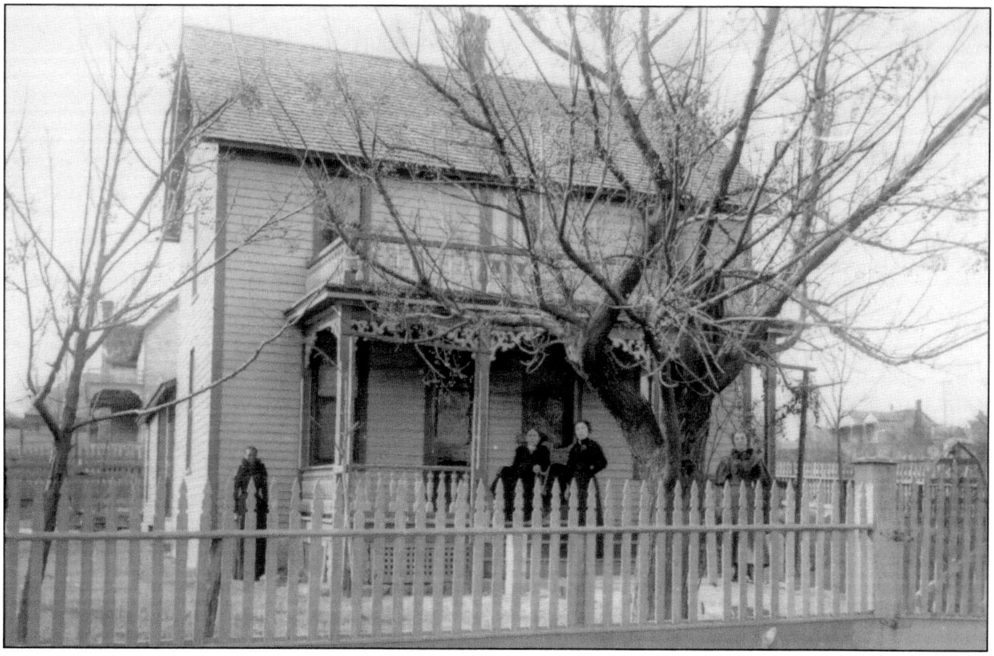

Rev. Thomas J. Hines became the presiding elder of the Weatherford District of the Methodist Episcopal Church, South in 1876. He would also pastor the Weatherford congregation before his death in 1881. This photograph of the Hines residence at Columbia and Alamo Streets includes, from left to right, Belle, the Hines's cook; Reverend Hines's widow, Marie Jane Hines; and two of his daughters, Lula and Margaret Hines. (DHCC, Hillis Wise Collection.)

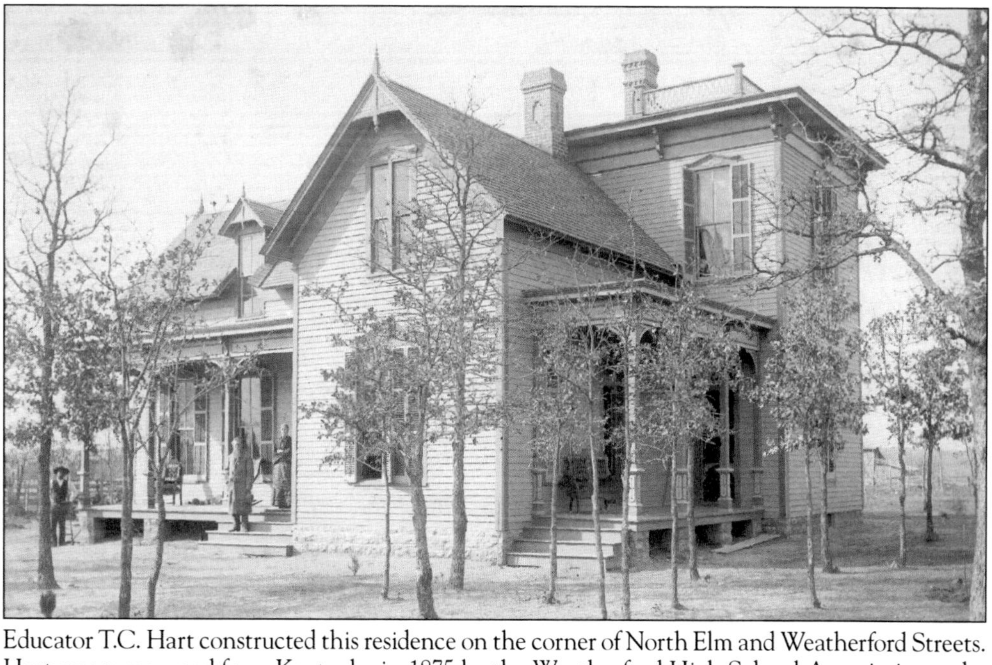

Educator T.C. Hart constructed this residence on the corner of North Elm and Weatherford Streets. Hart was summoned from Kentucky in 1875 by the Weatherford High School Association to be the principal of the Masonic Institute. Hart left his estate, including this home, to the Church of Christ upon his death in 1923. A 1931 fire primarily damaged the second floor. (WPL.)

Henry Oscar Barthold inherited a sense of style from his father, Charles, owner of a men's haberdashery from 1877 until 1927. He inherited a sense of design from his mother, Jane, a gifted artist who created colored-glass decorations for the family garden. Barthold grew exotic flowers used in arrangements he created at the Barthold-Harris Floral Shop, located next to his home on South Waco Street. (BSM.)

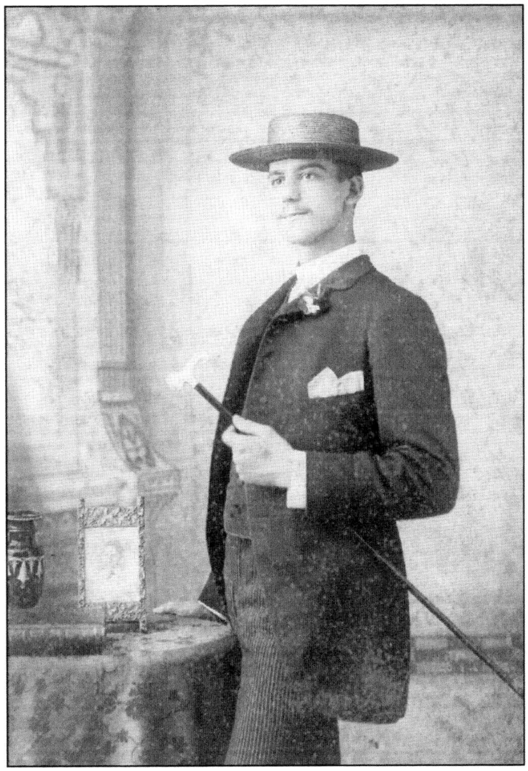

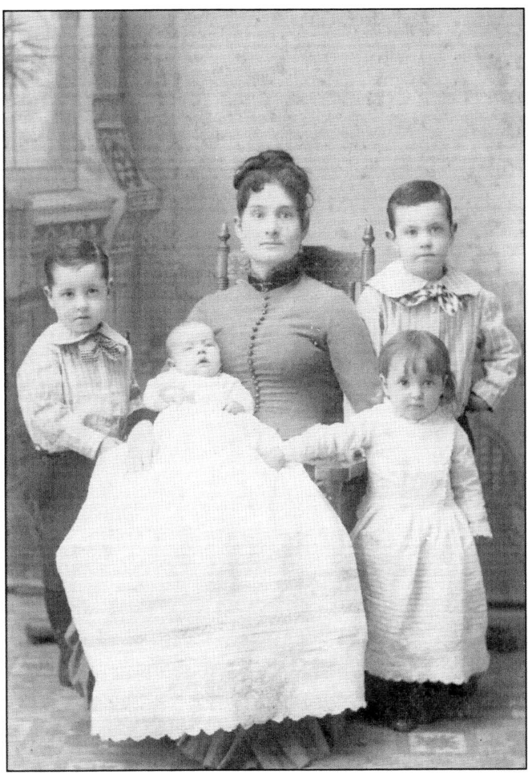

Walter Scott Fant married Frances "Fannie" Murphy in Jacksboro in 1882. The couple soon moved to Weatherford. Fant worked in several business endeavors before being employed by First National Bank in 1887. Fannie is pictured with her four oldest children, from left to right, Charles, Lillian, Louise, and George, around 1889. Walter S. Fant was later elected cashier and then president of First National Bank. (MW.)

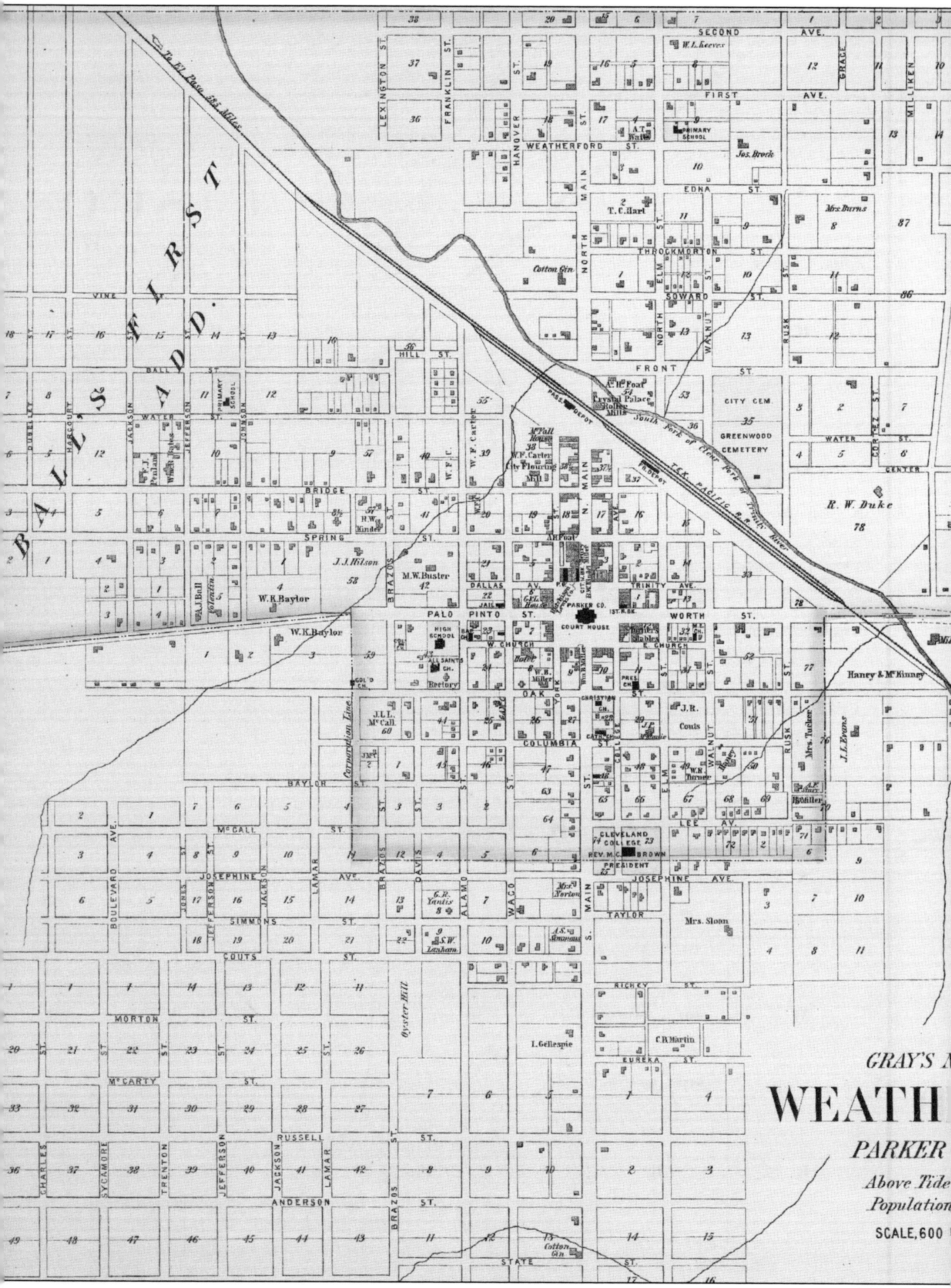
GRAY'S
WEATH
PARKER
Above Tide
Population
SCALE, 600
BALL'S FIRST ADD.
To El Paso 585 Miles
SECOND AVE.
FIRST AVE.
WEATHERFORD ST.
EDNA ST.
THROCKMORTON ST.
SOWARD ST.
FRONT ST.
HILL ST.
BALL ST.
WATER ST.
BRIDGE ST.
SPRING ST.
DALLAS AV.
PALO PINTO ST.
WORTH ST.
TRINITY AVE.
W. CHURCH
E. CHURCH
OAK
COLUMBIA ST.
BAYLOR ST.
LEE AV.
McCALL ST.
JOSEPHINE AVE.
PRESIDENT
TAYLOR
SIMMONS ST.
COUTS ST.
RICHEY ST.
MORTON ST.
EUREKA ST.
McCARTY ST.
RUSSELL ST.
ANDERSON ST.
STATE ST.
VINE
LEXINGTON ST.
FRANKLIN ST.
HANOVER ST.
NORTH MAIN ST.
ELM ST.
WALNUT ST.
RUSK ST.
GRACE
MILLIKEN
CORTEZ ST.
CENTER
BRAZOS ST.
DAVIS ST.
ALAMO
WACO
YORK
COLLEGE
LAMAR
JACKSON
JEFFERSON
JOHNSON
HARCOURT
DUBELLEY
JONES
BOULEVARD AVE.
CHARLES
SYCAMORE
TRENTON
S. MAIN
PRIMARY SCHOOL
Jos. Brock
W. L. Keever
T. C. Hart
Mrs Burns
Cotton Gin
Crystal Palace Roller Mills
CITY CEM.
GREENWOOD CEMETERY
PASS. DEPOT
FR. DEPOT
South Fork of Clear Fork of Trinity River
TEX. PACIFIC R.R.
R. W. Duke
W. F. Carter
City Flouring Mill
McFall House
R. W. Kinder
J. J. Wilson
M. W. Buster
W. K. Baylor
A. J. Ball
JAIL
COURT HOUSE
PARKER CO.
1ST. N. BK.
HIGH SCHOOL
ALL SAINTS CH.
Rectory
Corporation Line
J. L. L. McCall
J. R. Couts
Mrs. Tucker
J. L. Evans
Haney & McKinney
CLEVELAND COLLEGE
REV. M. C. BROWN
Mrs. Norton
G. R. Yantis
S. W. Lanham
A. S. Simmons
Mrs. Sloan
Oyster Hill
I. Gellespie
C. B. Martin
Cotton Gin

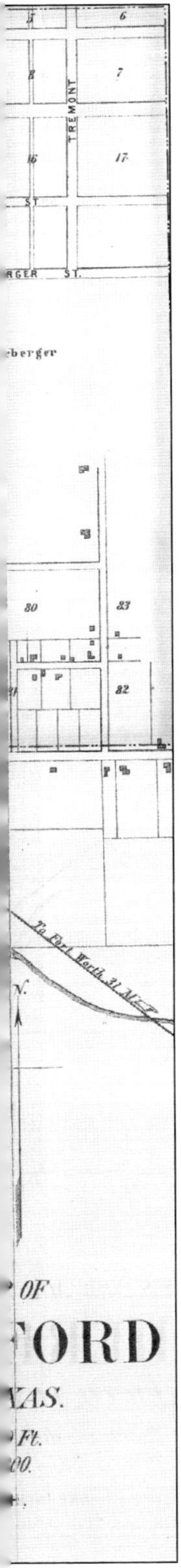

Philadelphia cartography firm O.W. Gray and Son published *Gray's New Map of Weatherford* in 1885. Important buildings pinpointed on the map include the Methodist Episcopal Church on East Church Street, destroyed in 1886; Cleveland College at College and Lee Streets; the passenger and freight depots of the Texas & Pacific Railway straddling North Main Street; and prominent downtown businesses. A new subdivision, Ball's First Addition, is also charted. (UTA.)

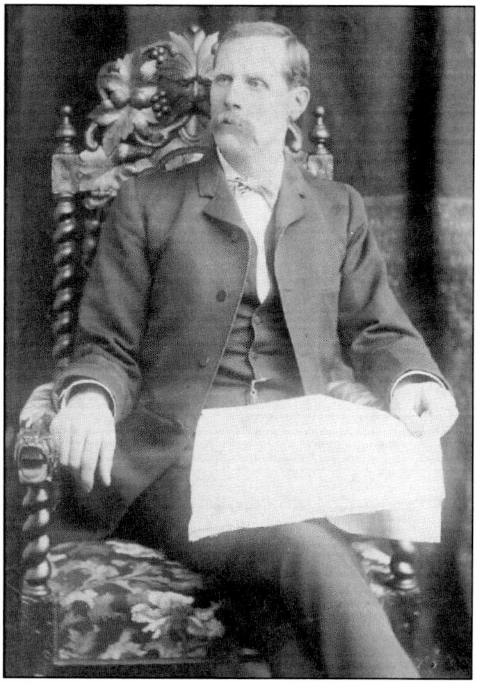

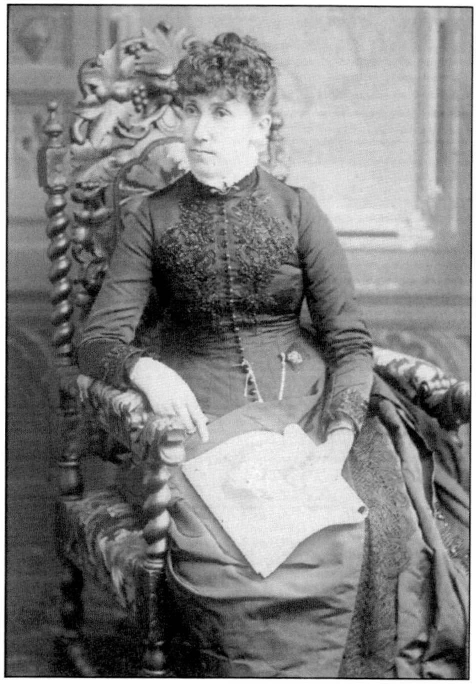

Retired sea captain Hiram E. Swain, his wife, Mary, and their adopted daughter Katie arrived in Weatherford in 1875. Swain invested in real estate, the Crystal Palace Flouring Mill, and First National Bank. When Swain died in San Francisco in 1883, his body was returned home and interred in this elaborate mausoleum built for the family years earlier. Mary (right) married Robert H. Foat (left) in 1887. Foat owned a hardware store on North Main and Spring Streets. His stock included Mitchell wagons, McCormick grain self-binders, toys, kettles, stoves, and furnaces. His many investments included Merchants & Farmers National Bank, Crystal Palace Flouring Mill, and the Franco-Texan Land Company. (All, WPL.)

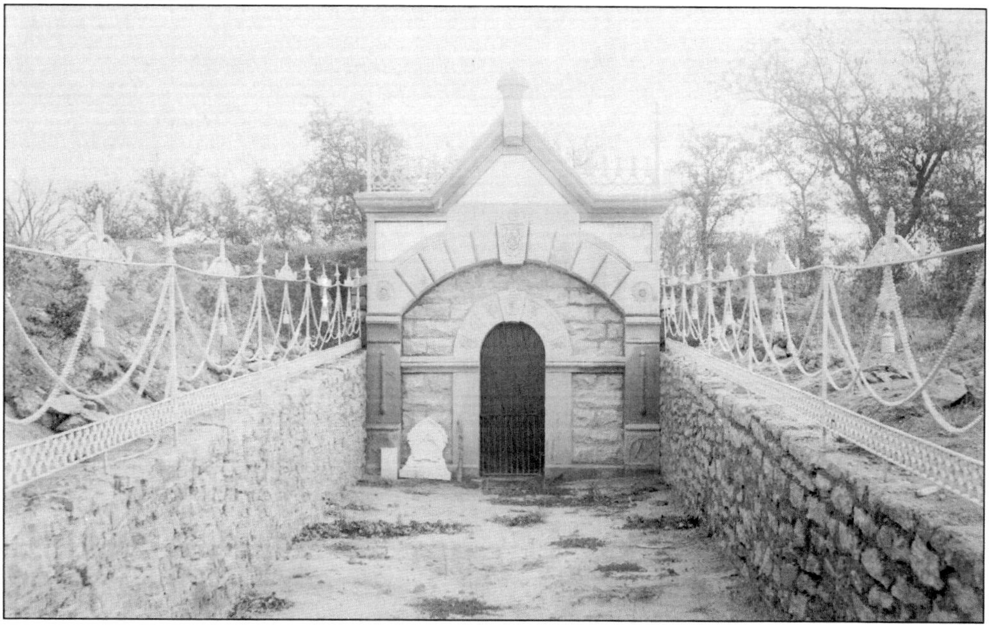

Three

1890–1899

Great Expectations

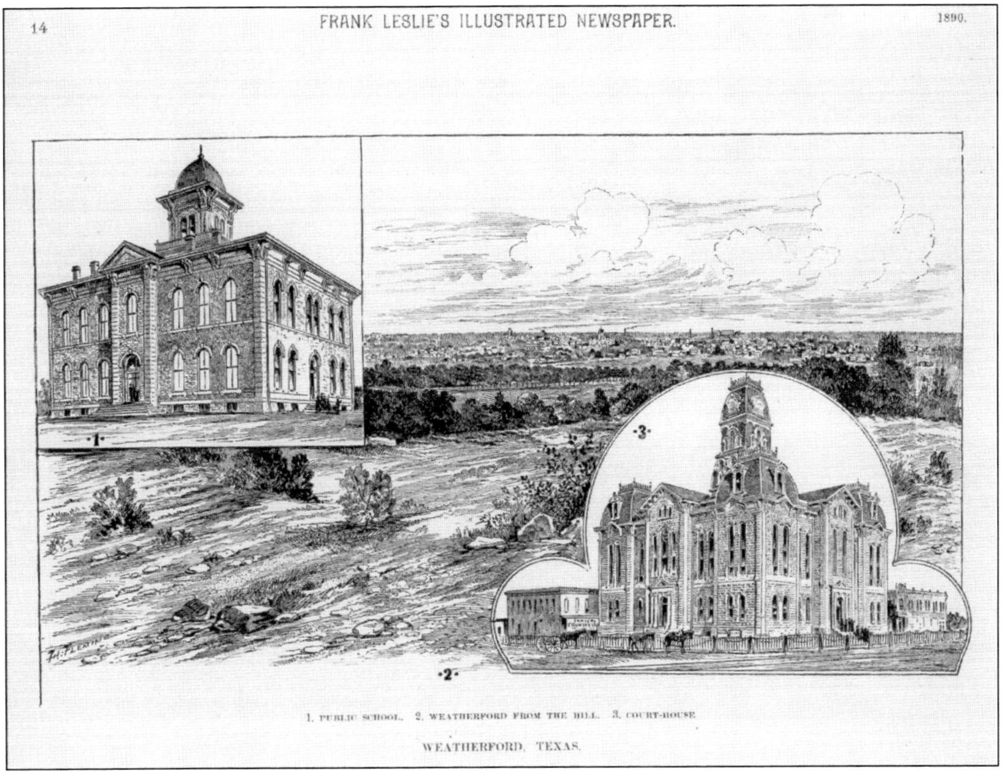

National attention was cast on Weatherford when this collage of town views was published in *Frank Leslie's Weekly Newspaper* in 1890. Editors of the popular weekly literary and news magazine highlighted prominent, recently completed buildings the Central High School and Parker County Courthouse and a picturesque view from one of the surrounding hills. (BSM.)

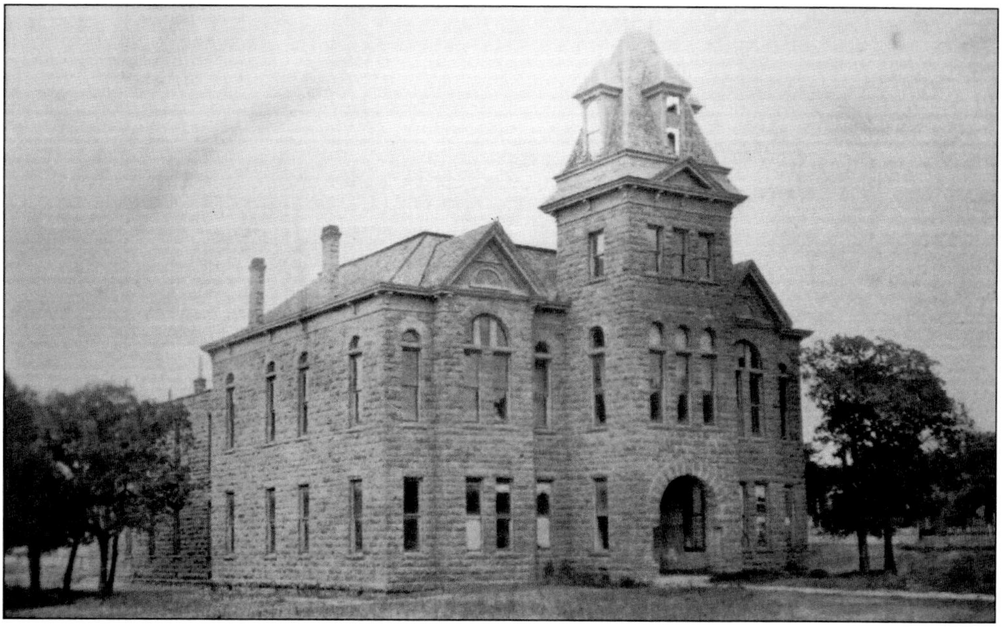

The Weatherford District of the Methodist Episcopal Church, South acquired the Masonic Institute property in June 1889 through the generosity of the citizens of Weatherford. The church consolidated its existing Granbury College with the Masonic Institute to form Weatherford College. The charter was transferred, and president David S. Switzer and the faculty were reassigned. Classes began September 15, 1889, with an enrollment of 227 students. The college prospered under Switzer's leadership with his wife, Rebecca, at his side. In 1894, the landmark Old Main building (above) was added to the old Masonic Institute, as was an astronomical observatory. Switzer, affectionately termed the "Father of Weatherford College," guided the school through December 1901. Weatherford College faculty seated in front of Old Main, pictured sometime between 1894 to 1901, included, from left to right, Josie Middlebrook, Grace Switzer, Reverend Burkhead, N.E. Adams, David S. Switzer, Rebecca Switzer, unidentified, Dr. Edwin Rankin, and Davida Switzer. (Both, WC.)

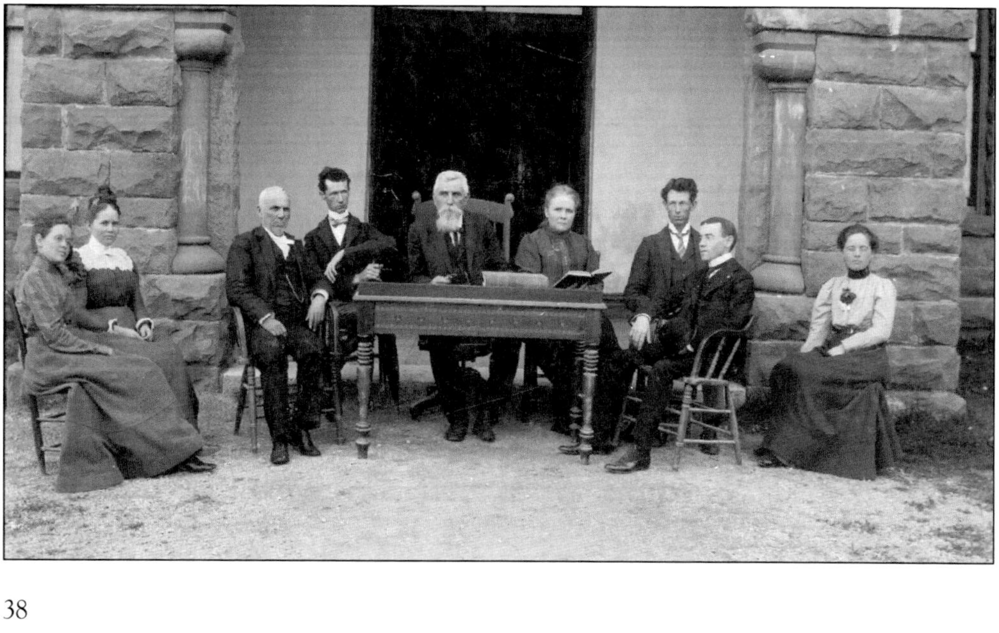

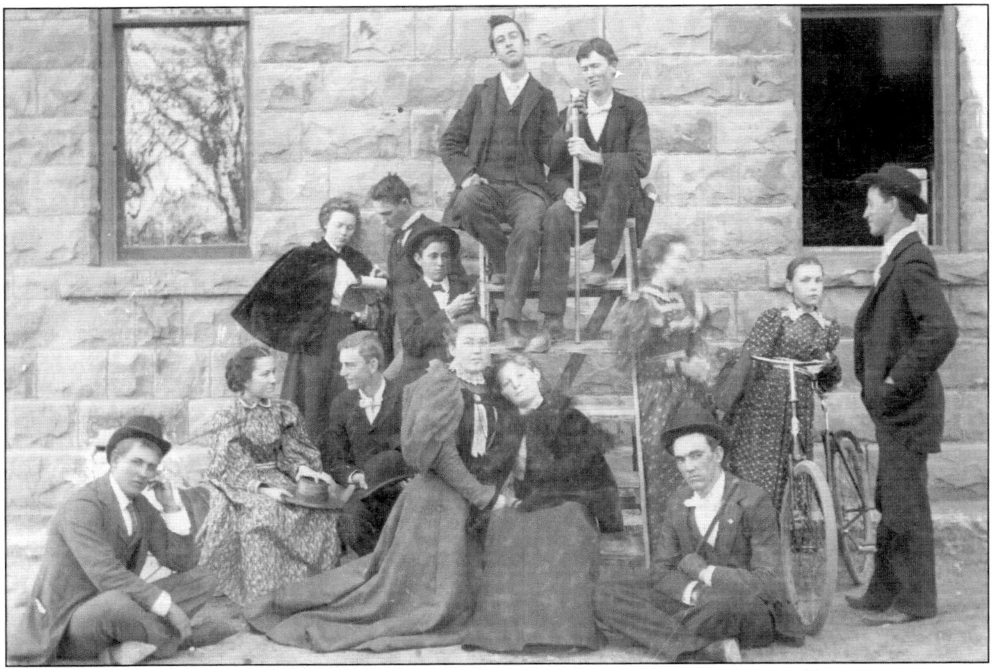

Weatherford College offered study in primary, intermediate, preparatory, and college departments. College coursework included Greek, Latin, English, modern languages and literature, oratory and elocution, mental and moral philosophy, mathematics and astronomy, natural sciences, business, history, pedagogy, music (piano, voice, and stringed instruments), and art. Oratory students posed for this photograph in 1897. (WC.)

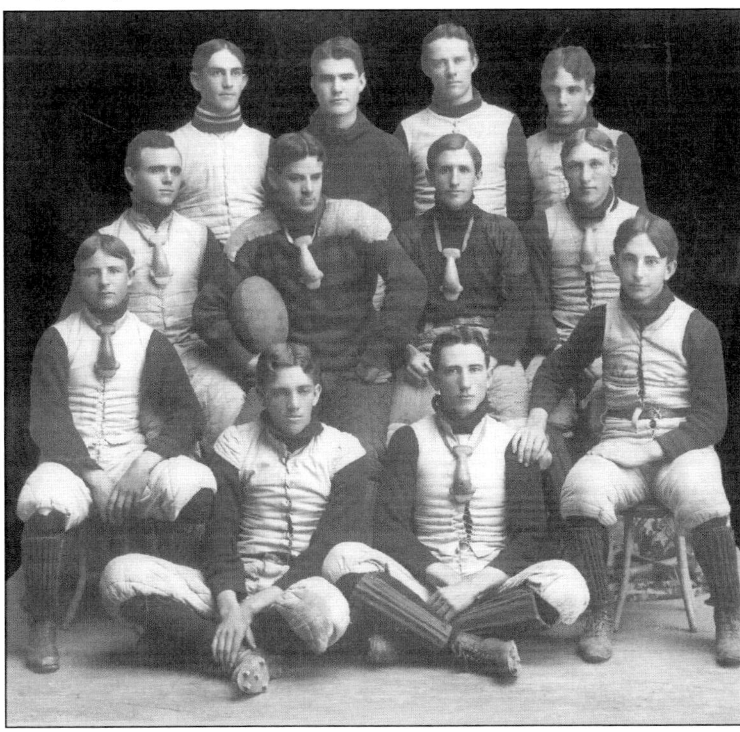

Although the focus of Weatherford College was clearly academics, the school sported this football team in the 1898–1899 school year. Compared to today, the players were lightly protected from the rigors of the game with simple padded vests and pants, shin guards, cleated shoes, and a combination noseguard and mouthpiece. (WC.)

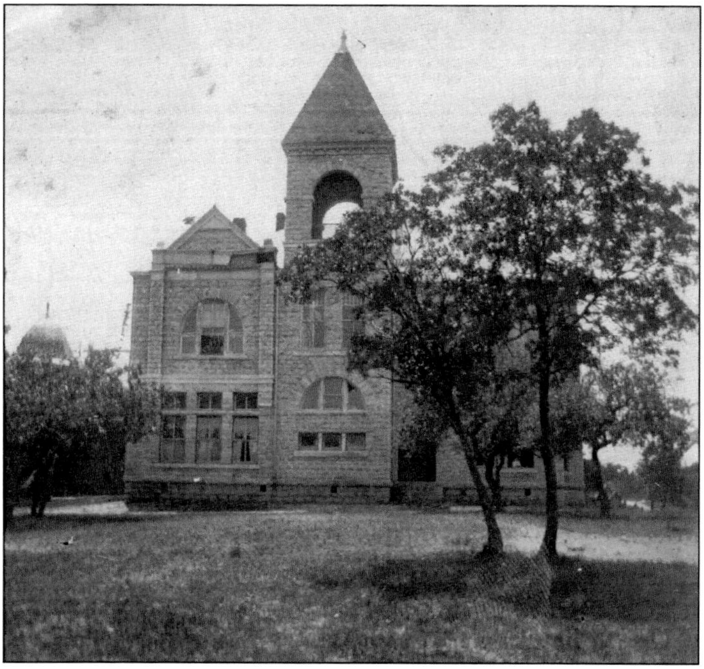

In 1887, leading citizens of Weatherford initiated a movement to establish a school for girls. Land was purchased, and buildings were erected by private subscription ranging from $100 to $800. On March 6, 1890, the Texas Female Seminary was chartered by the synod of the Cumberland Presbyterian Church. Original campus buildings included an 11-room classroom building with a chapel and cloakroom, as well as a commodious dormitory for boarding students. (WC.)

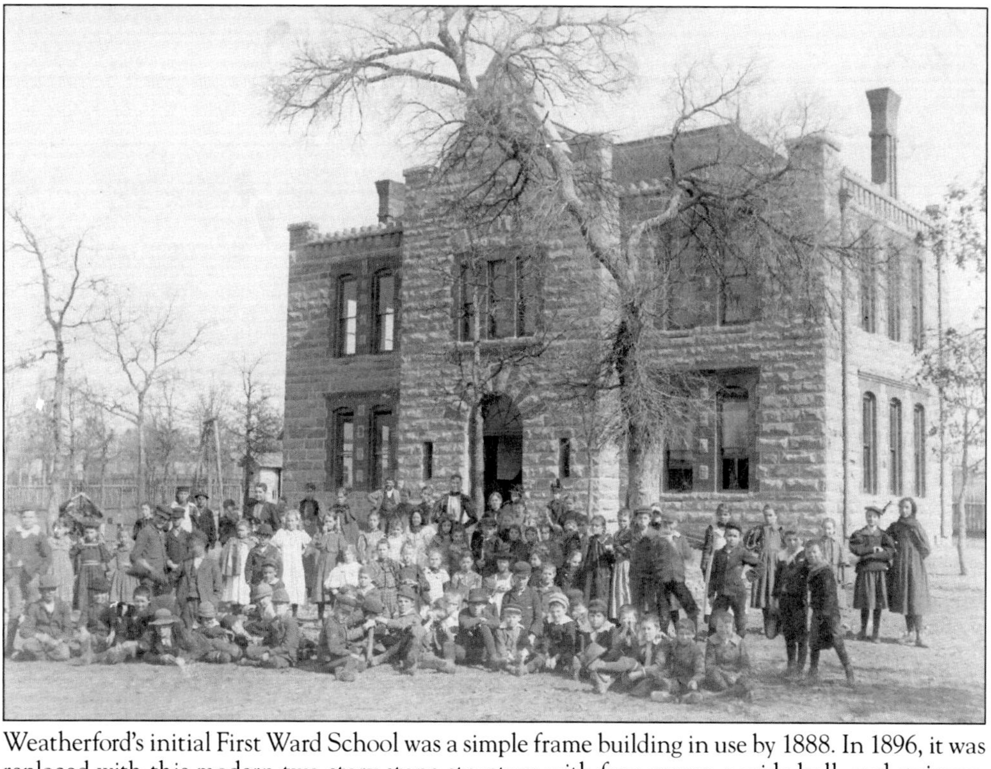

Weatherford's initial First Ward School was a simple frame building in use by 1888. In 1896, it was replaced with this modern two-story stone structure with four rooms, a wide hall, and stairway. The school was, in later years, also known as the North Side School and the James Bowie School. This photograph records the new school building, its students, and faculty sometime in the late 1890s. (WPL.)

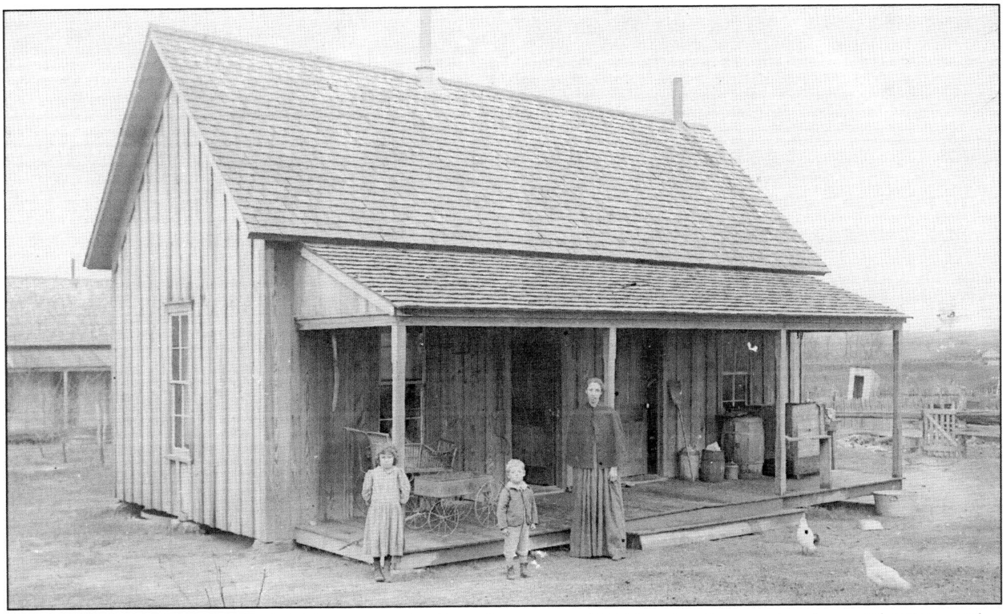

Thomas R. and Laura Sisk Waters made their home at 406 Eureka Street in the mid-1890s. The Waters family led a simple life in a wood-frame home that featured a full front porch as well as a gated garden and chickens in the yard. Laura Waters is pictured here with children Ruth Lee (far left) and Berry Lloyd. (WPL.)

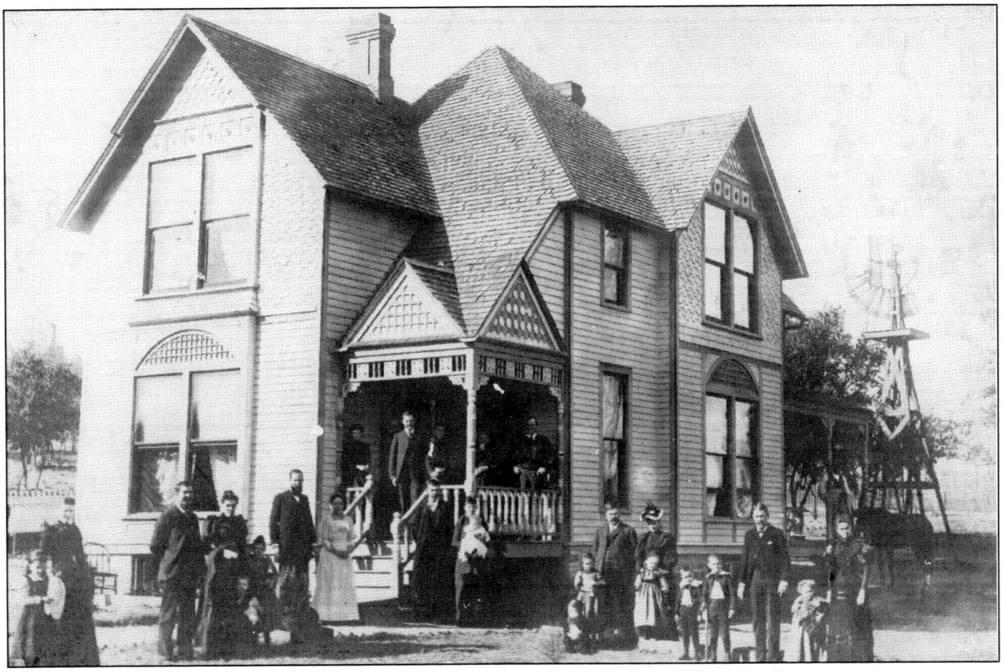

Rowland and Ann Lewis celebrated Christmas 1893 at their Park Avenue home in the company of their children and grandchildren. First-floor windows were opened to accommodate the fair weather. The couple moved from Minnesota to Texas in 1876 at the urging of their son John R. Lewis. They followed him again to Weatherford around 1884. Daughters Ellen and Jennie were among the first graduates of Texas Female Seminary. (WPL.)

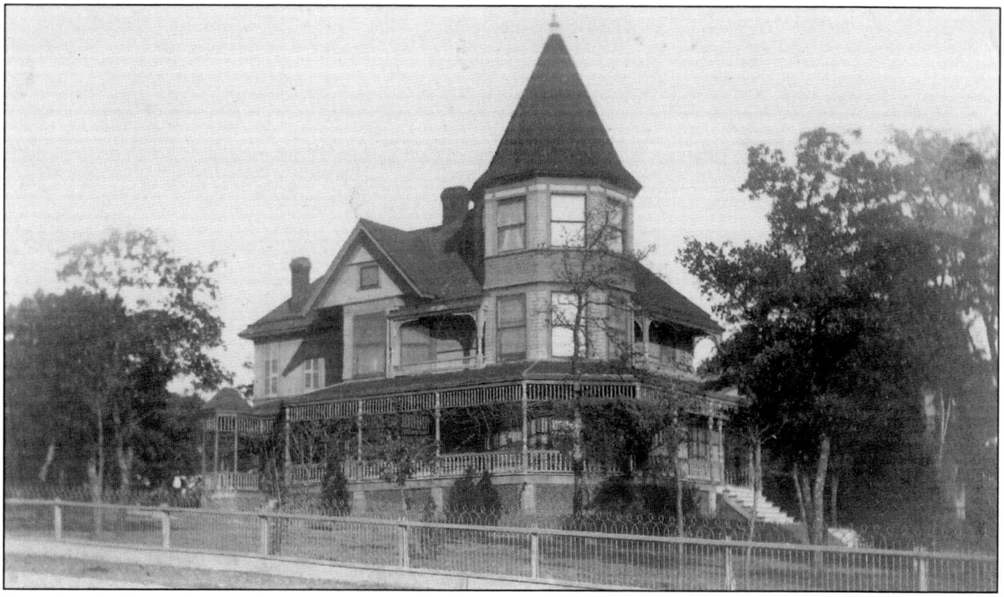

Weatherford banker and entrepreneur William H. Eddleman built this fashionable two-story Queen Anne residence at 508 South Lamar Street in 1887. Its design featured a wraparound porch with delicately turned columns and spindled balustrades and friezes. The three-story tower was removed for safety reasons by Asa N. Grant, the home's subsequent owner, after the Eddleman family moved to Fort Worth in 1905. Original outbuildings included servants' quarters, stables, and a barn. The Eddleman home shared a full block with that of Robert H. Foat, immediately to the north. Eddleman's daughter Carrie hosted a backyard tennis game (below) for family and friends. Carrie Eddleman and her first cousin Dora Eddleman are pictured standing to the far right of the group of tennis players in this undated photograph. The Foat dwelling, along with its greenhouse, is prominent in the background. (Both, HFW.)

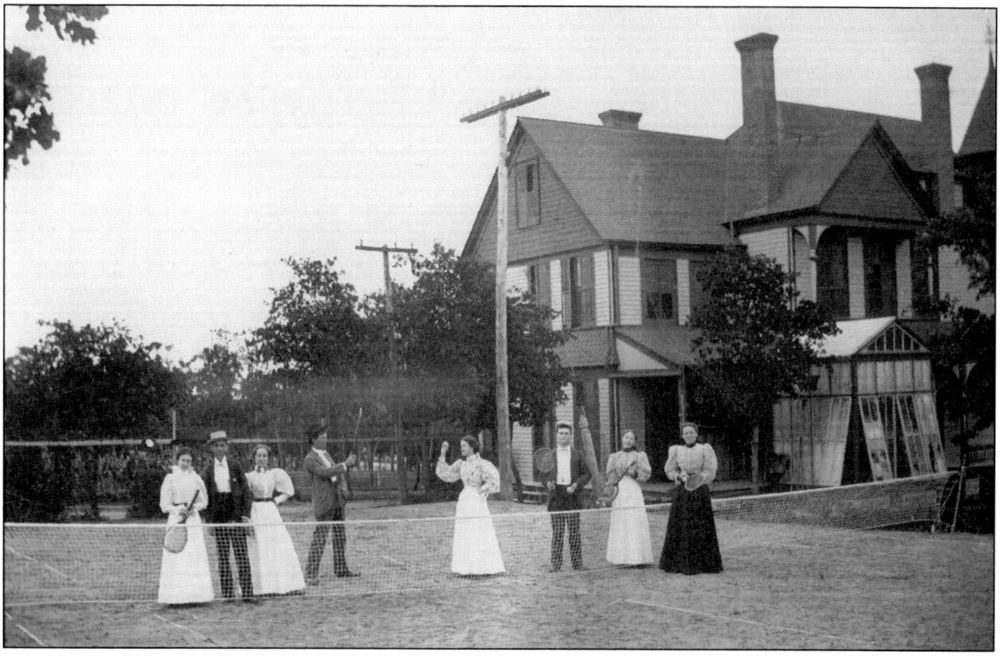

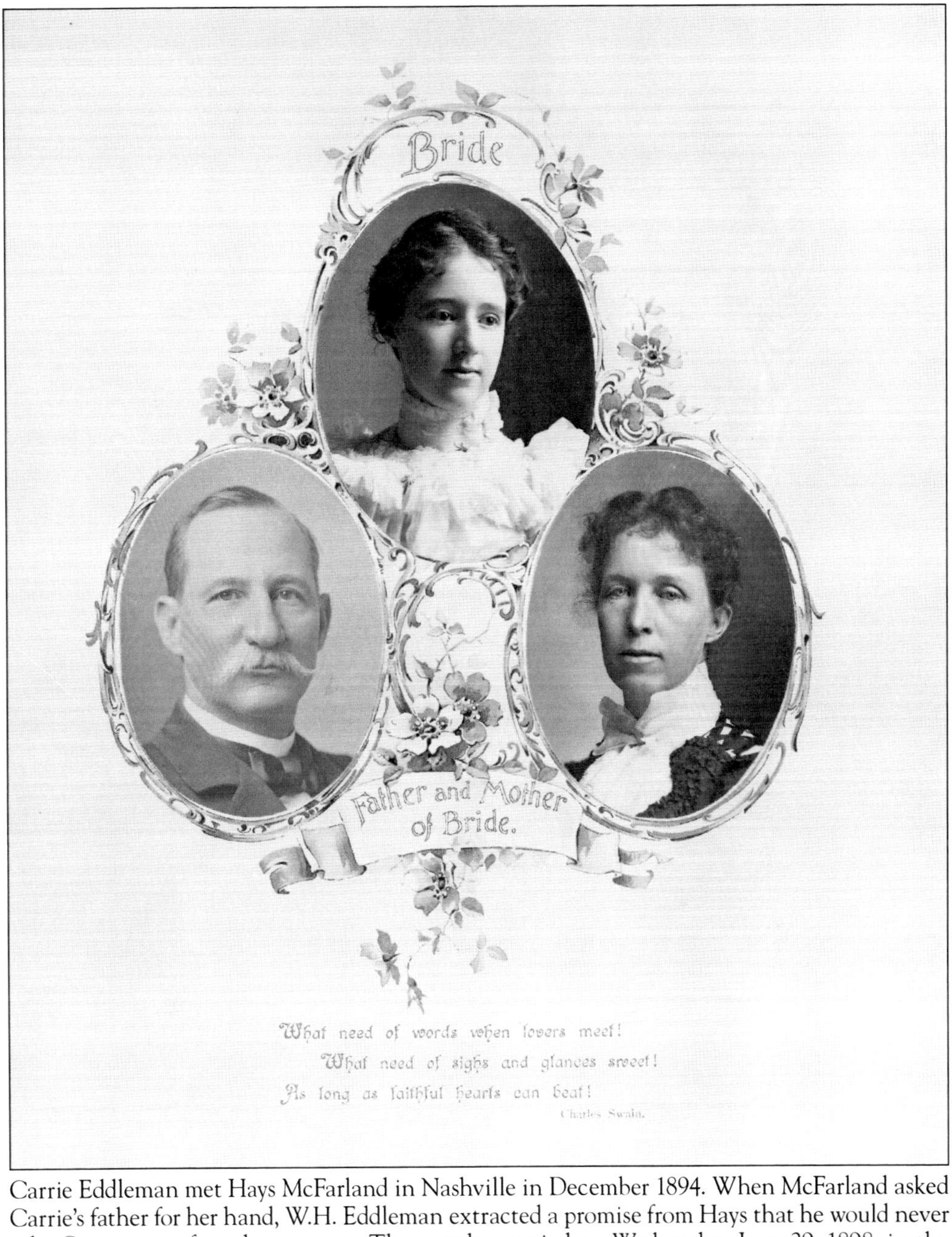

Carrie Eddleman met Hays McFarland in Nashville in December 1894. When McFarland asked Carrie's father for her hand, W.H. Eddleman extracted a promise from Hays that he would never take Carrie away from her parents. The couple married on Wednesday, June 29, 1898, in the Eddleman home. A small but distinguished group of guests attended, including Congressman S.W.T. Lanham, Robert H. and Mary Foat, Asa and Susie Grant, and Charles and Eloise McFarland. The bride recorded details of her wedding in a dainty embroidered cloth album. Gifts included a silver tea service, brass bed, chiffonier, French dressing table, $500 check, and a souvenir spoon. This album page features portraits of the bride and her parents, William H. and Sarah Conger Eddleman. The newlyweds did set up residence in the Eddleman household, an arrangement that lasted until William H. Eddleman's death in 1932. (HFW.)

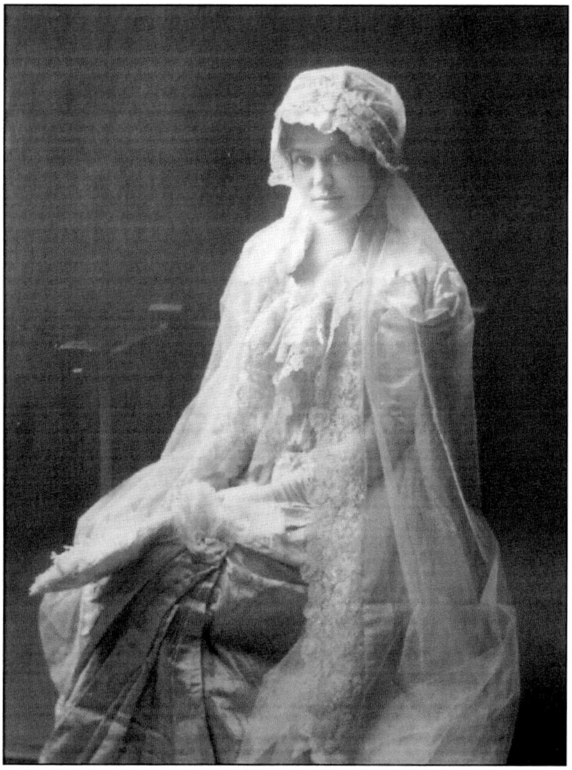

Margaret Couts, daughter of banker J.R. Couts, married Hillery Link Moseley on May 9, 1891, wearing this exquisite cream-colored silk brocade gown with a cut V-neck and elbow-length sleeves. This bridal portrait shows their daughter Hillery Moseley, named after her father, beautifully attired in her mother's wedding gown as she wed Claude McCabe Maer on October 16, 1916. (CMFC.)

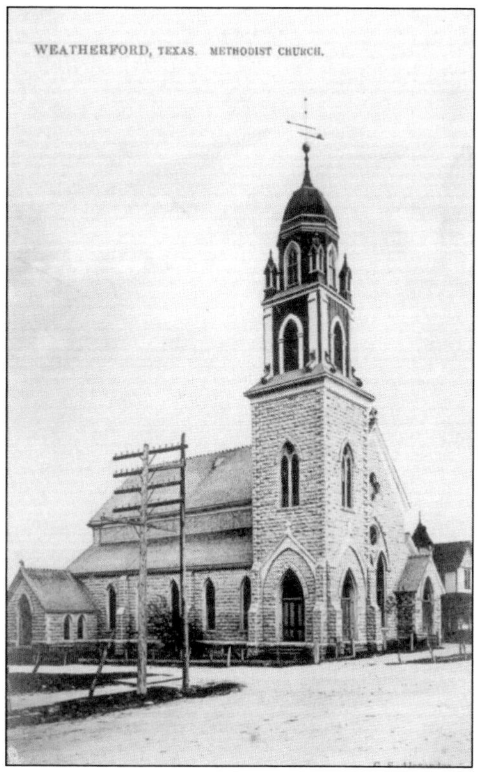

Over the years, Weatherford became known as the "City of Churches" for the beautiful places of worship that lined its streets. Churches were popular subjects for early 1900s postcards, such as the one pictured here and the two on page 45. First Methodist Church, designed by Weatherford architect George Godfrey, was established in 1889 but not completed until 1891, since the congregation did not want to incur any debt. Located at 301 South Main Street, the Victorian Gothic limestone edifice still greets its flock. (BSM.)

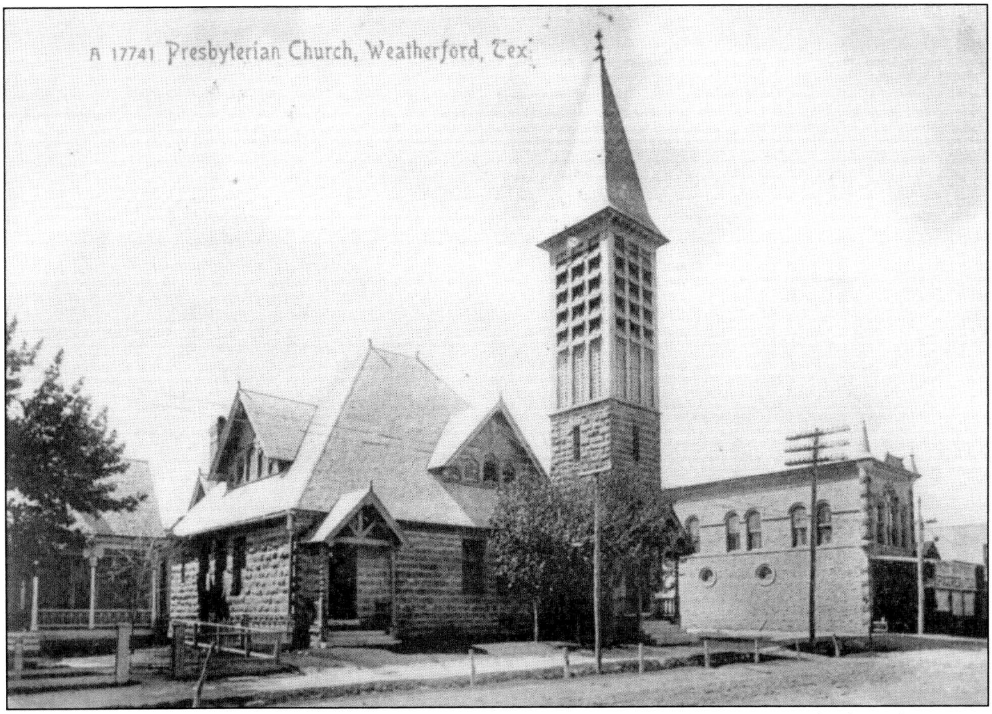

First Presbyterian Church, located at 200 South Main Street, was constructed of sandstone in 1896. Designed by Los Angeles architect L.B. Volk, it utilized an Akron floor plan that allowed flexible seating. The statuesque steeple was lowered after suffering repeated lightning strikes. Across Oak Street to the north is the Masonic Lodge building, the meeting place of the Phoenix Masonic Lodge No. 275 from 1891 until 1987. (BSM.)

The First Baptist Church, organized in 1856, has worshipped on the block bounded by Church, Alamo, Palo Pinto, and Waco Streets since the early 1870s. A small frame church with bell cupola, constructed at Alamo and Church, was the first edifice. From 1896 to 1959, this rock building facing Palo Pinto Street at Alamo, housed the congregation. A parsonage and tabernacle were also erected on the block. (BSM.)

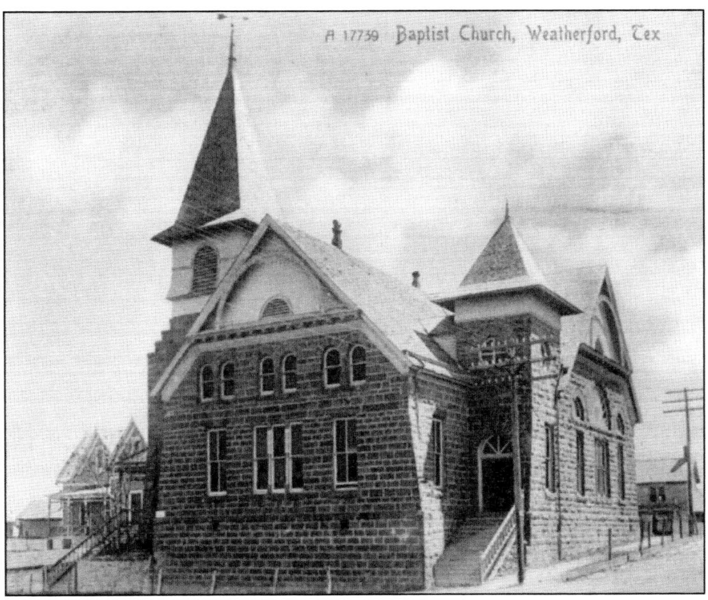

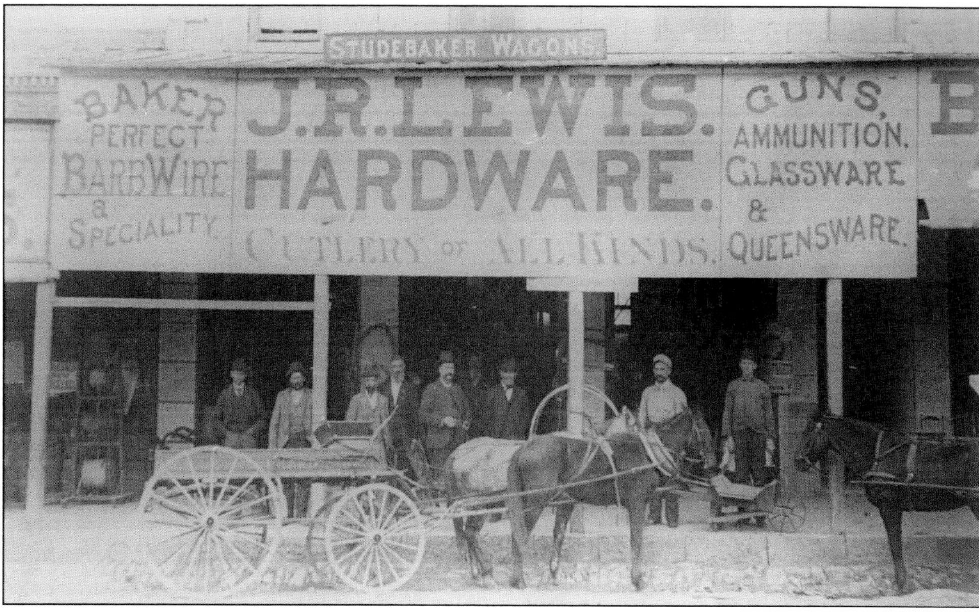

During the first years John R. Lewis spent in Texas, he worked as a cowboy, drilled water wells for the railroads, and ginned cotton. When he moved to Weatherford in 1884, he tried his hand as a tinsmith before adding hardware to his stock and commencing business at 120 North Main Street in 1885. Lewis prospered and became one of the major hardware merchants in the city. Like many of his business associates, he was civically active, serving on city council and school board and as a trustee of the Texas Female Seminary. J.R. Lewis (center, with mustache) stood in front of his hardware store around 1895. This building burned in 1901. (WPL.)

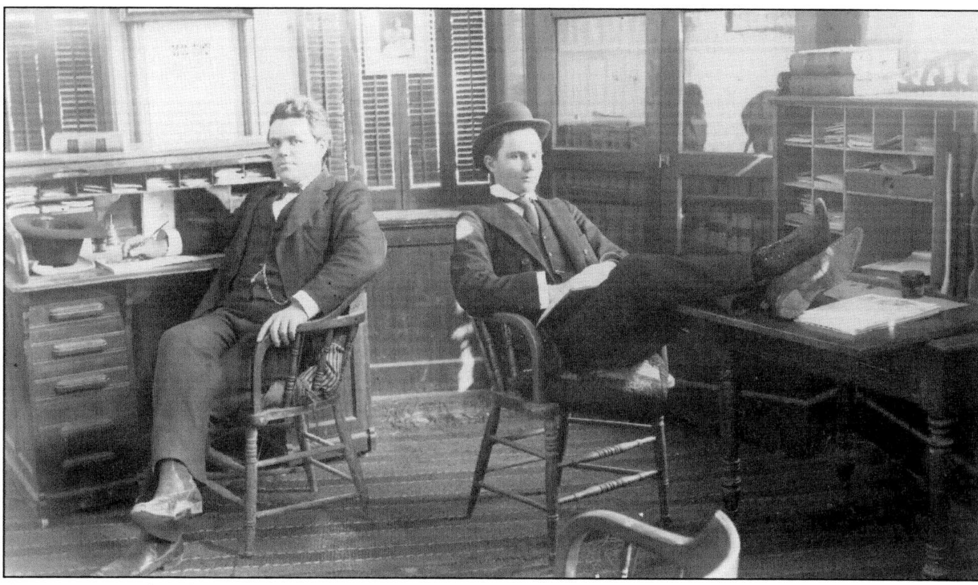

Attorneys Richard Bartow Hood (left) and Preston Martin jauntily posed in Hood's courthouse office in 1897. Hood had twice been elected to the Texas Legislature while attending law school and was serving his second term as county attorney. Martin was the doting father of Hollywood star Mary Martin. The duo often represented opposite sides of a legal matter. They were adversaries in the courtroom, but friends out in the hall. (WPL.)

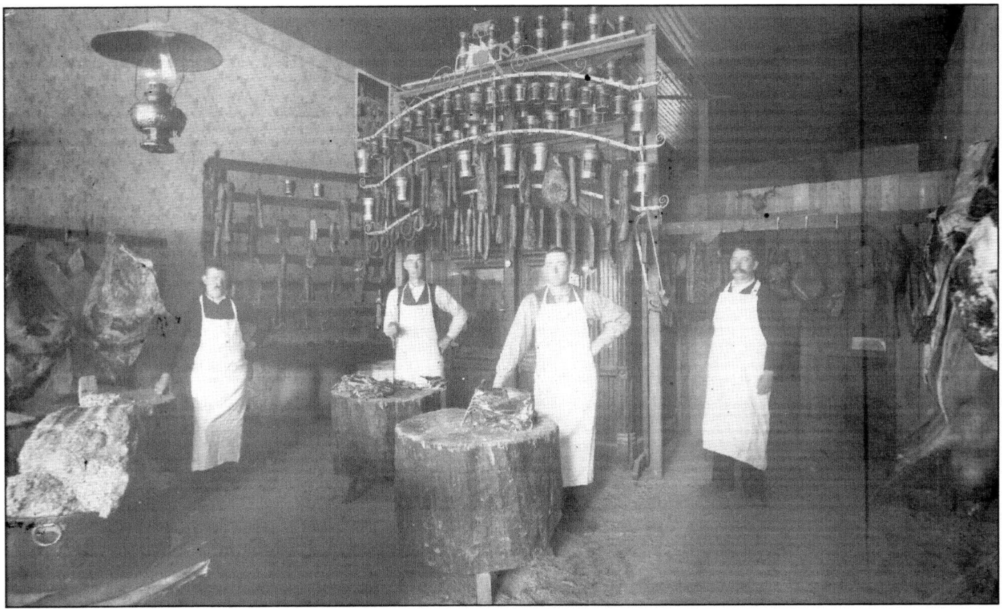

Sausage, lard, and fresh cuts of beef and pork were available to customers of the Waldock Meat Market, long in business on North Main Street. The four butchers, pictured in the 1890s, are, from left to right, Harry Waldock, Chris McCarty, William Waldock, and John Bitner. William Waldock was fire chief from 1906 to 1914 and served on city council. (WPL.)

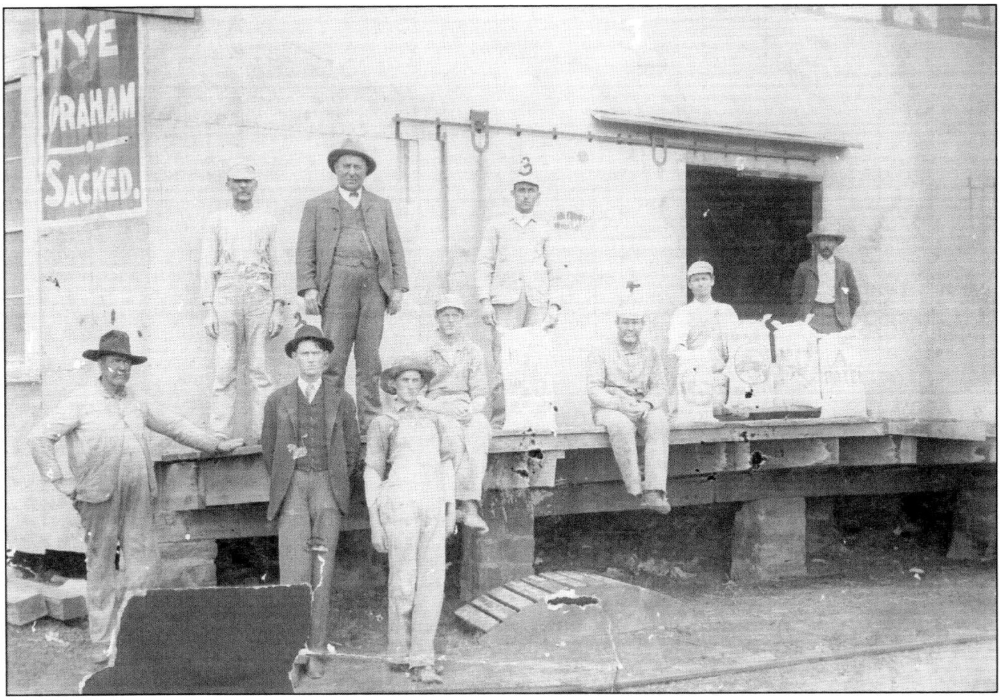

Men standing on the railroad platform of the Crystal Palace Flouring Mill proudly displayed samples of the sacked flour and meal produced by both the Crystal Palace and Parker County Roller Mills. Among them are Marion H. Darnell (1), John Frank Darnell (2), Bert Brownlee (3), and John H. Darnell (4). (BSM.)

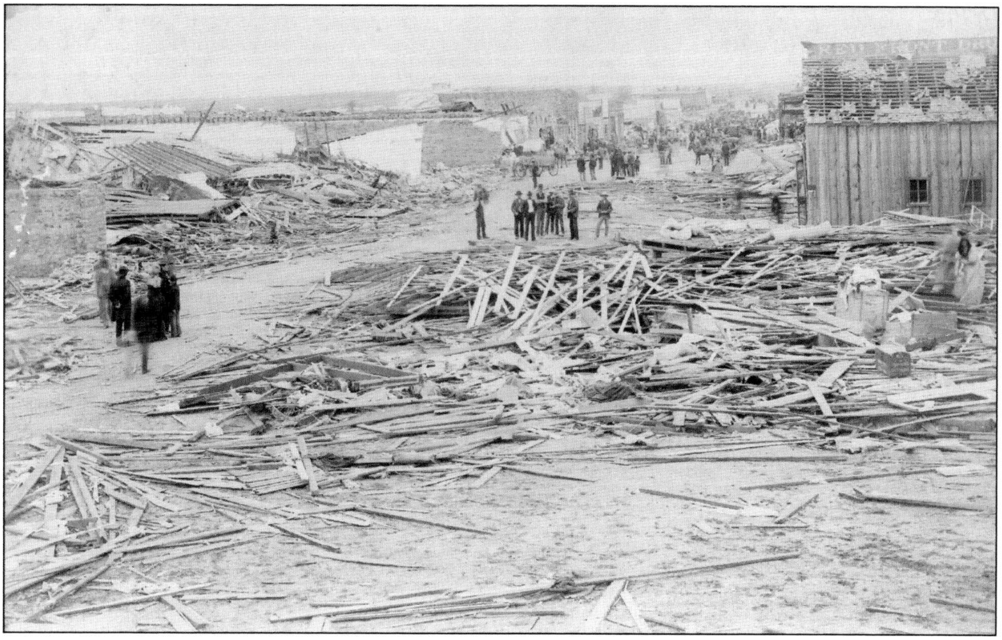

The town of Cisco, some 80 miles southwest of Weatherford, was leveled by tornadic winds on April 28, 1893, leaving 21 dead and hundreds injured. Weatherford citizens quickly raised over $2,000 in cash and shipped more than $500 in provisions of clothing, food, and tents. In addition, a relief corps of 27 men removed debris, and 13 women nursed the sick and distributed clothing. (WPL.)

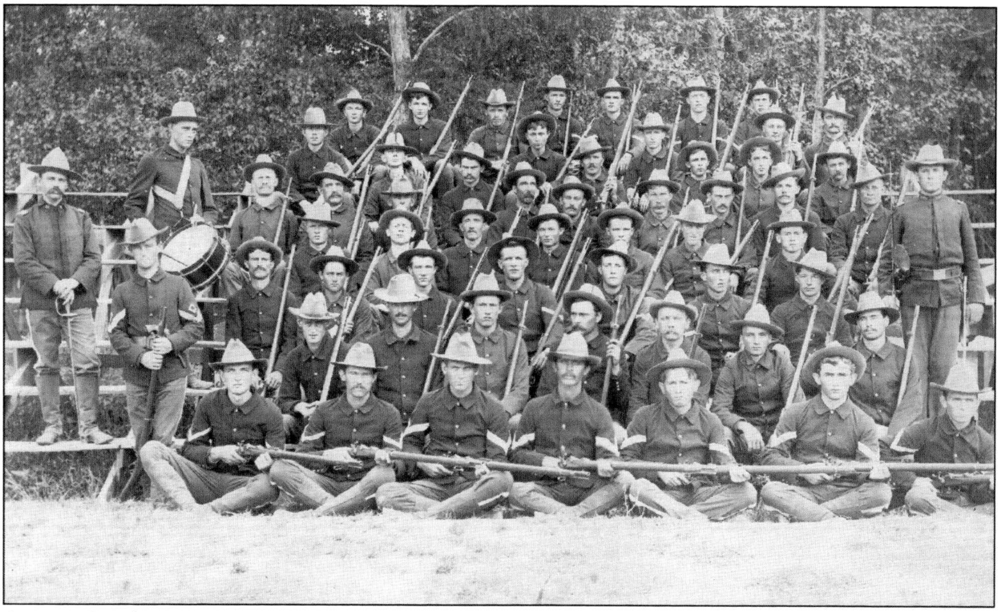

Some 85 Parker County men answered the call in 1899 to volunteer for service in the Spanish-American War. *Weatherford Democrat* publisher Hiram C. Baker, far left, resigned his position to command Company E, 39th United States Volunteer Infantry in the Philippines conflict. Before the company disbanded in 1901, two men had been killed in action, three died of illness, and Captain Baker was decorated for bravery in battle. (WPL.)

Four

1900–1909

A New Century

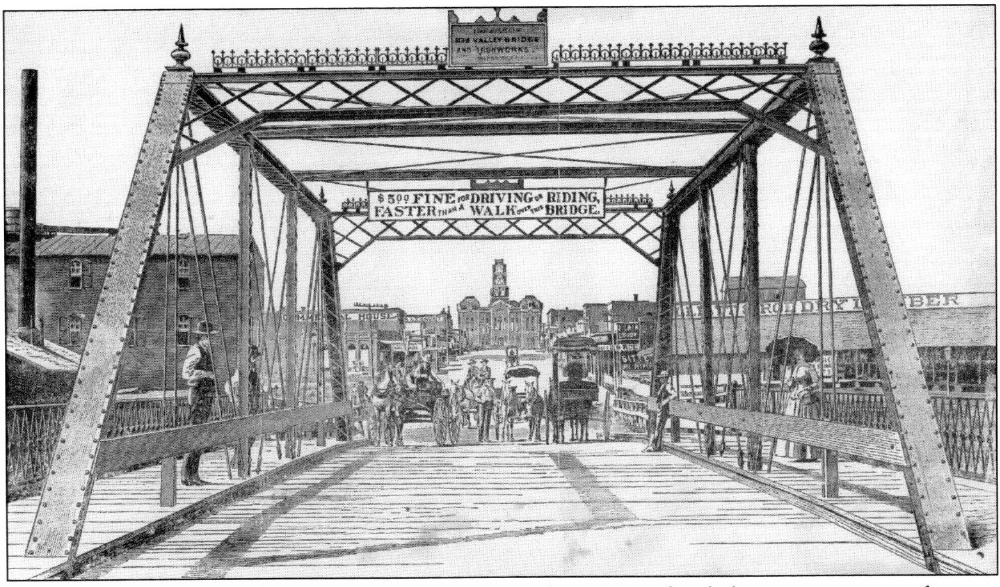

City voters approved a $5,000 bond election in July 1908 to fund the construction of a new concrete bridge on the North Main Street crossing of Town Creek. The new, heavily traveled bridge replaced a dangerous narrow chute that constricted traffic and required frequent replacement of its wooden plank roadway. The new street-wide bridge easily accommodated two-way vehicular traffic. (UTA, Roberts Family Photographs.)

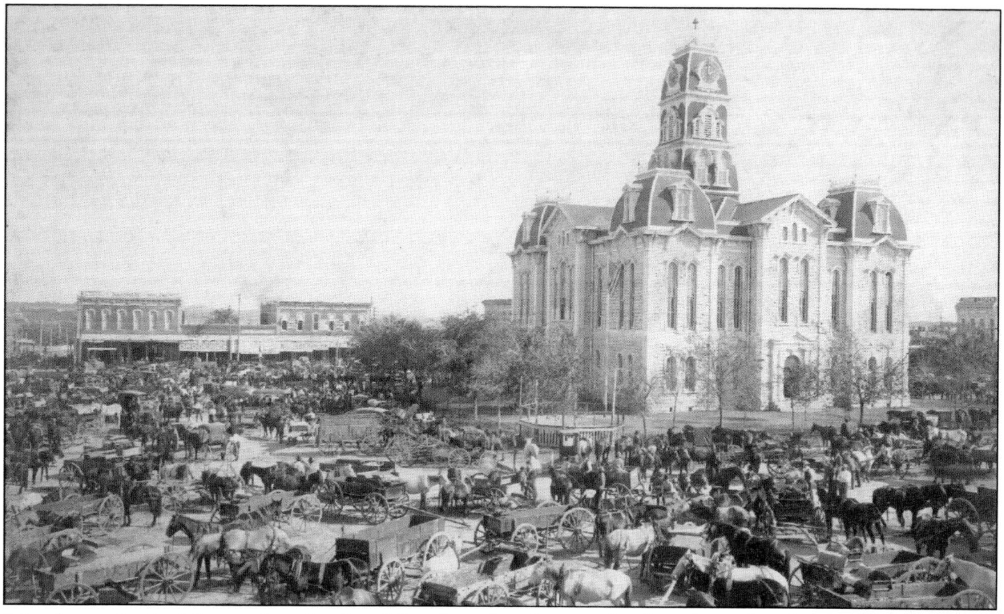

Merchants looked forward to the first Monday of each month when farm families and city dwellers filled the courthouse square to buy, sell, and trade stray and owned livestock, hay, and homegrown produce. A.H. Gernsbacher was the first merchant to advertise "Stray Day" bargains in 1900. Sale of livestock dominated this first Monday, November 7, 1904. Note the bandstand on the northwest corner of the courthouse. (WPL.)

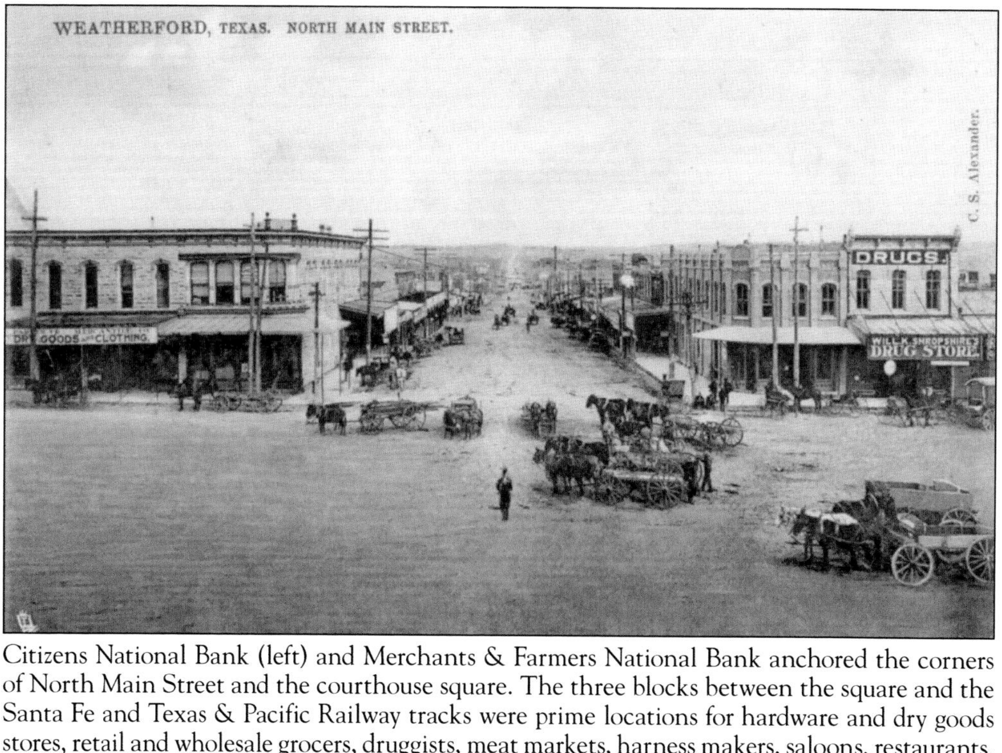

Citizens National Bank (left) and Merchants & Farmers National Bank anchored the corners of North Main Street and the courthouse square. The three blocks between the square and the Santa Fe and Texas & Pacific Railway tracks were prime locations for hardware and dry goods stores, retail and wholesale grocers, druggists, meat markets, harness makers, saloons, restaurants, hotels, and express companies. (BSM.)

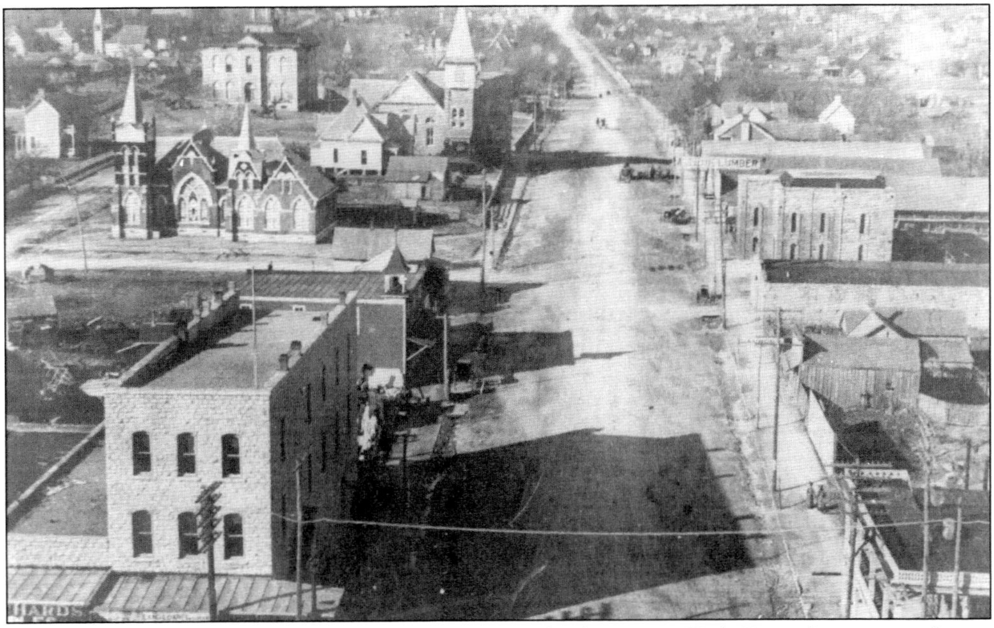

The courthouse roof provided a superb vantage point for this view of Palo Pinto Street meandering to the west in 1906. The Grace Cumberland Presbyterian Church, First Baptist Church, and the Central High School are notable behind J.B. Price Land Locators and the city firehouse in the left foreground. The county jail and A.J. Roe Lumber are visible beyond the Carson & Lewis House in the right foreground. (WPL.)

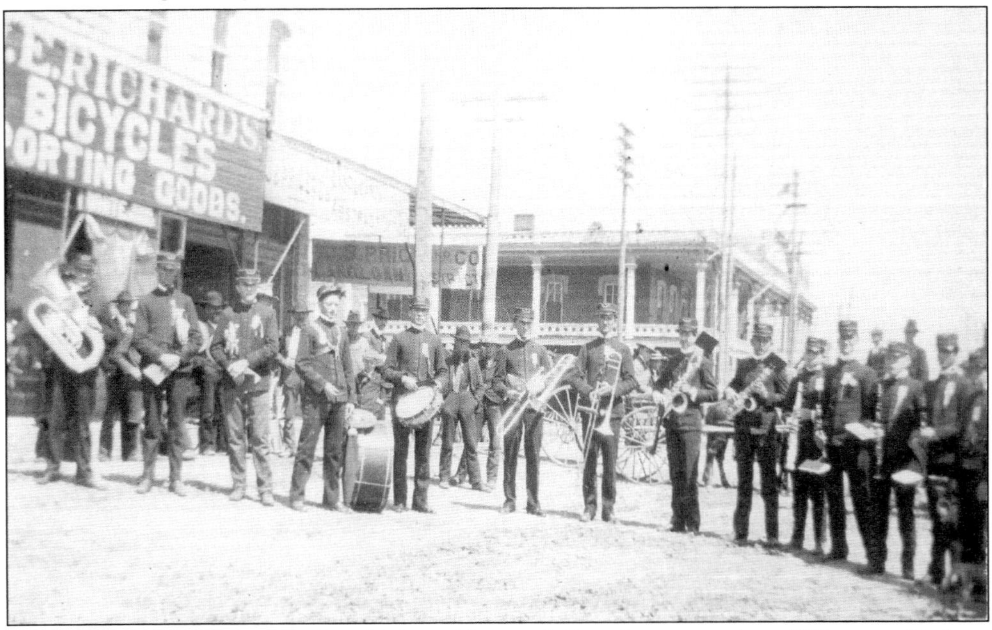

Weatherford's 4th Regiment Band, Texas National Guard, organized in 1903, assembled on the west side of the courthouse square to perform in a parade. An undated article reported the band to be comprised of 35 "gentlemanly young men" with full instrumentation, including flute, piccolo, oboe, bassoon, clarinet, and saxophone. Directed by Paul Harris, the highly acclaimed band played concert dates in venues from Dallas to Austin to Abilene. (WPL.)

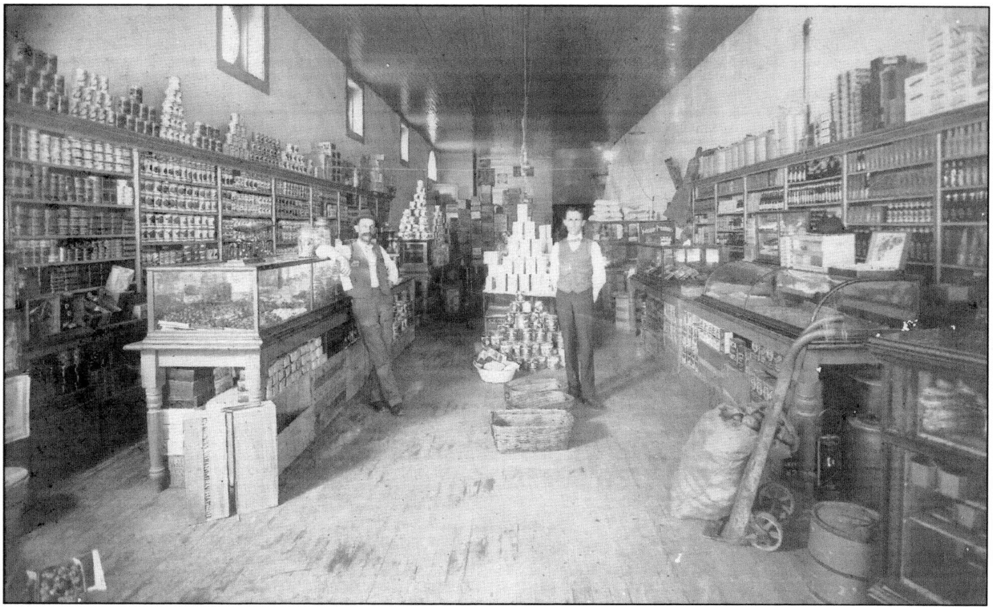

Derrell M. Hart Jr. was a green grocer as early as 1896. By 1902, he was conducting business in the Masonic Building on South Main Street. Louis A. Hart joined his brother in about 1904, and the business name was changed to Hart Brothers. The store offered staple and fancy groceries, as well as fresh poultry and eggs supplied by the Hart poultry farm three miles east of town. (UTA, Mary Kemp Collection.)

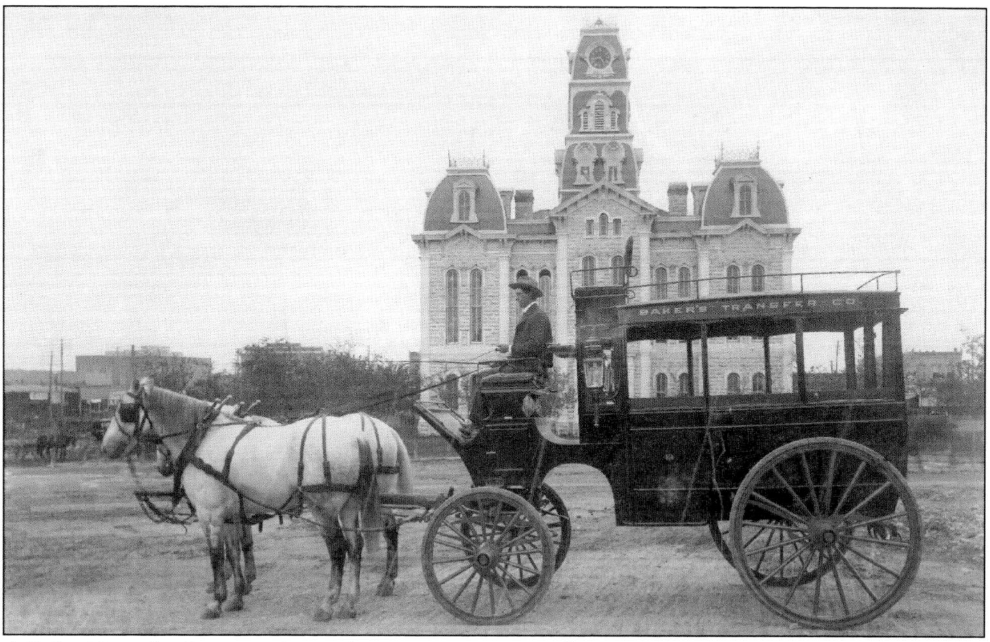

A Baker Transfer Company horse-drawn carriage awaited passengers across from the Parker County Courthouse in the early 1900s. Long headquartered at the Carson & Lewis House, the company provided transport services to and from city hotels and railroad stations beginning in 1879. The company maintained a barn on Spring Street and later on Dallas Street, offering a variety of vehicles to move people, household goods, freight, or pianos as needed. (WPL.)

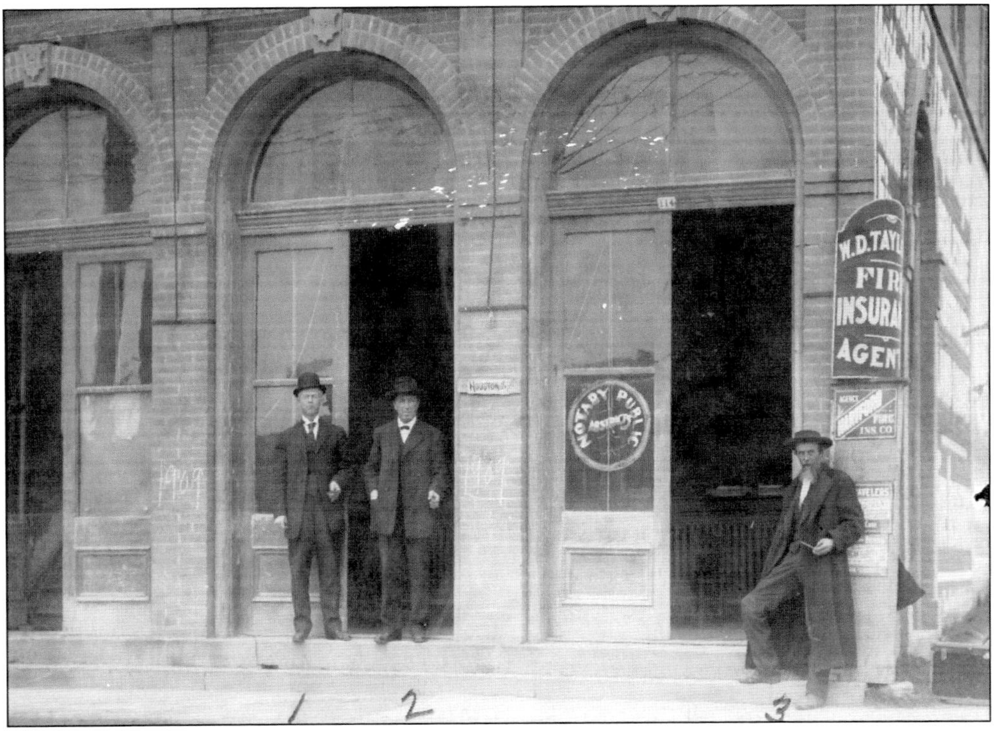

Ira Taylor and son Wright D. Taylor comprised the firm of Taylor and Taylor, a general real estate, loan, and abstract business dating to 1879. Wright Taylor also operated W.D. Taylor and Company, an insurance agency. The companies shared offices at 114 Houston Avenue, the original site of Citizens National Bank. From left to right, Wright Taylor, Bill Hawkins, and an unidentified man stood in front of the Taylor building in 1909. (WPL.)

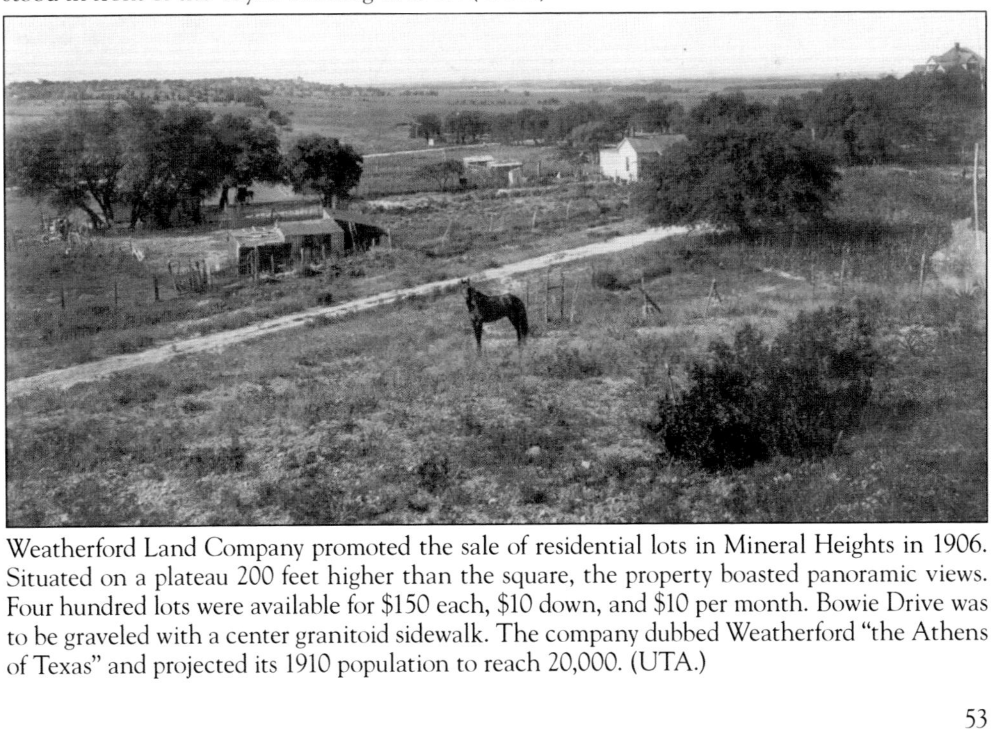

Weatherford Land Company promoted the sale of residential lots in Mineral Heights in 1906. Situated on a plateau 200 feet higher than the square, the property boasted panoramic views. Four hundred lots were available for $150 each, $10 down, and $10 per month. Bowie Drive was to be graveled with a center granitoid sidewalk. The company dubbed Weatherford "the Athens of Texas" and projected its 1910 population to reach 20,000. (UTA.)

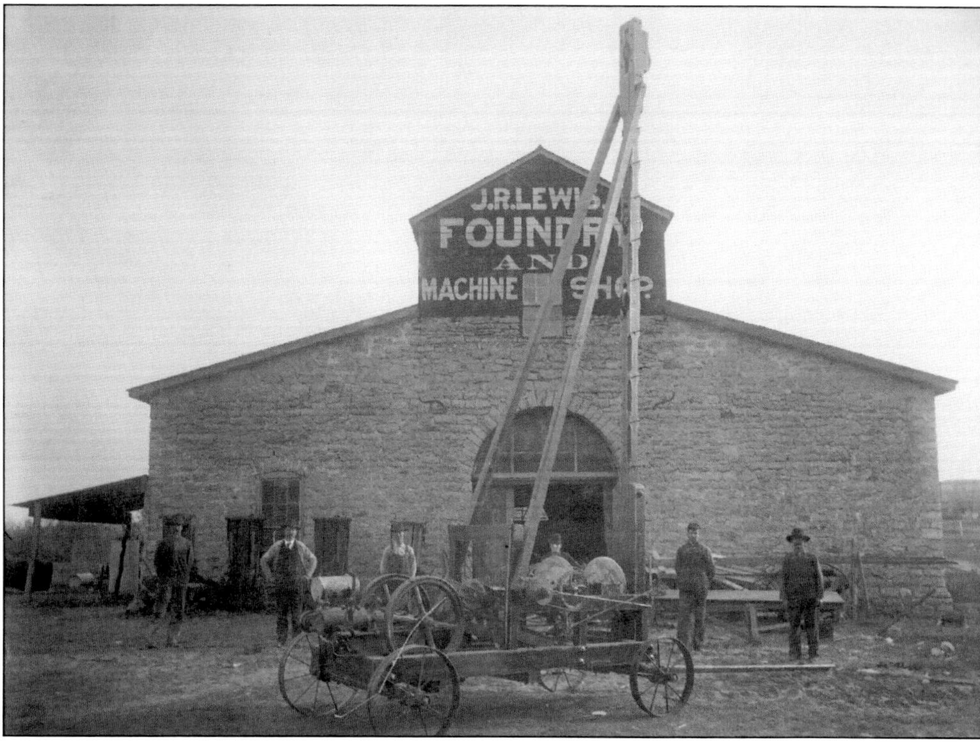

The J.R. Lewis Foundry and Machine Shop on Front and North Elm Streets manufactured gasoline engines, well-drilling machinery, iron storefronts, and weighted window sashes. J.R. Lewis, left, Henry Pipkin, and a Mr. Beck are pictured in 1908. Through the years, the building housed the Kindel castor oil plant (around 1868), the Watermelon Ku Klux Klan Klavern (around 1925), and American Legion and Rotary Club meetings (around 1936). (WPL.)

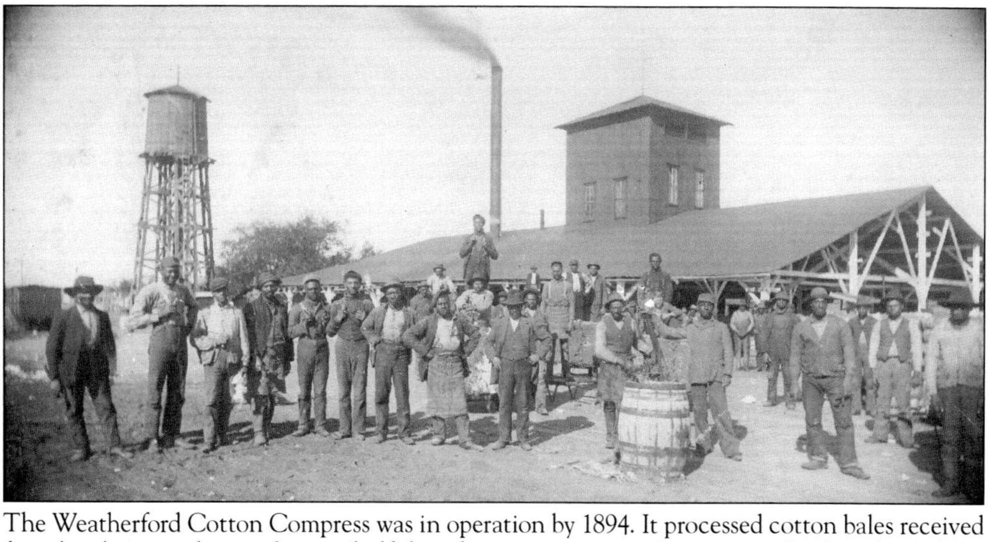

The Weatherford Cotton Compress was in operation by 1894. It processed cotton bales received from local gins, reducing them to half their former size to ease shipment and reduce fire risk. In 1920, the compress employed 25 to 50 workers for six months with an average annual production of 100,000 bales. By 1939, Parker County cotton production had dwindled to 846 bales due to insects, dry weather, and economic factors. (WPL.)

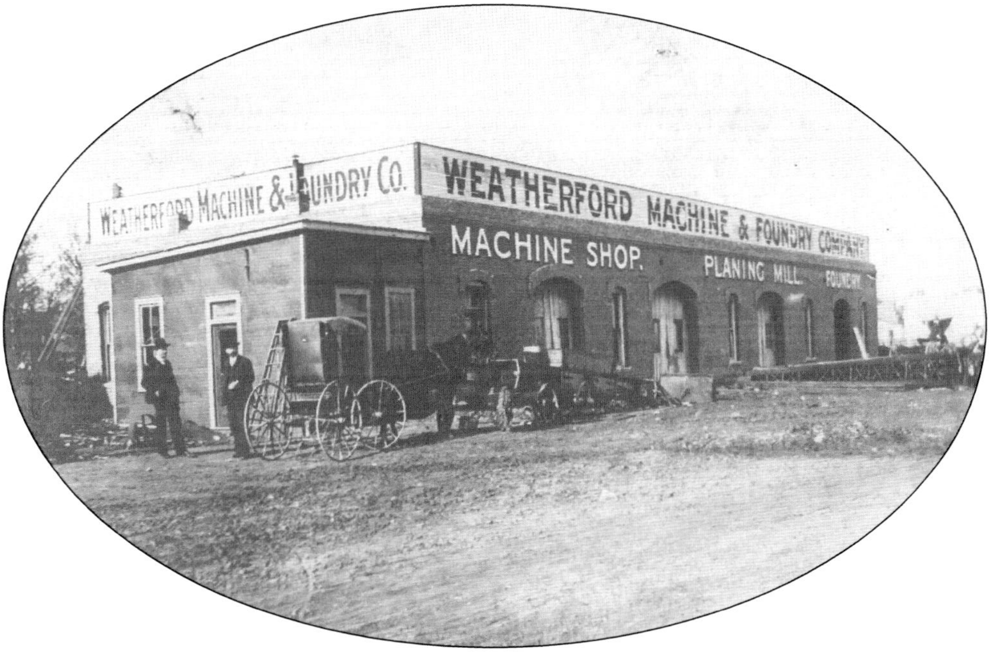

Weatherford Machine and Foundry was established near the Texas & Pacific Railway station in about 1904. The machine shop made gasoline engines and well drills, and repaired automobiles and intricate machinery. The foundry forged iron and brass castings for machinery, sills, lentils, columns, and andirons. Extensive millwork for the Pythian Home was an early job for the planing mill. Mitchell & Pigg bridges were also manufactured by the company. (MEDA.)

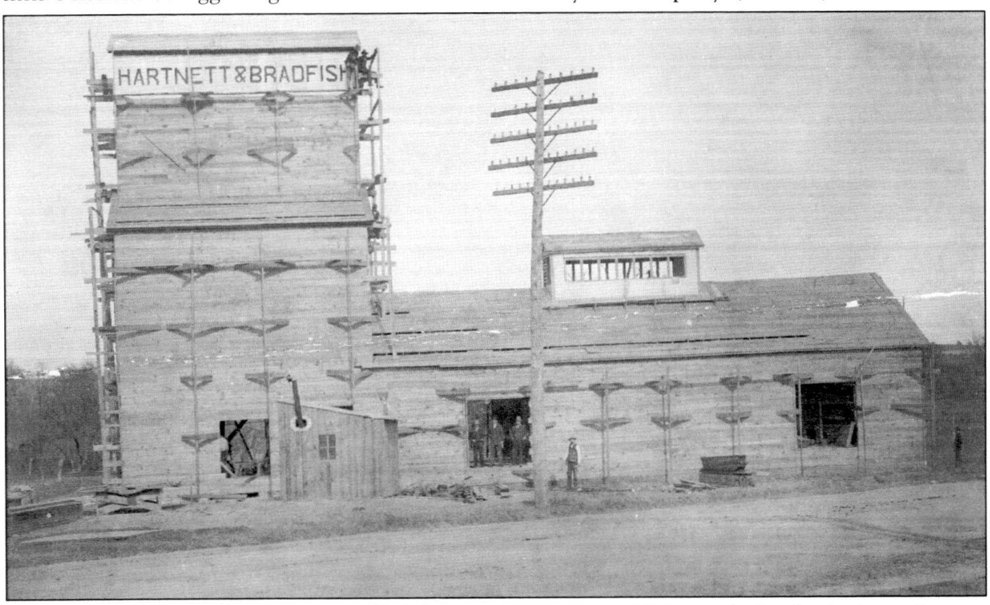

Dan D. Hartnett and Henry J. Bradfish became partners in 1903 as wholesale dealers of grain, hay, mill products, wood, and coal. The construction of this 20,000-bushel elevator and granary between the Santa Fe and Texas & Pacific tracks on Fort Worth Street was completed in 1907. The facility was rebuilt after a 1924 fire and stood until it was demolished to make way for the Albertson's store in 2001. (UTA, Ancellin-Hartnett Family Papers.)

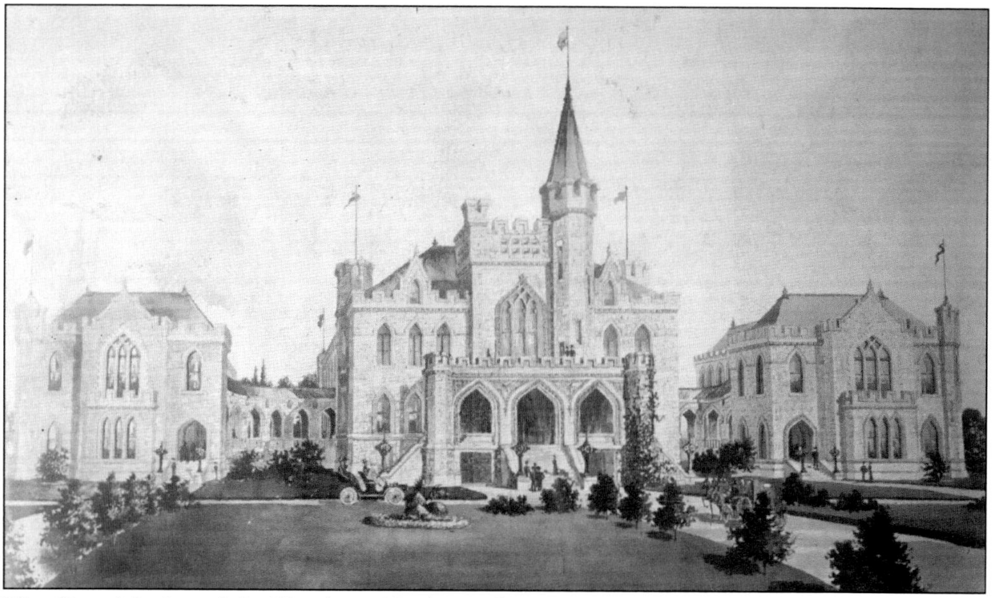

The Grand Lodge of the Knights of Pythias of Texas met in Mineral Wells from April 25 to April 27, 1905, primarily to select a location from nine proposed sites for a Widows and Orphans Home and Industrial School. Members of Weatherford's Lone Star Lodge No. 4 arranged for a train to transport 143 Pythian representatives to Weatherford to inspect their offering of a 200-acre gently sloping parcel of land east of the city. The train is seen arriving at the Texas & Pacific depot (below). When the Lodge reconvened in Mineral Wells, Weatherford was selected on the fifth ballot, beating semifinalist Fort Worth. Houston architect Charles H. Page Jr. was commissioned to design the main building and two future dormitories. The 52-room main building, with capacity to house 250 individuals, opened March 1, 1909. (Above, UTA, Fort Worth *Star-Telegram* Collection; below, WPL.)

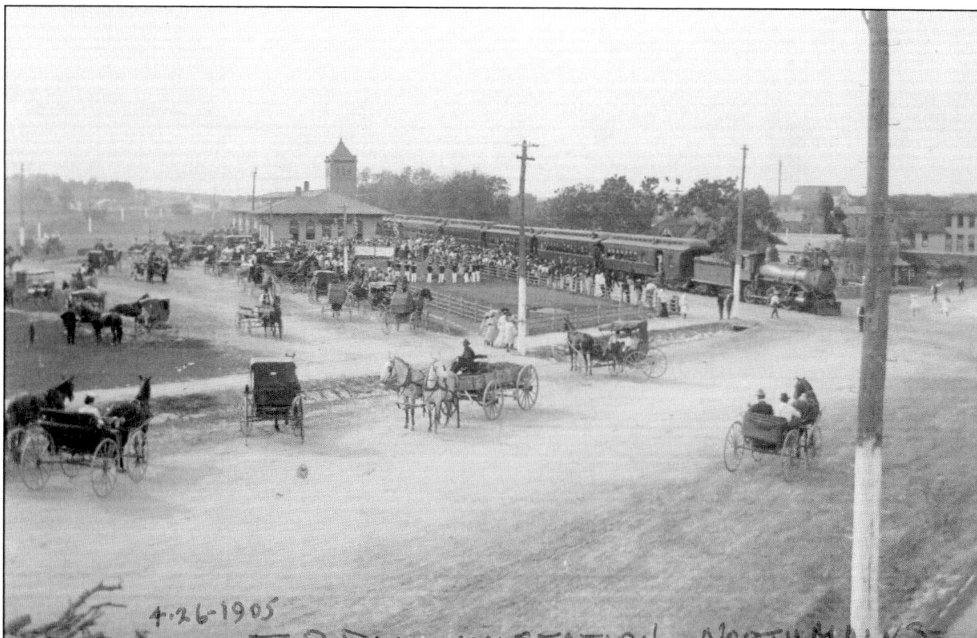

Organized in 1857, the Cumberland Presbyterian Church worshiped in a white frame church on East Church Street from the late 1870s until this elegant redbrick sanctuary was completed at Waco and Palo Pinto Streets in 1901. Designed by Weatherford architect George G. Orr, the building was constructed for $8,000. The name was changed to Grace Presbyterian Church when the Cumberland and USA Presbyterian Churches merged in 1906. (BSM.)

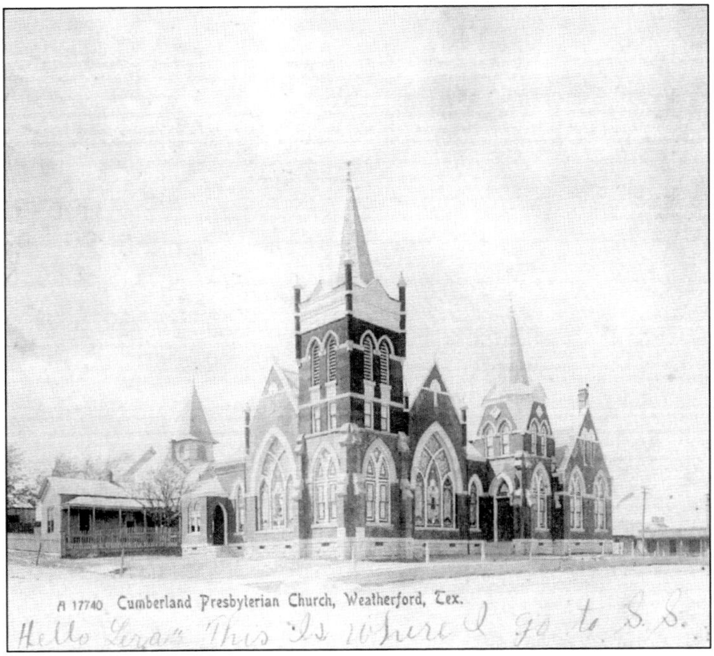

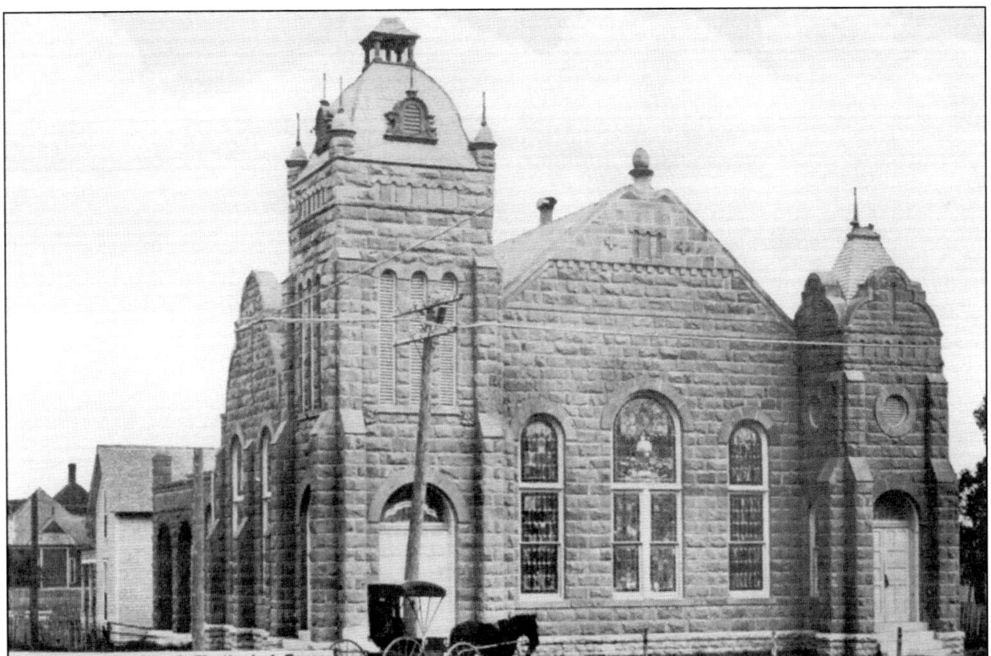

The Christian Chapel, also dating to 1857, began meeting in a frame church at 201 South Main Street in 1886. A debate over playing an organ during services split the congregation in 1894. This new sandstone building was dedicated in 1904. It was comprised of an auditorium, two classrooms, and a baptistery under the pulpit stage. The church is still in use as the South Main Church of Christ. Neighboring St. Stephen Catholic Church, at 211 South Main Street, was constructed in 1903. (WPL, BSM.)

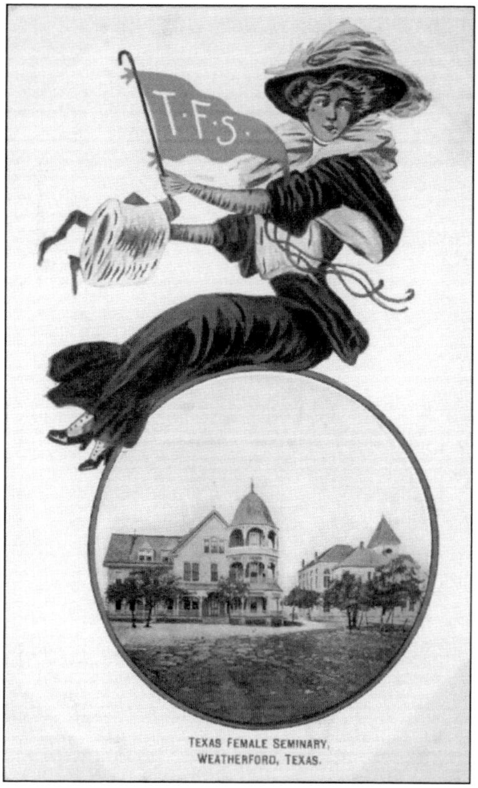

Perhaps a member of the early 1900s Texas Female Seminary graduating class (below) selected this cheery postcard to share with family and friends. The school's dormitory for boarding students and classroom building are clearly pictured in the inset photograph. When the Cumberland Presbyterian Church merged with the Presbyterian Church USA in 1909, seminary students requested that the name of their school be changed to Texas Fairemont Seminary. *Fairemont* combined two French words to indicate the school was a monument to Christian-educated womanhood. The intricate wooden student domicile was replaced by a modern redbrick dormitory in 1911. (Left, BSM; below, WPL.)

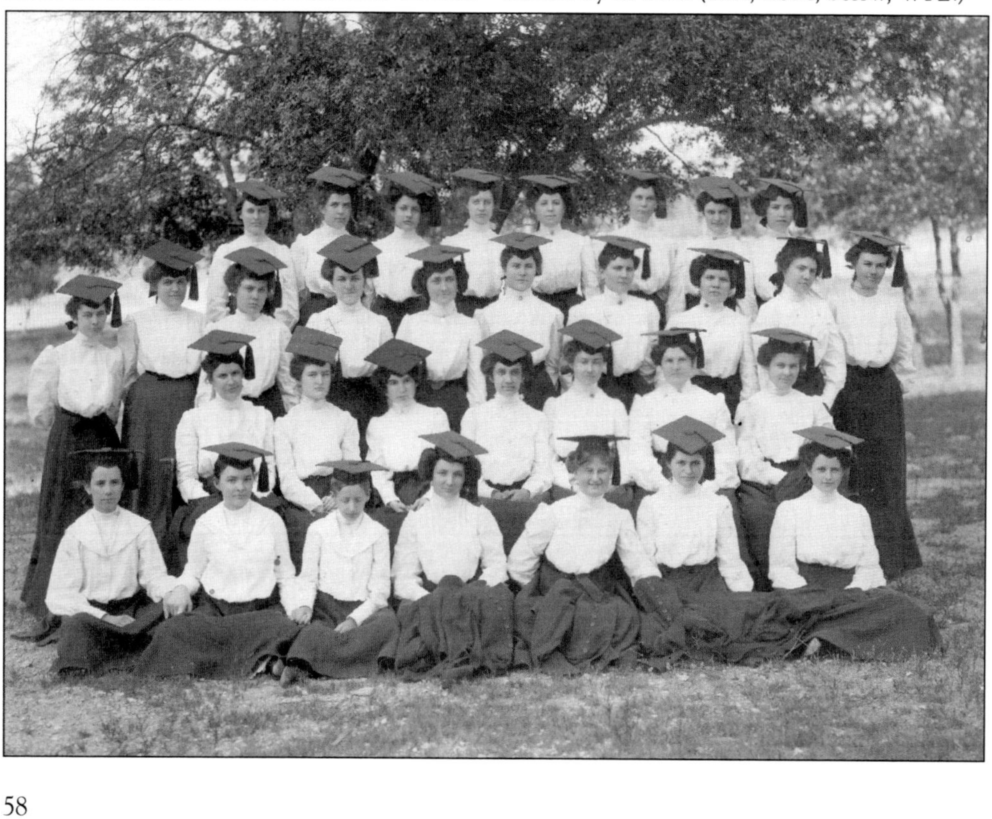

Commencement exercises for the Weatherford High School Class of 1904 were held at the Haynes Opera House on May 20. An admission fee was charged: 10¢ per child and 15¢ per adult. Class members were T.A. Wythe Jr., Robert Scott, Beulah Veldora Cox, Agnes Louise Fant, Elvie Alice Freear, Hannah Gernsbacher, Rosa Haas, Elloie Patterson, Augusta Lee Roberts, Lady Grace Rowlett, and Alice Van Gieson. (WPL.)

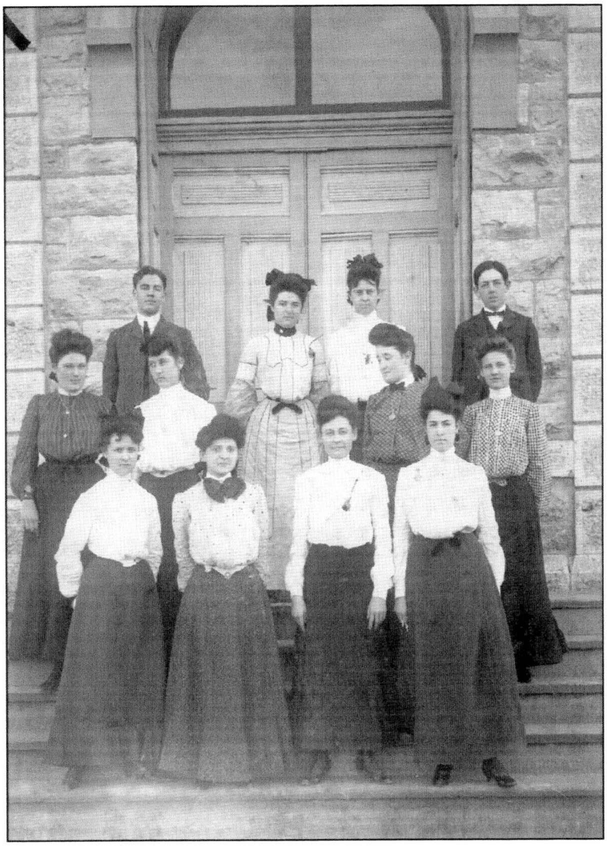

Trustees voted to change the curriculum of Weatherford College to that of a training school for boys and girls in May 1902. A year later, Allen H. Hughey and John P. Turner took charge as coprincipals of the Hughey-Turner Training School. W.E. Richards (third row, third from left) coached the school's 1903 football team. Future Army three-star general Hood Simpson (second row, far left) was a team member. (WC.)

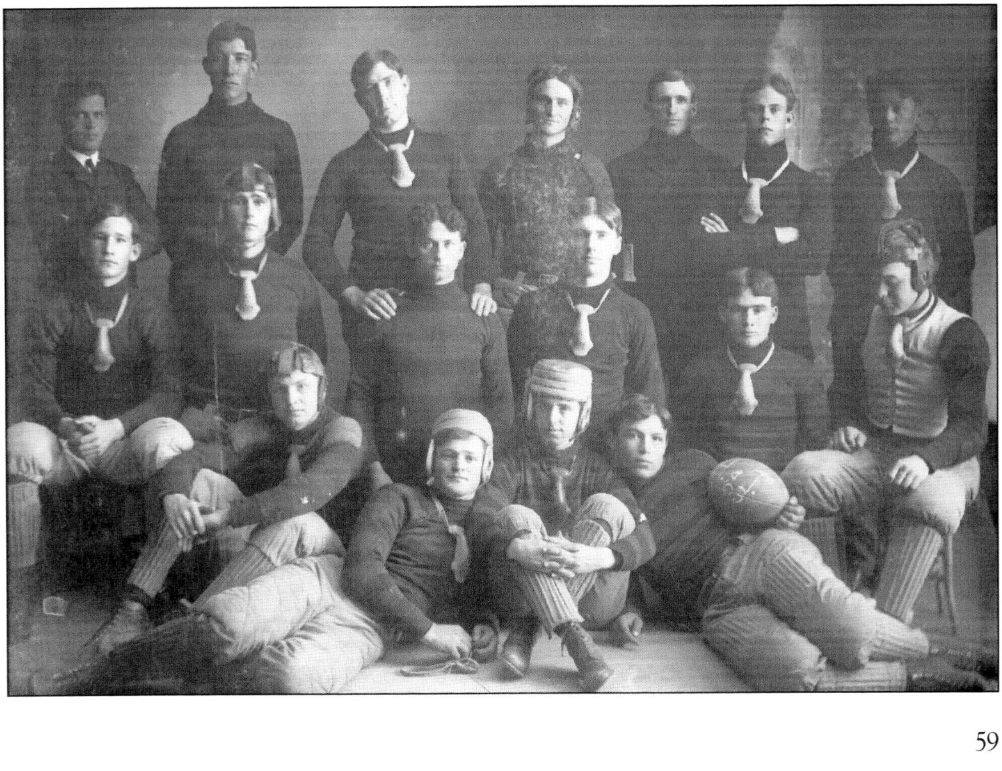

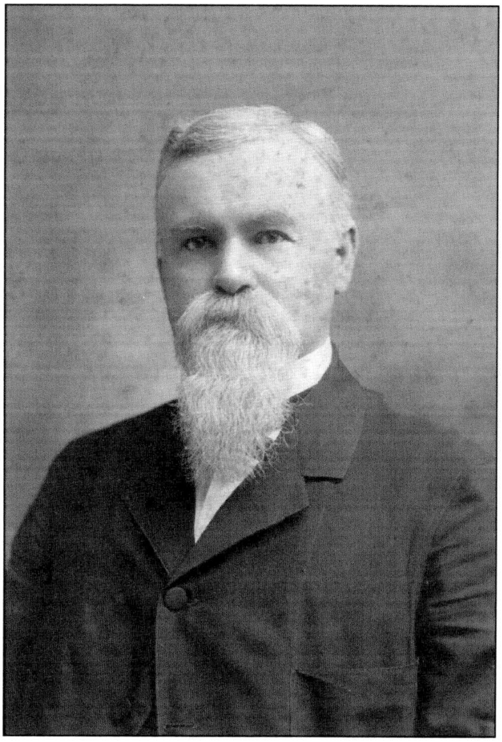

In November 1882, S.W.T. Lanham was elected to the US Congress from Texas District 11—called the "Jumbo District" because it comprised 98 counties. He served a total of five terms. Following an unsuccessful bid for the Texas Democratic gubernatorial nomination in 1894, Lanham returned to Congress from 1897 to 1903, representing the Eighth District. Congressman Lanham addressed issues such as cattlemen interests, Indian depredation claims, and state and international boundary questions. In 1902, Lanham succeeded in his gubernatorial bid. He served two terms as governor, from 1903 to 1907, and was the last Confederate veteran to hold the office of governor of Texas. Greatly beloved by the people of Weatherford, Lanham returned to private life in ill health. He is pictured at his home on South Alamo Street sometime during his tenure as governor (below). (Both, UT, S.W.T. Lanham Papers.)

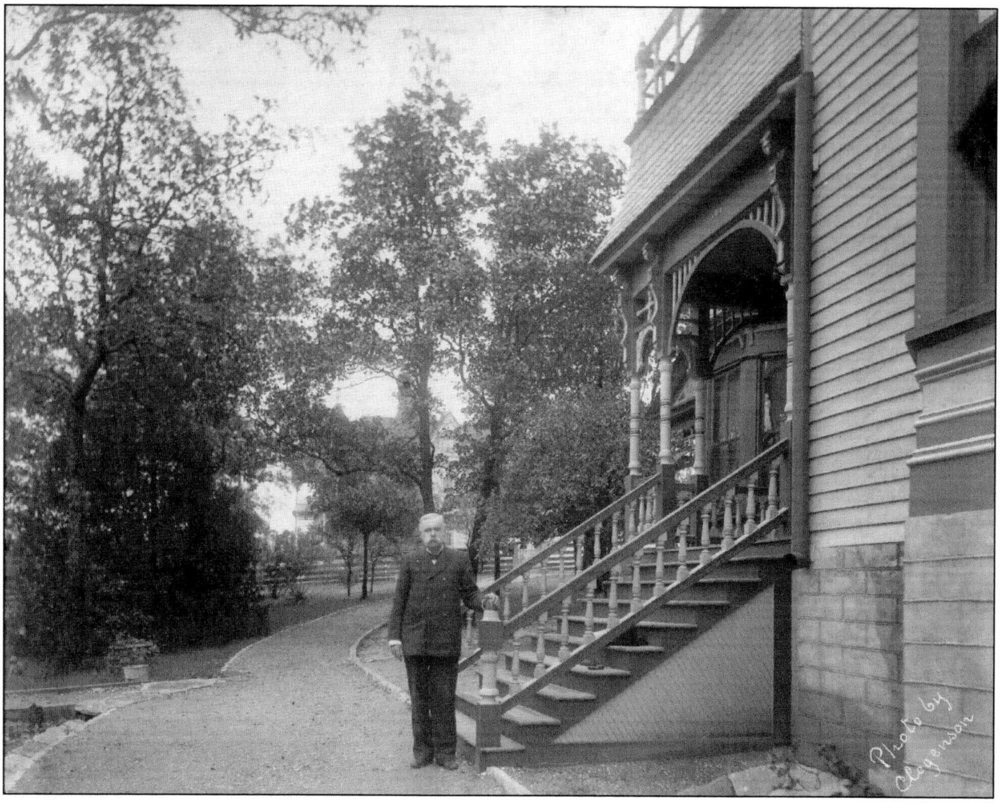

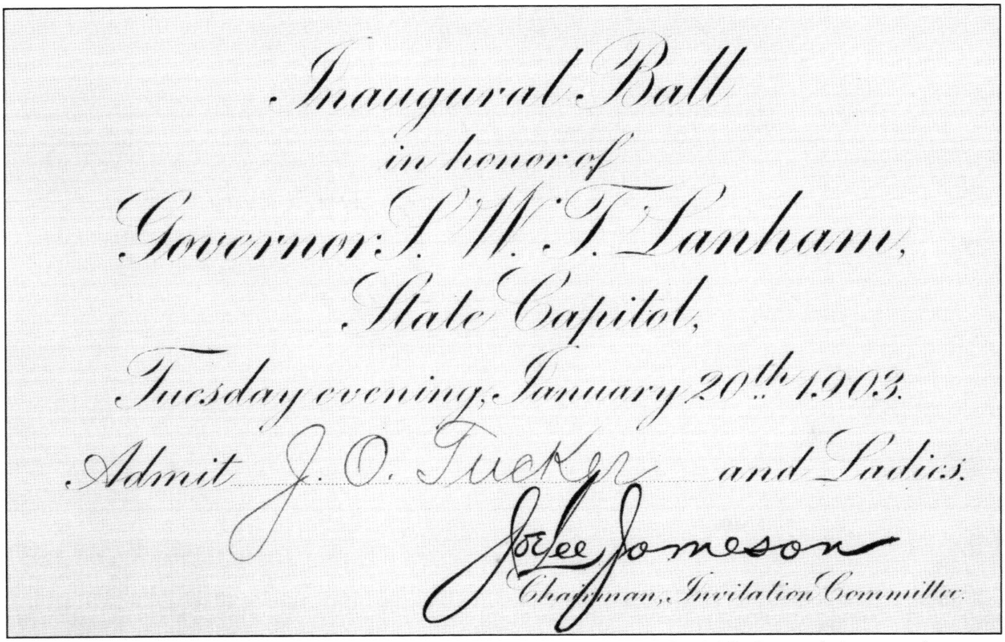
Inaugural Ball
in honor of
Governor S. W. T. Lanham,
State Capitol,
Tuesday evening, January 20th 1903.
Admit J. O. Tucker and Ladies.
Jo Lee Jameson
Chairman, Invitation Committee.

S.W.T. Lanham was inaugurated as Texas governor on January 15, 1903. Several thousand guests, including Weatherford friends such as J.O. Tucker, were invited to the inaugural ball in the Texas State Capitol, slated for 9:00 p.m. on January 20. Dancing began at 11:00 p.m. with a grand march led by Governor and Mrs. Lanham and lasted almost until morning. During his tenure as governor, Lanham presided over successful legislation requiring filing of campaign expenses and uniform primaries for major political parties. In addition, an important antitrust law was enacted, and two higher education institutions opened: the College of Industrial Arts in Denton and Southwest Texas Normal School in San Marcos. Governor Lanham is seated in his private office (below) on the first floor of the Texas State Capitol with an unidentified guest. (Above, BSM; below, UT, S.W.T. Lanham Papers.)

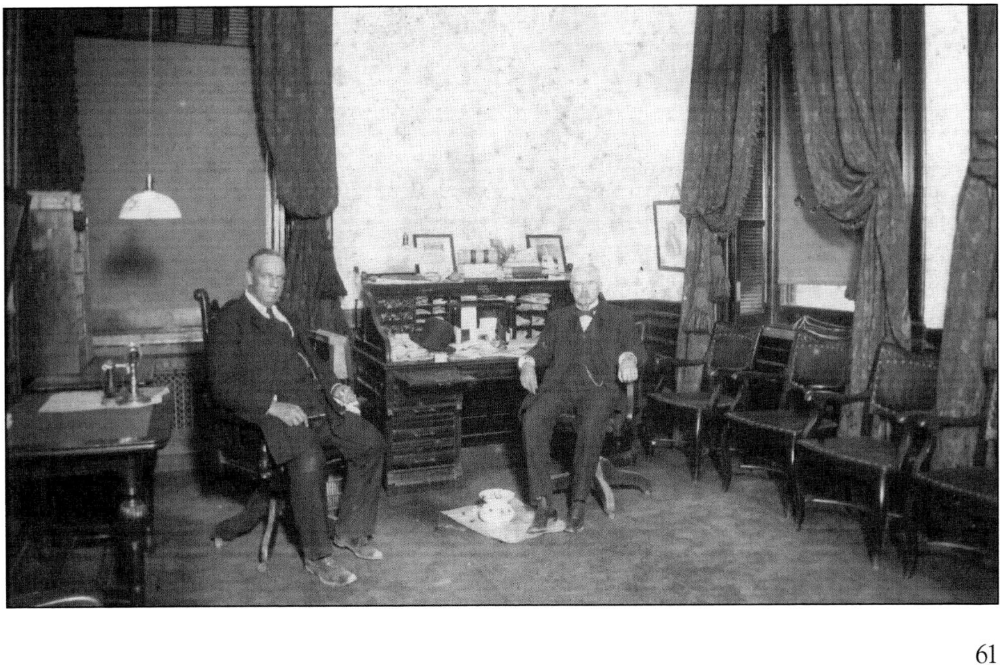

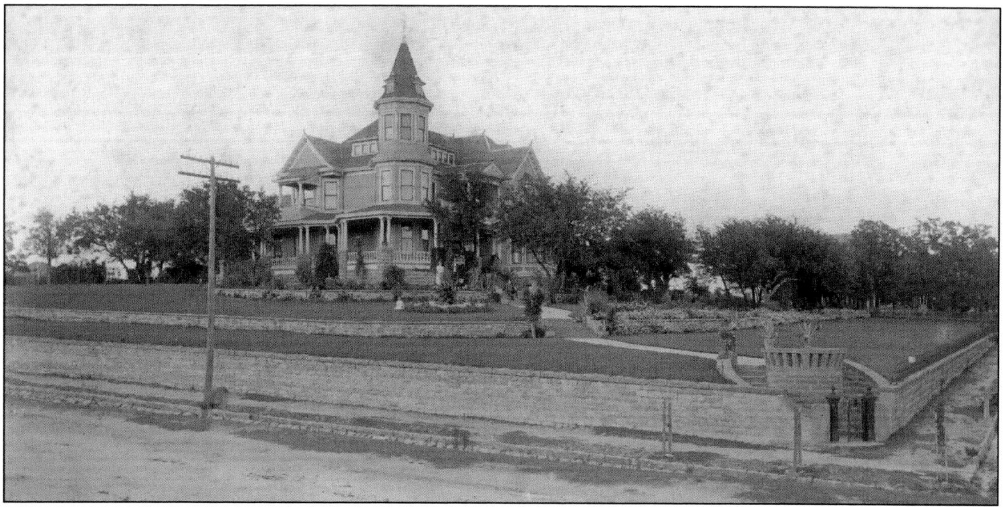

Native Scotsman Col. George Morland Bowie and his wife, Margaret, built a 24-room Queen Anne mansion on the corner of North Main and Soward Streets in 1900. Their multistoried home featured a turret-topped wraparound porch, fancy-shaped stained-glass portholes, and bay windows. Visitors approached the beveled-glass front entrance via four flights of concrete steps. Two peacocks strutted across the elegant grounds that included a terraced lawn, a strawberry bed, a grape arbor, a grove of live oak trees, and a tennis court. Family members gathered on the front steps of the house on December 26, 1908, from left to right, include (first row) Donald Bowie, Ellen Bowie, Margaret Bowie, Col. George Bowie, George Brannan (child), Benjamin W. Fouts, and Edith Bowie Brannan Fouts; (second row) William Bowie and Sallie Bowie. (Both, UTA, Bowie and Holland Family Papers.)

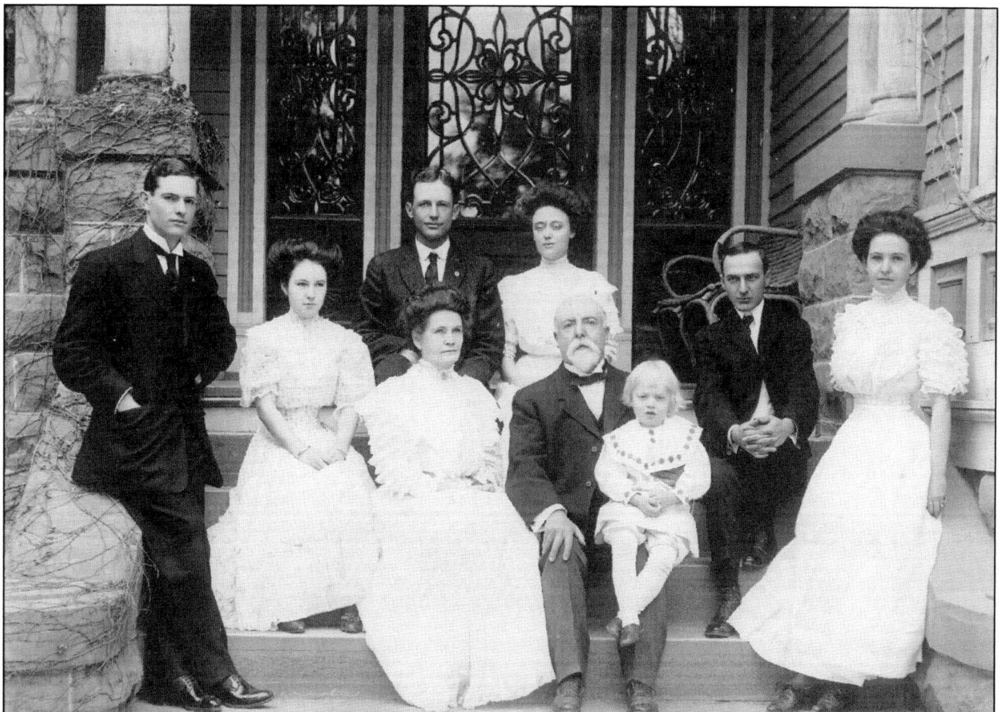

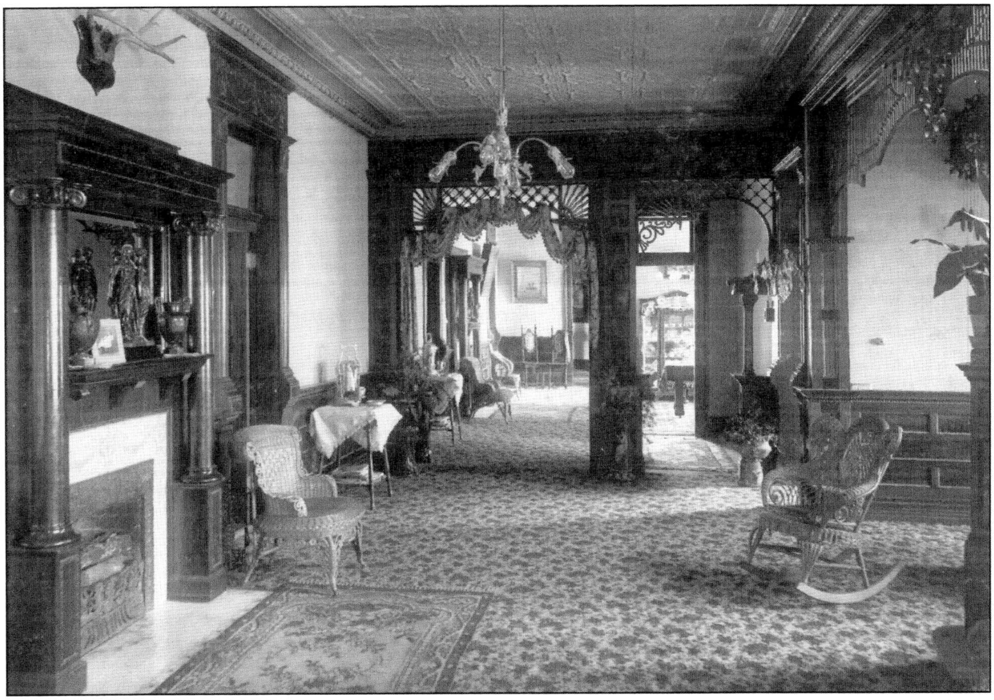

Margaret Bowie meticulously decorated each of the two dozen rooms in her new home. The spacious entry hall flowed into two adjoining rooms appointed with identical fireplace mantels, wicker chairs, rockers, side tables, electric ceiling lights, and objects d'art. These three rooms also shared a tin ceiling, floral wall-to-wall carpet, and burled cypress wainscoting personally selected by Colonel Bowie, a lumber executive who appreciated fine woods. Colonel Bowie's first floor study was furnished with a large rolltop desk and glass-front bookcases that stored his business documents and books. He composed correspondence on an Elizabethan table embellished with gargoyles at each corner. A tufted leather couch and armchair with family portraits lining the room completed Colonel Bowie's personal domain. (Both, PPHM.)

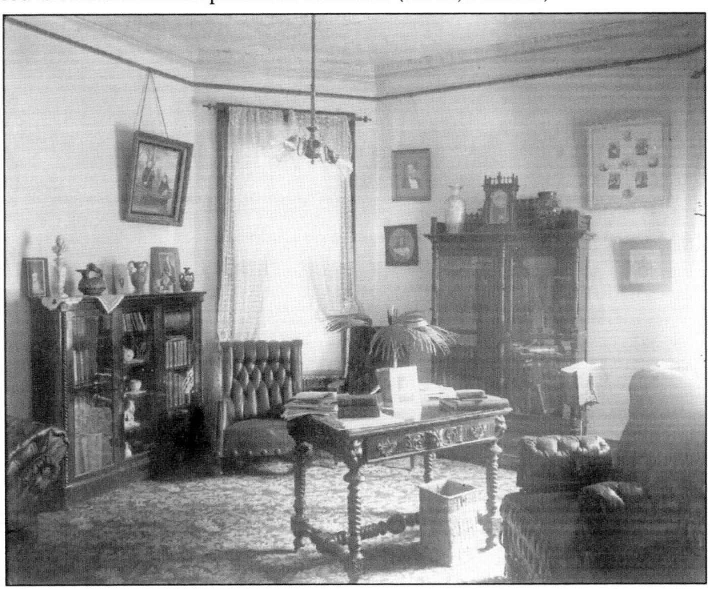

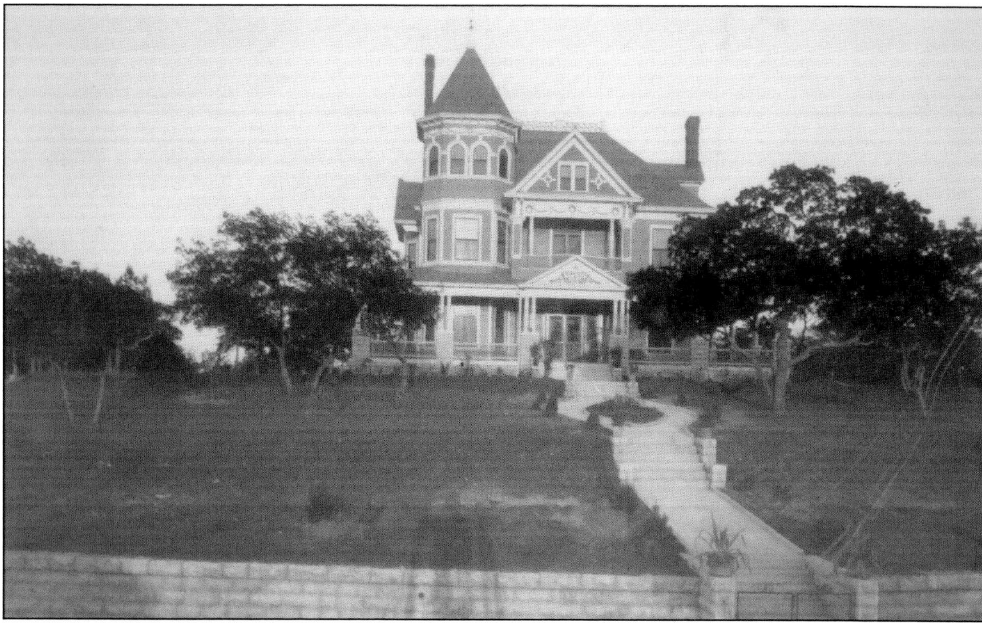

Aledo cattle rancher Charles T. McFarland purchased 23.4 acres just south of Weatherford in 1901. He designed and built an impressive 22-room, three-story Queen Anne home poised atop a prominent hill. McFarland, his wife, the former Eloise McAfee, and their seven children occupied the house in 1902, a move made necessary so that the older children (including boys) could attend the neighboring Texas Female Seminary. (DHCC, McFarland Family Papers.)

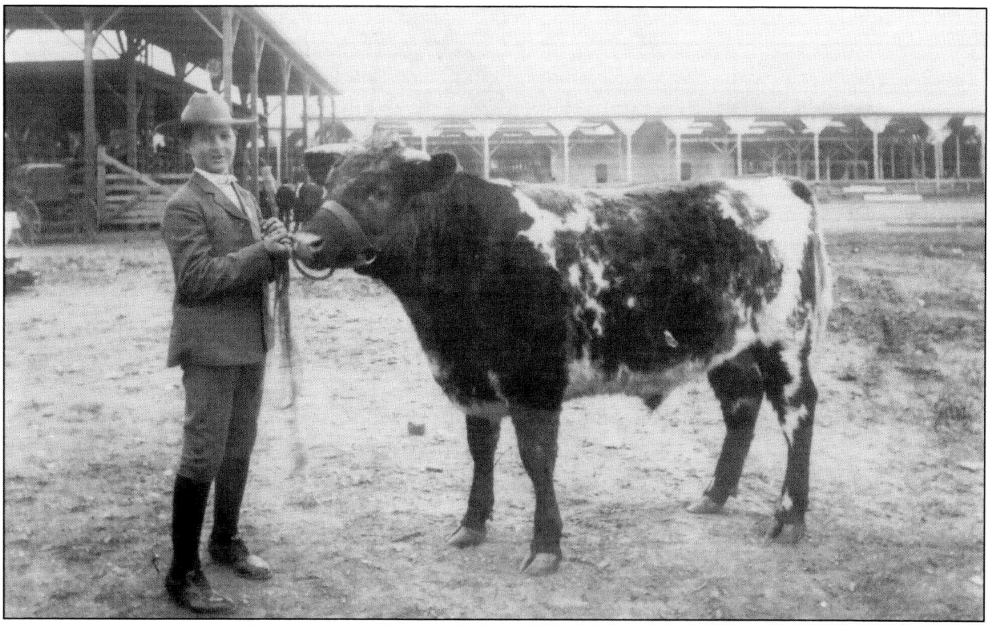

In 1896, Charles McFarland suggested to Fort Worth Stockyards executive C.C. French that an exhibition of fat cattle and blooded lines would help develop the industry. The first Fort Worth Fat Stock Show, held that year under a tree along Marine Creek, continues today as the Southwestern Exposition and Livestock Show. Charles McFarland Jr. showed his shorthorn at the 1905 Stock Show. (DHCC, McFarland Family Papers.)

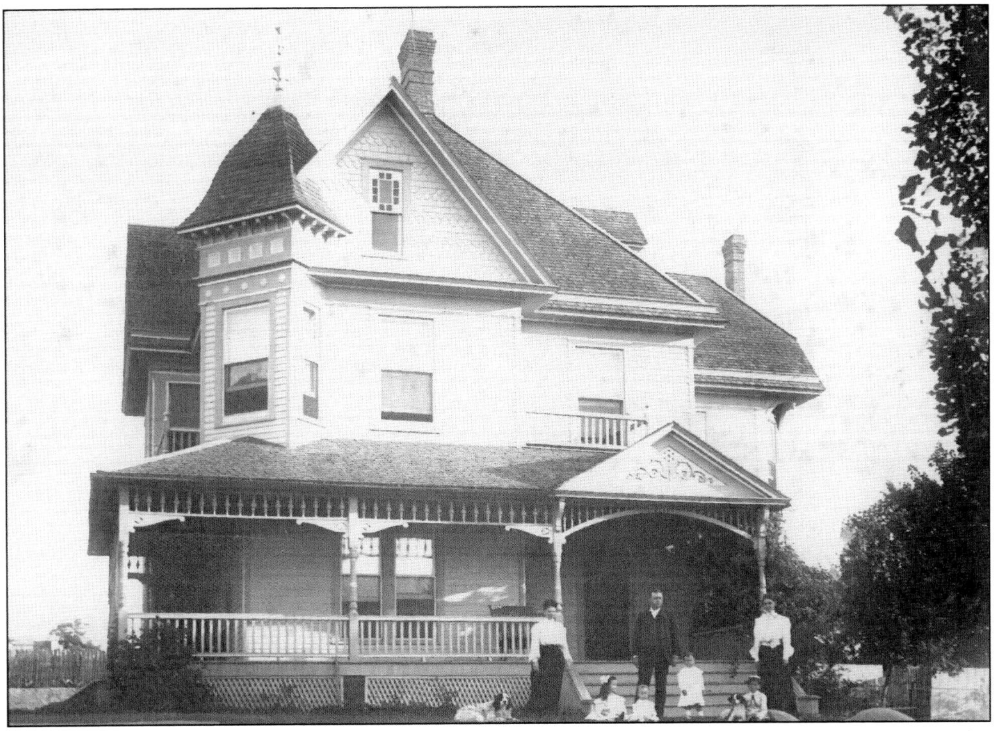

The Blair residence on the northeast corner of Palo Pinto and Lamar Streets is depicted in the early 1900s. The Blair family members are, from left to right, children Kathleen, Jim, Edwin, and Wiley Jr. and adults Maggie Blair, a milliner and dressmaker; her husband, Wiley Blair, a grocer; and Josephine Blair. The facade of this home is very similar to that built by banker Walter S. Fant Sr. at 401 Palo Pinto Street. (WPL.)

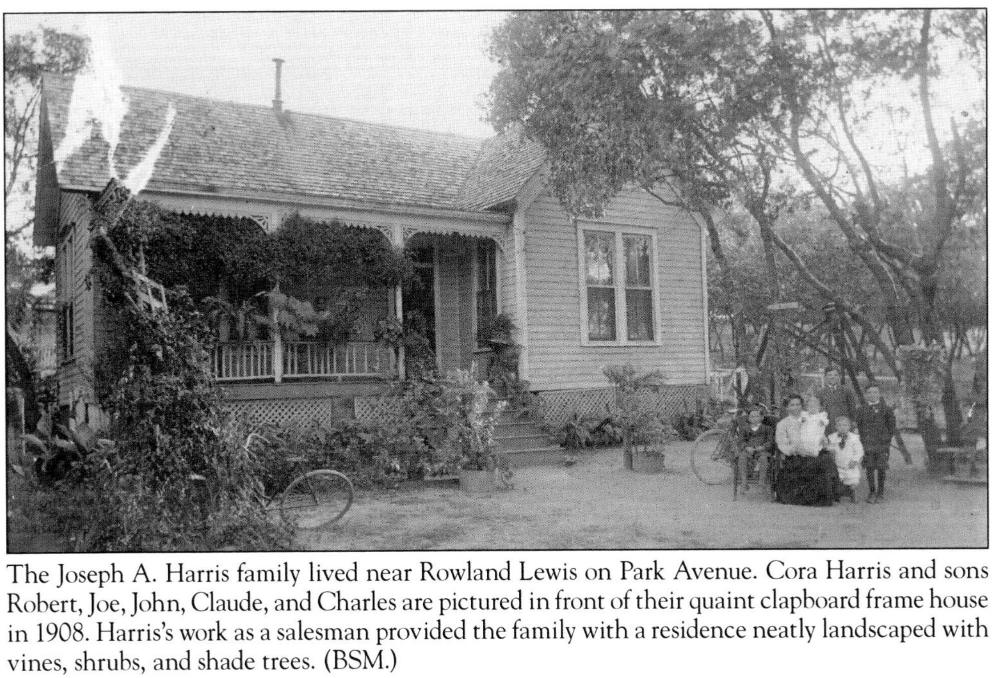

The Joseph A. Harris family lived near Rowland Lewis on Park Avenue. Cora Harris and sons Robert, Joe, John, Claude, and Charles are pictured in front of their quaint clapboard frame house in 1908. Harris's work as a salesman provided the family with a residence neatly landscaped with vines, shrubs, and shade trees. (BSM.)

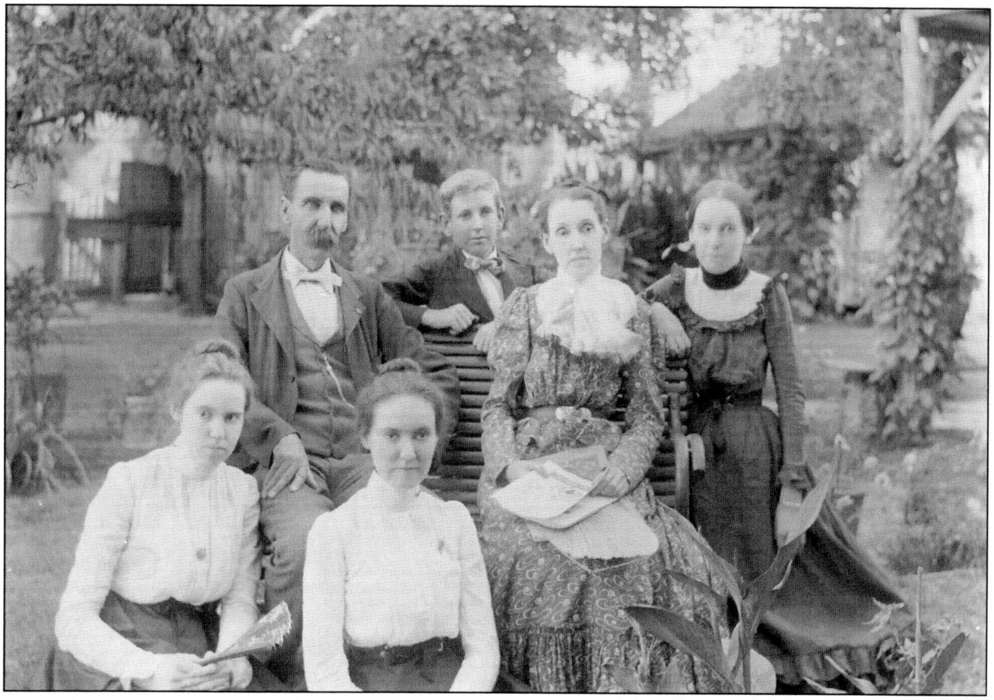

The Chauncey Cyrus Baker family was integral to the cultural development of Weatherford. Baker owned Baker Transfer Company and named company vehicles after his daughters Mary, Lucy, and Bessie. The sisters taught violin, voice, and piano in the family home on Spring Street. Their brother Carson Cullum Baker belonged to the 4th Regiment Band. The siblings often accompanied one another during performances at the opera house and courthouse bandstand. (WPL.)

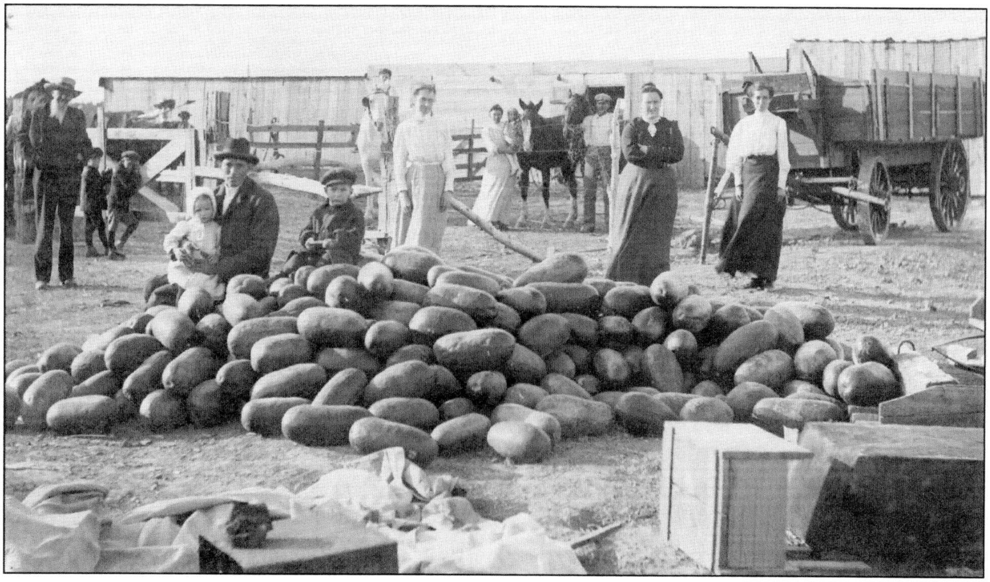

Parker County received world notoriety after 12 local watermelons, weighing from 96 to 106 pounds each, were awarded first prize at the 1904 St. Louis World's Fair. Demand for the flavorful melons increased yearly, and local farmers shipped watermelons to all parts of the United States. This farming family had its watermelons stacked ready for market. (WPL.)

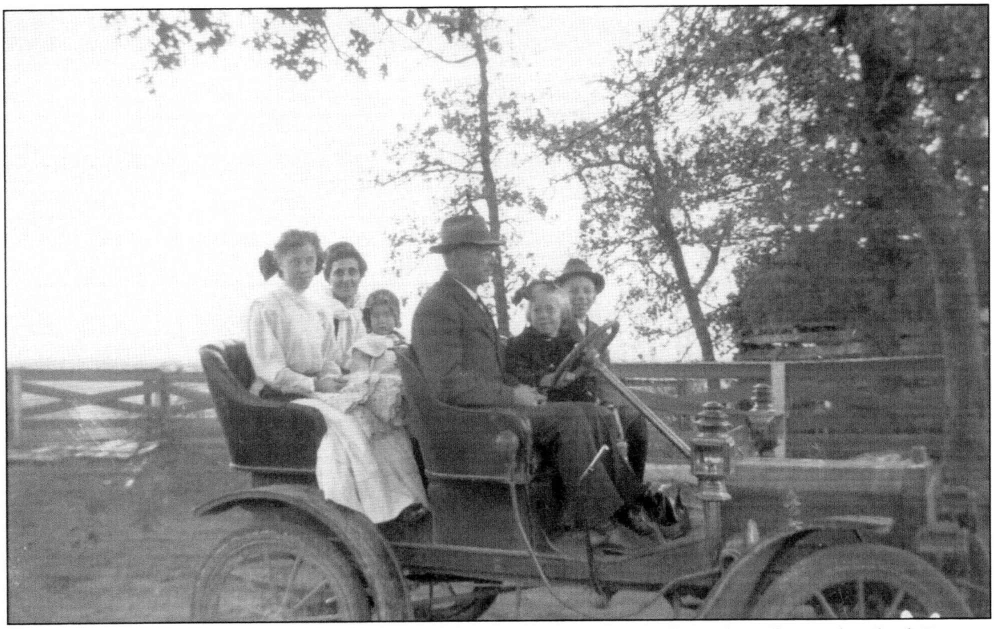

William H. Eddleman, president of Merchants & Farmers National Bank and Weatherford Cotton Compress, is credited with owning the first automobile in town, a 1901 Locomobile or a 1902 curved dash Oldsmobile. Ezra A. Frantz, a machinist extraordinaire and inventor of the Frantz bale wire buckle, took his family for a drive around 1909. From left to right are Florence Brubaker and Mary, Nellie, Ezra, Ruby, and Ray Frantz. (MEDA.)

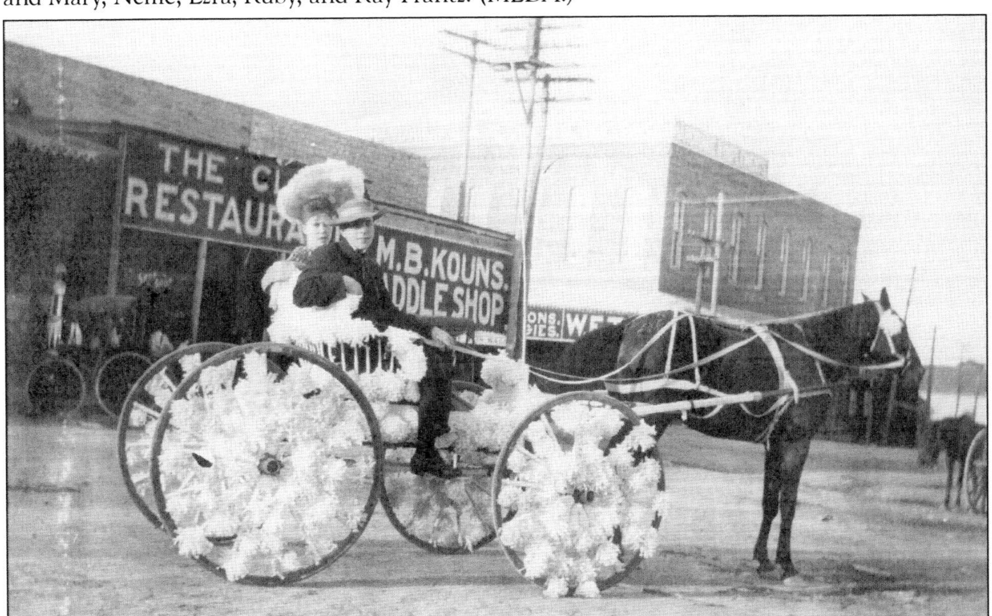

The couple in this decorated horse-drawn buggy pause in the northeast quadrant of the square to smile for the camera. The Club Restaurant and M.B. Kouns Saddle Shop in the background help date this photograph around 1905 to 1910. The Club Restaurant, operated by Patrick and George Bavousett, could seat around 55 people. M.B. Kouns was one of the prominent harness and saddle makers in Parker County. (WPL.)

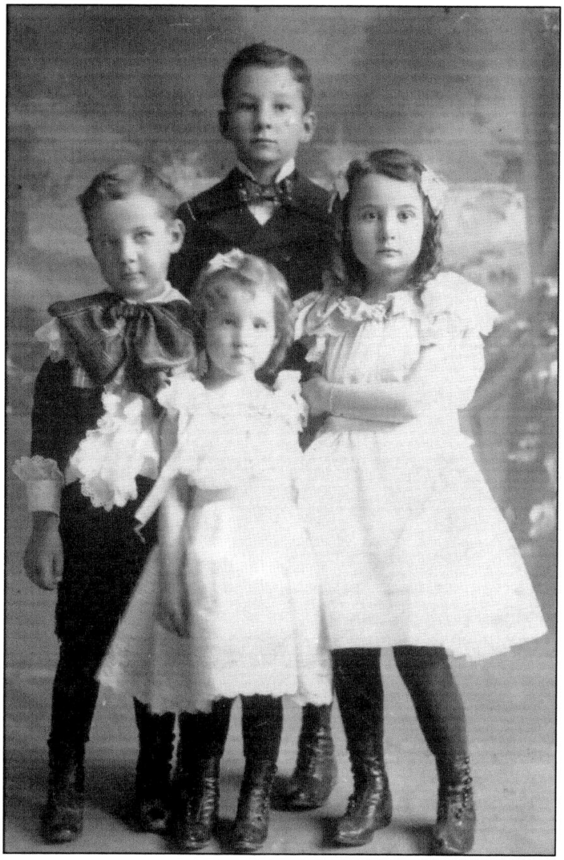

The children of Charles and Eloise McFarland may have attended the juvenile operettas directed by Mollie Steele at the Haynes Opera House. Pictured here around 1900, the children are, clockwise from top, James Porter McFarland, Eloise McFarland, Eulalia Jane McFarland, and Charles McFarland Jr. (DHCC, McFarland Family Papers.)

Thomas S. Carter purchased the J.R. Lewis Hardware Company at 120 North Main Street after a devastating May 1901 fire. Carter rebuilt the structure and reopened the business as T.S. Carter Hardware Company. William T. Ivy was briefly involved with the enterprise when it incorporated in 1907 as Carter-Ivy Hardware Company. Generations of the Carter family served the hardware needs of Weatherford until the business closed in 2004. Carter is pictured here with his wife, Mary. (WPL.)

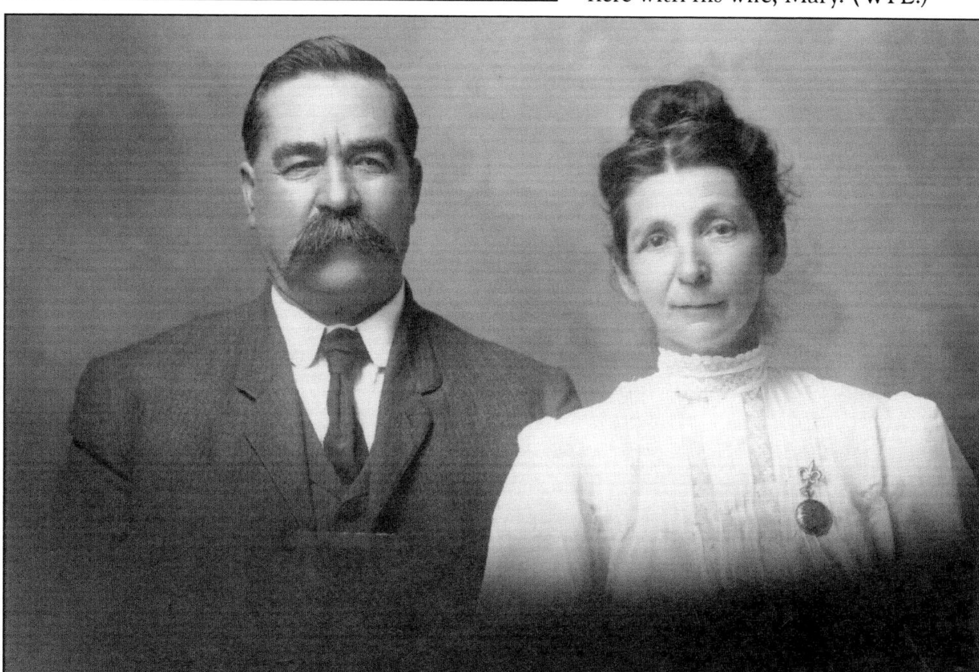

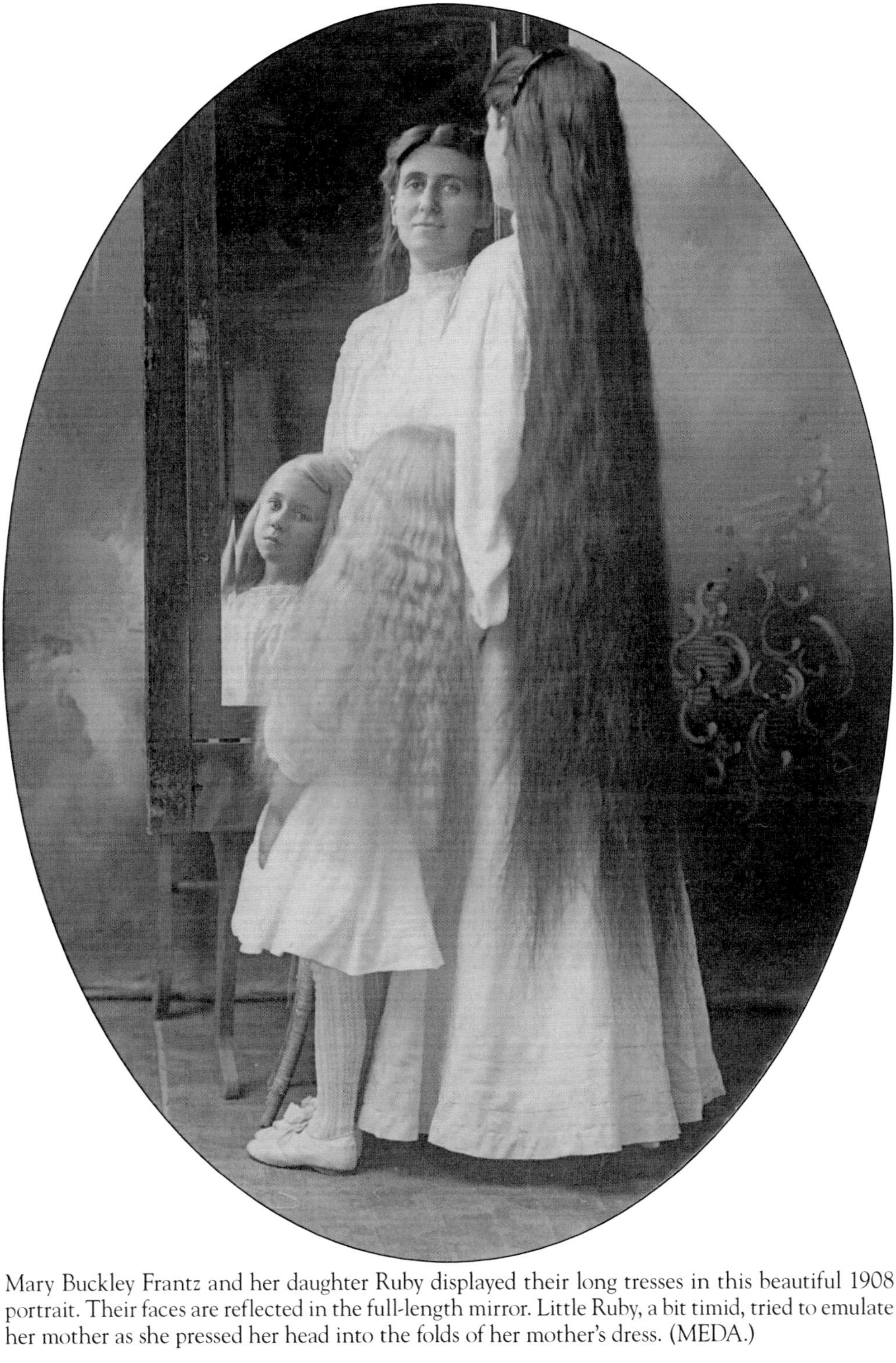

Mary Buckley Frantz and her daughter Ruby displayed their long tresses in this beautiful 1908 portrait. Their faces are reflected in the full-length mirror. Little Ruby, a bit timid, tried to emulate her mother as she pressed her head into the folds of her mother's dress. (MEDA.)

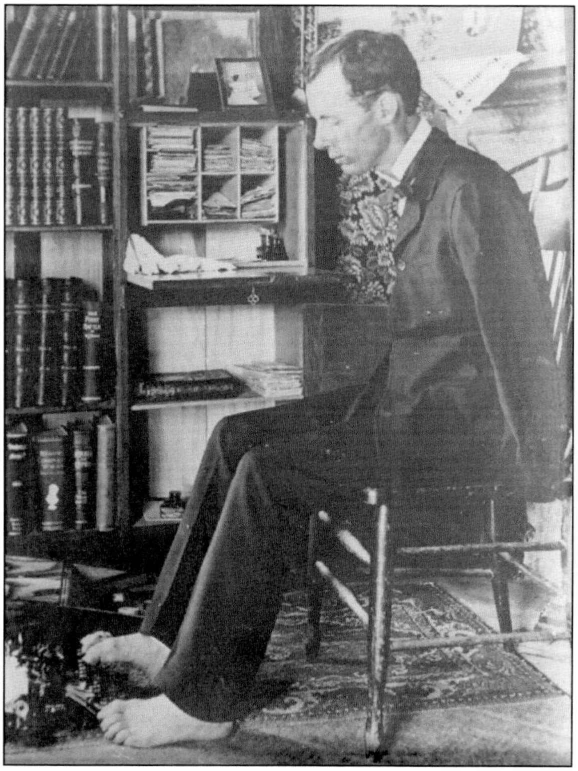

Aaron Smith, though armless since birth, learned to write and type with his toes. An attorney, his most notable achievement was as a newspaper and trade magazine publisher. After purchasing the weekly *Weatherford Democrat* newspaper, Smith moved his family to Weatherford in 1899. Always an ardent crusader, he devoted many editorials in 1901 to the topic of liquor prohibition by local option. The *Weatherford Democrat* was the only one of four local newspapers to take a stand in favor of prohibition. (WPL.)

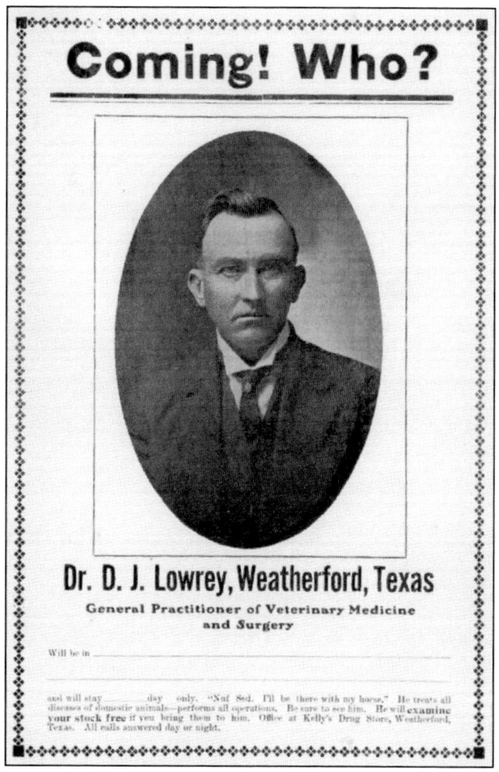

Veterinarian David J. Lowrey maintained his office at Kelly's Drug Store in Weatherford but also scheduled appointments around the county. In 1902, he published *Private Prescriptions and Lectures*, a handbook on the diseases of livestock. Lowrey also manufactured veterinary patent medicines—a liniment for wire cuts, bruises, sprains, and enlargements of the joints and a blood, liver, and kidney remedy for horses and cattle. (UTA.)

German native Henry J. Bradfish immigrated to Illinois with his parents as a toddler. Orphaned by the age of seven, he began making his own living early in life. Working in railroads and then in life insurance, Bradfish made his way to Weatherford in 1894. He was a bookkeeper for the Dan D. Hartnett grocery for nine years before partnering with Hartnett in the grain and elevator business in 1903. (UTA, Ancellin-Hartnett Family Papers.)

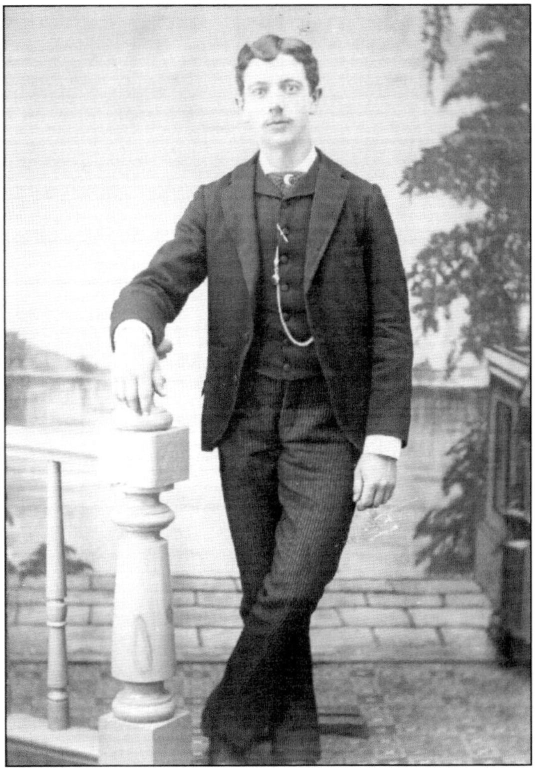

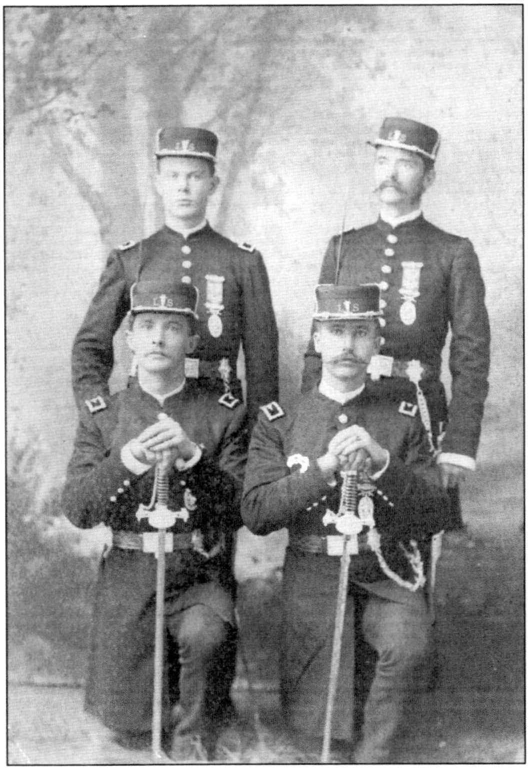

These four gentlemen, pictured in 1904, were members of the Lone Star Lodge No. 4, Knights of Pythias. As members of the Uniformed Rank of the Knights, they performed military-style drills for parades and other official functions. Edward Porter Sawtelle, kneeling left, was a partner in the mercantile firm of Porter, Grant, and Sawtelle, located on the southeast corner of the square and South Main Street. (UTA, Montfort, Sawtelle, and Gilbert Family Papers.)

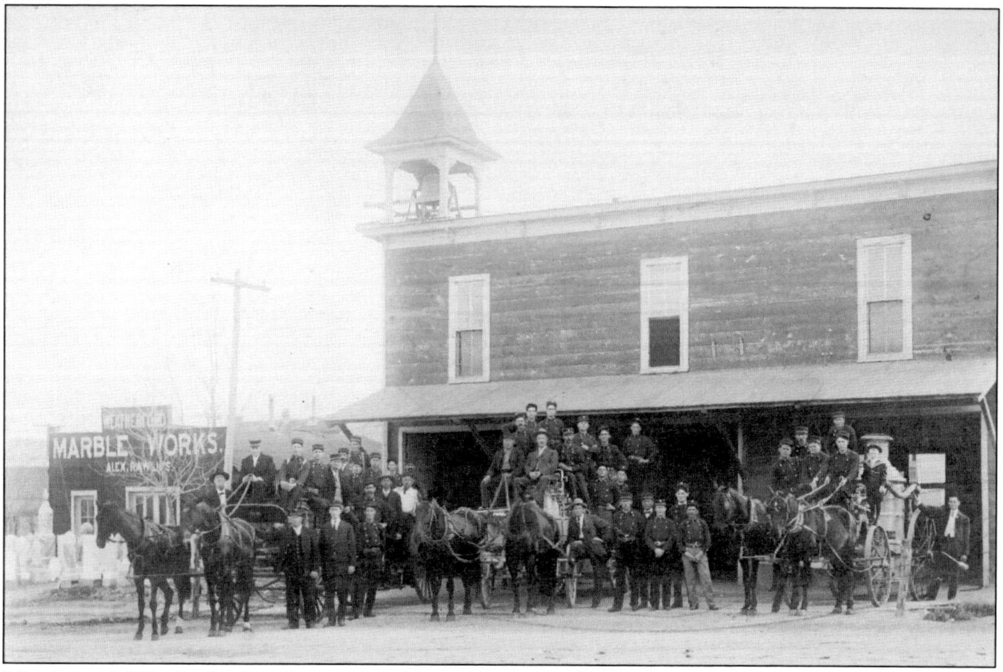

Members of Weatherford's volunteer fire department assembled to have their picture taken on January 24, 1909. Three companies of horse-drawn fire wagons, including the Silsby steam pumper on the far right, stood ready in front of the firehouse on Palo Pinto Street. The firehouse bell sounded the alarm in emergencies. The Weatherford Marble Works is visible on the left. Peace officers joined the volunteer fire department for the group photograph below. Notable visages include former fire chief Col. George M. Bowie, city marshal John R. Brown, and volunteer fire chief William Waldock, pictured second, fourth, and sixth from left to right in the second row. (Both, WPL.)

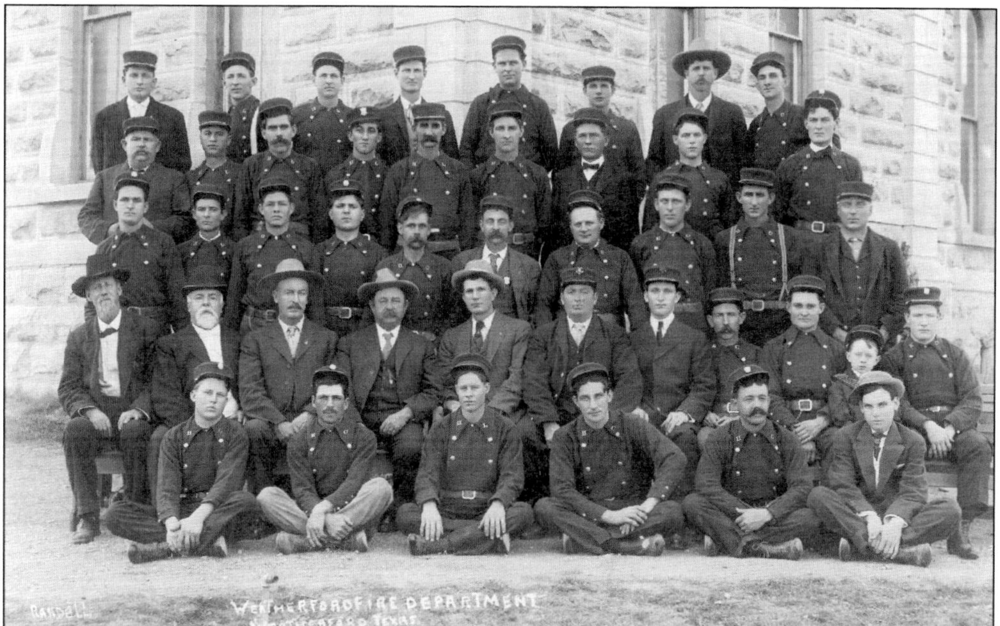

Five

1910–1919

On the Home Front

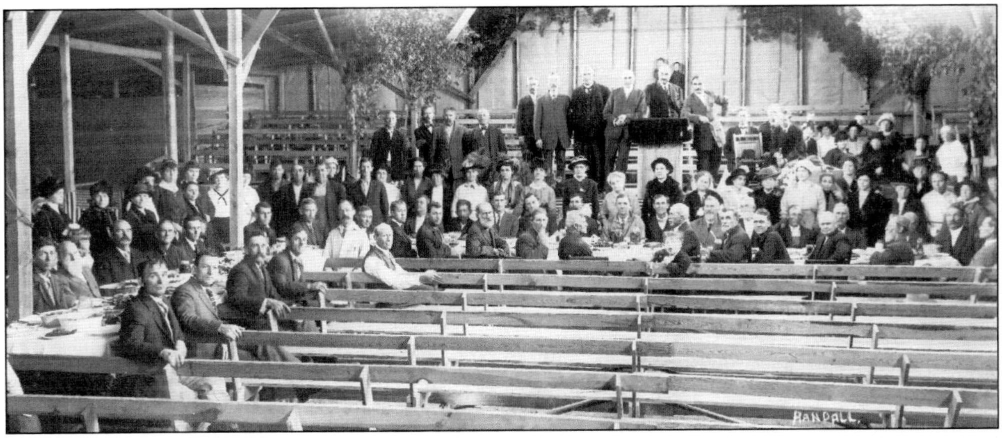

Rev. Mordecai Ham and his music minister William J. Ramsay brought their revival to Weatherford in November 1914. This tabernacle was constructed on the grounds of Weatherford College because permission could not be obtained to hold the revival on the public square. The structure had to be enlarged to accommodate the large attendance. On November 30, with three weeks remaining, 42,850 souls had attended the "evangelistic campaign." (WPL.)

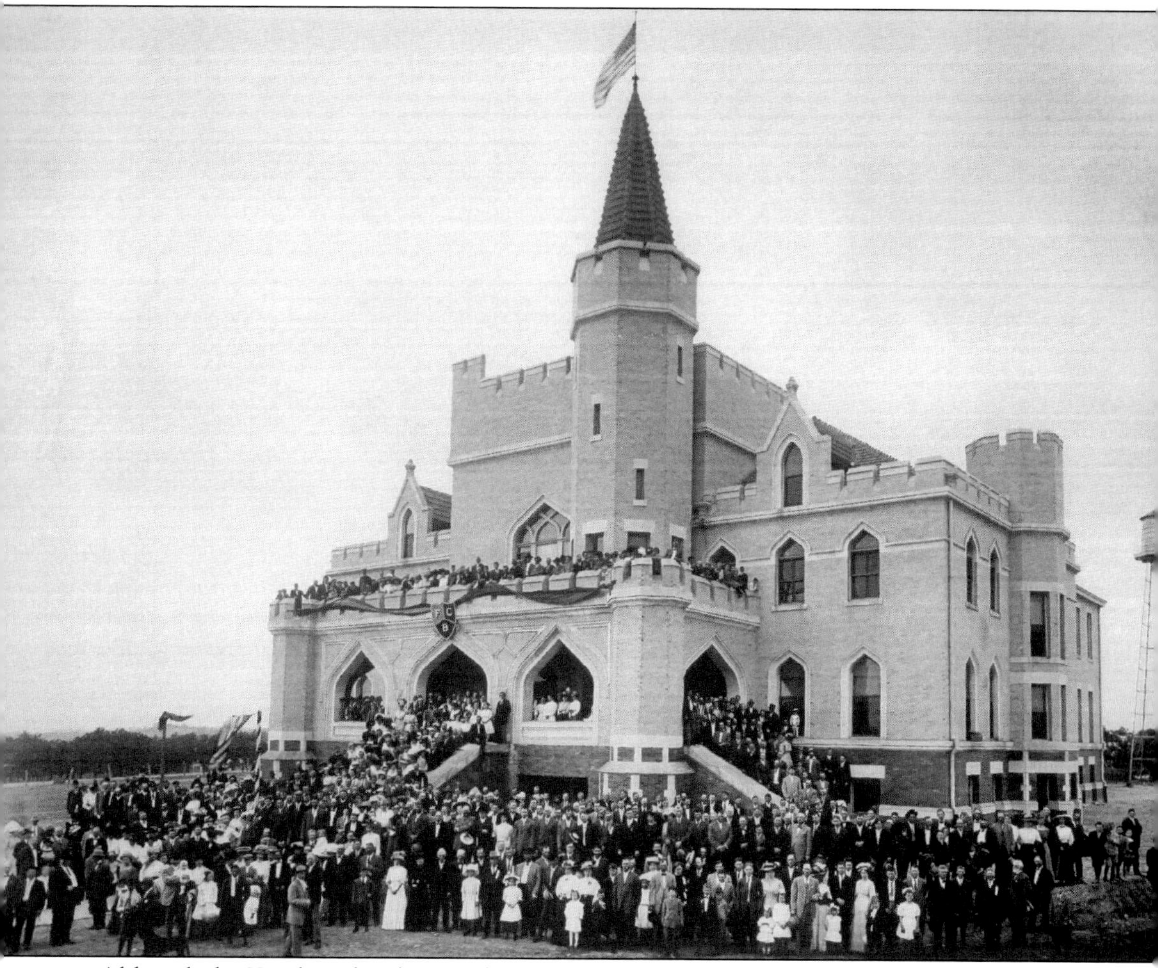

Although the Knights of Pythias Widows and Orphans Home and Industrial School opened in 1909, the facility was not formally dedicated until April 23, 1911. A special Fort Worth train brought 500 Pythians to the "castle on the hill" for dedication ceremonies. At that time, the administrator's family, 62 orphans, and three widows were in residence. Ancillary facilities included a barn and stables, blacksmith shop, pump house, laundry house, and a coal house. A boys' dormitory (1914), girls' dormitory (1924), and hospital (1930) were later added. A new name for the home, the Pythian Home, was adopted in 1915. (TPH; UTA, Fort Worth *Star-Telegram* Collection.)

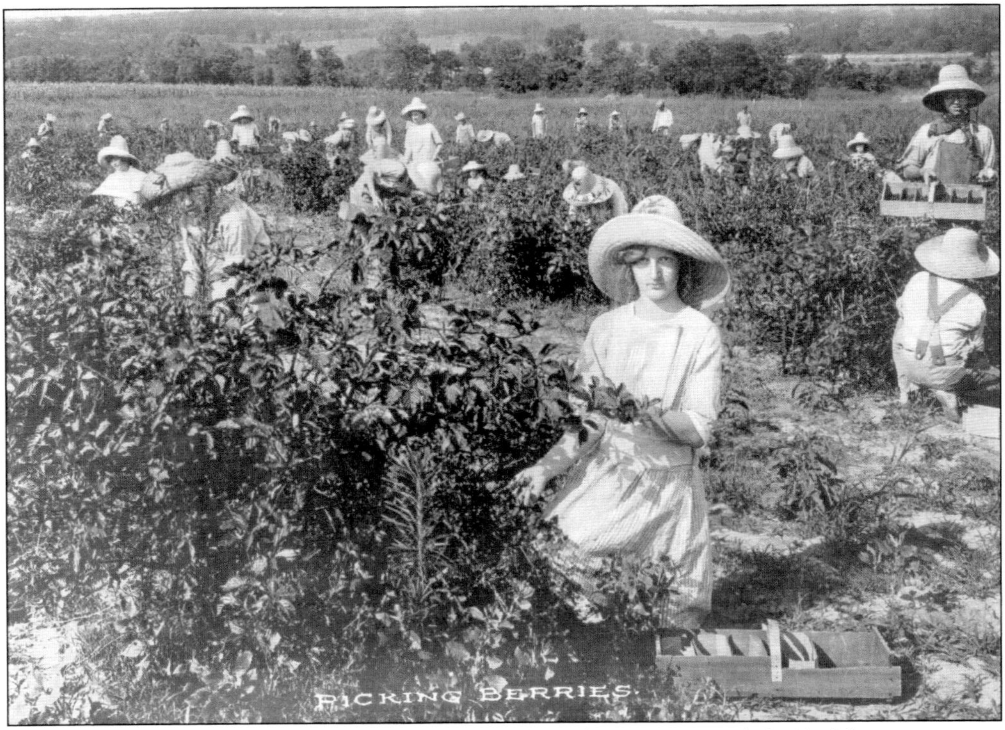

The 200-acre site of the Pythian Home was fully fenced. Approximately half of the acreage was under cultivation to raise crops for onsite consumption; any surplus was sold. Horses and mules, cows and calves, goats, hogs, and chickens were also raised on the property. *The Pythian Home*, published by the noted Albertype Company around 1916, featured beautiful views of the grounds and interiors of the Home. Berry picking and outdoor preserving were among the activities documented in this pictorial work. (LC.)

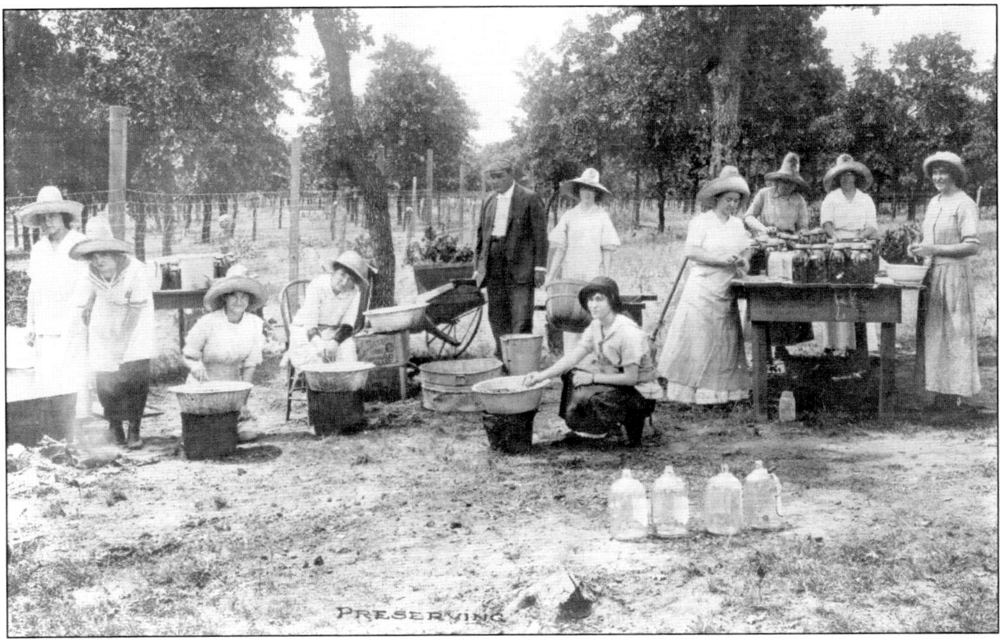

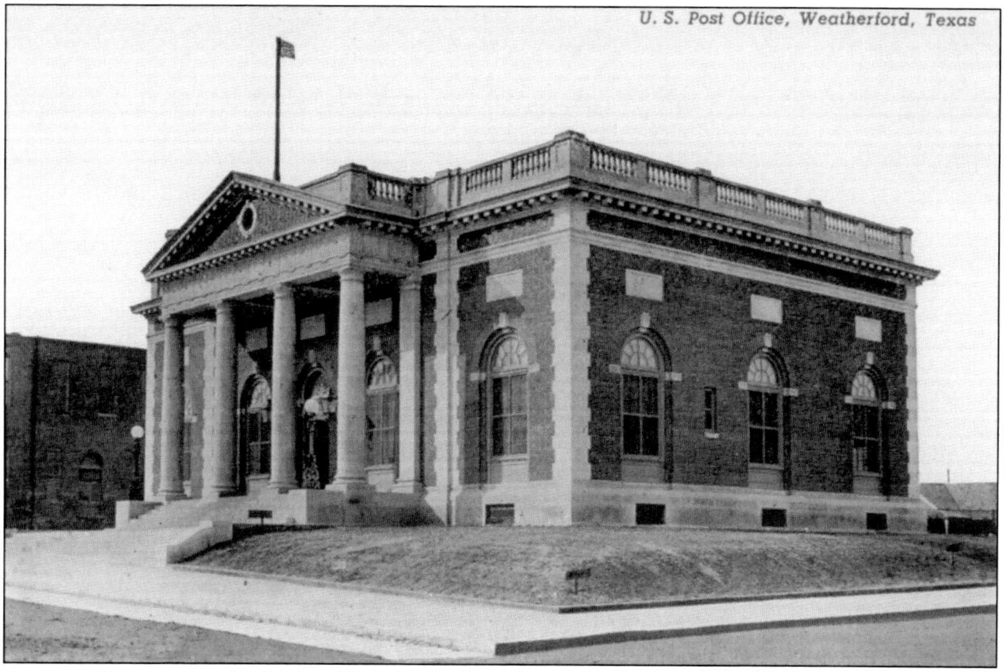

A post office was established in Weatherford on September 18, 1856, with David O. Norton as postmaster. It moved among several early locations on the square and on York Avenue. From December 26, 1914, until 1996, the post office occupied this Georgian Revival building at 117 Fort Worth Street, the site of an early wagon yard. Remodeled in 1999, the historic building is now utilized for district court functions. (BSM.)

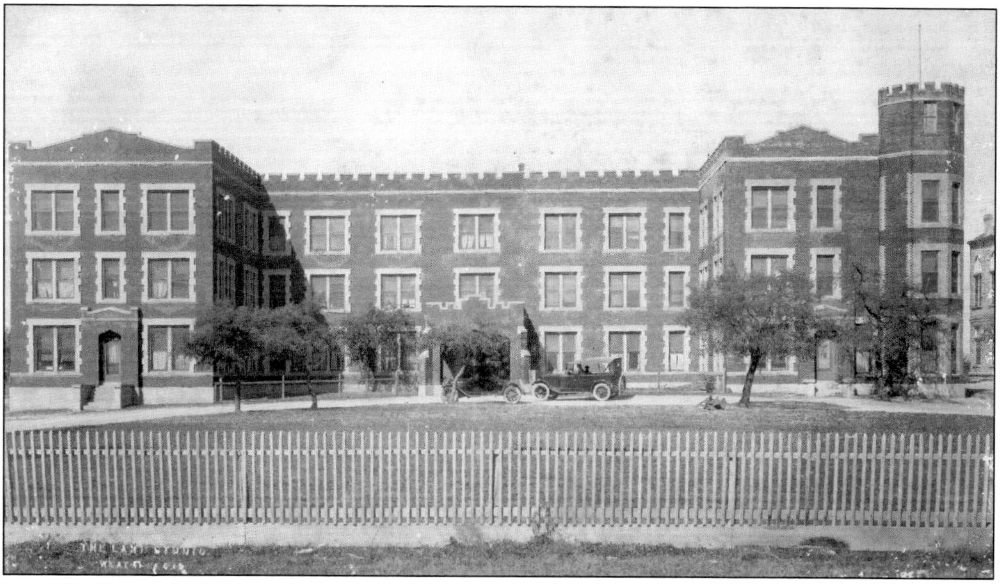

In 1911, this redbrick dormitory was constructed at the Texas Fairemont Seminary, replacing the Victorian wooden residence for boarding students. After the seminary closed around 1920, the dormitory housed the Weatherford Sanitarium and Training School for Nurses under the leadership of Dr. Hubert F. Leach. By 1930, it reverted to its former purpose as a men's dormitory for Weatherford College. The site is now the Emmanuel Baptist Church. (DHCC.)

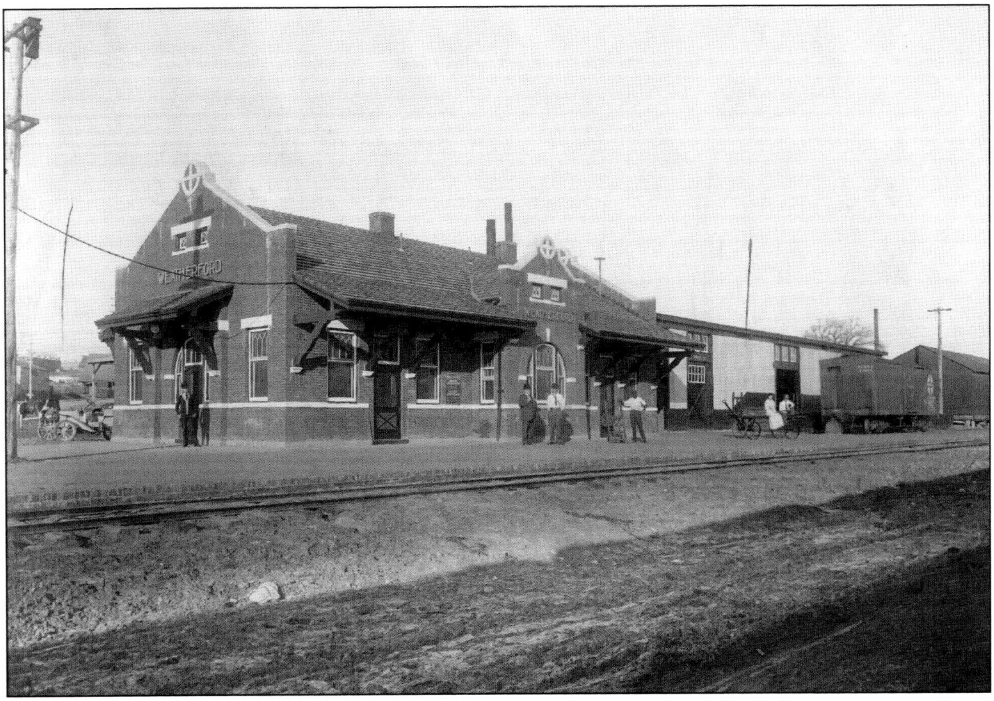

The new Gulf, Colorado & Santa Fe Railway passenger depot on Fort Worth Street was completed in November 1910. Jim Crow laws dictated separate passenger waiting rooms based on gender and color. The historic red pressed-brick depot now houses the Weatherford Chamber of Commerce and continues to welcome visitors to the city. (UTA, Fort Worth *Star-Telegram* Collection.)

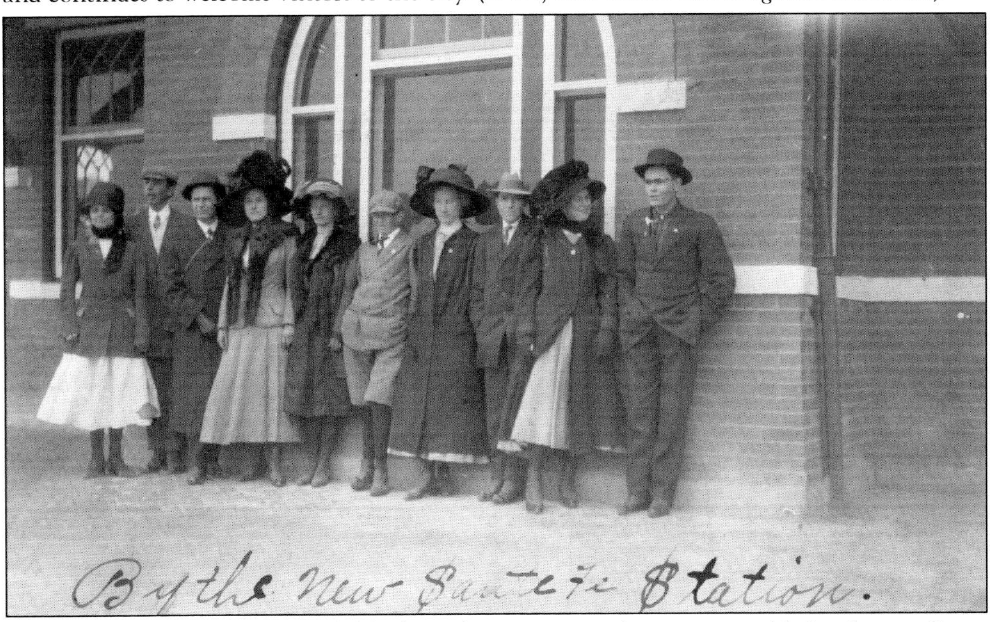

It was a chilly day when these stylishly dressed young men and women assembled at the new Santa Fe railroad station. Their names or purpose in gathering in unknown; perhaps they await the arrival of a special friend or family member. This postcard, mailed in April 1911, was penned by Gladys Howard to her older brother, Will, aboard the USS *West Virginia* in San Francisco. (BSM.)

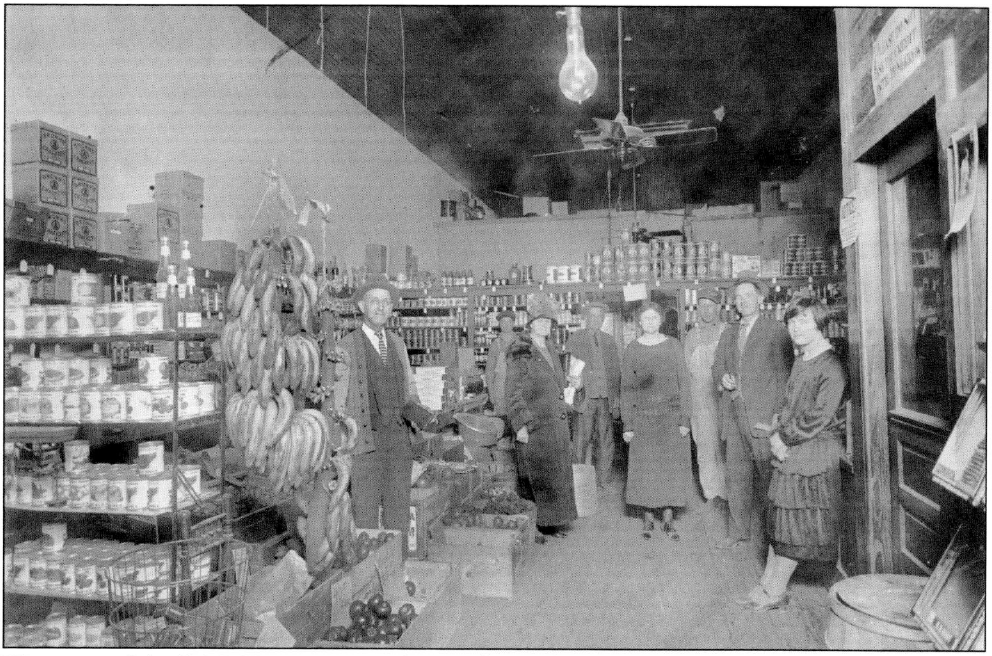

This view of the D.M. Hart grocery, after it relocated to North Main Street, was taken around 1916. Bananas were shipped in tall boxes cushioned by excelsior and then hung from the ceiling, where customers could pick them. A sign above the door implored, "Please do not ask for credit until tomorrow." D.M. Hart is pictured on the far left. (BSM.)

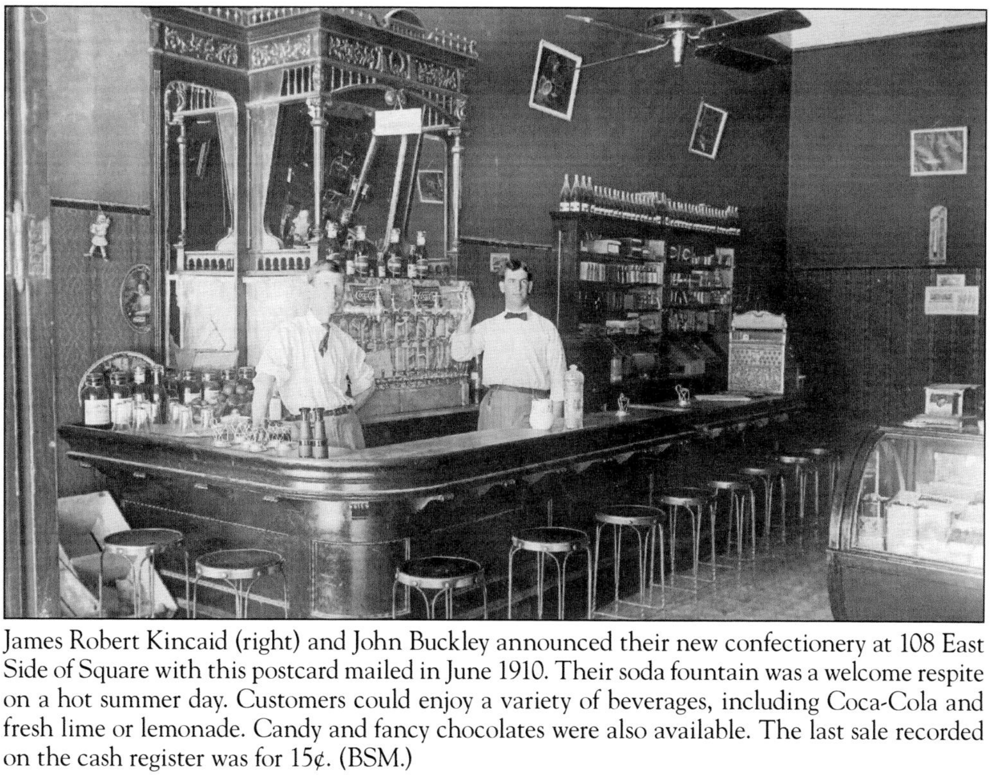

James Robert Kincaid (right) and John Buckley announced their new confectionery at 108 East Side of Square with this postcard mailed in June 1910. Their soda fountain was a welcome respite on a hot summer day. Customers could enjoy a variety of beverages, including Coca-Cola and fresh lime or lemonade. Candy and fancy chocolates were also available. The last sale recorded on the cash register was for 15¢. (BSM.)

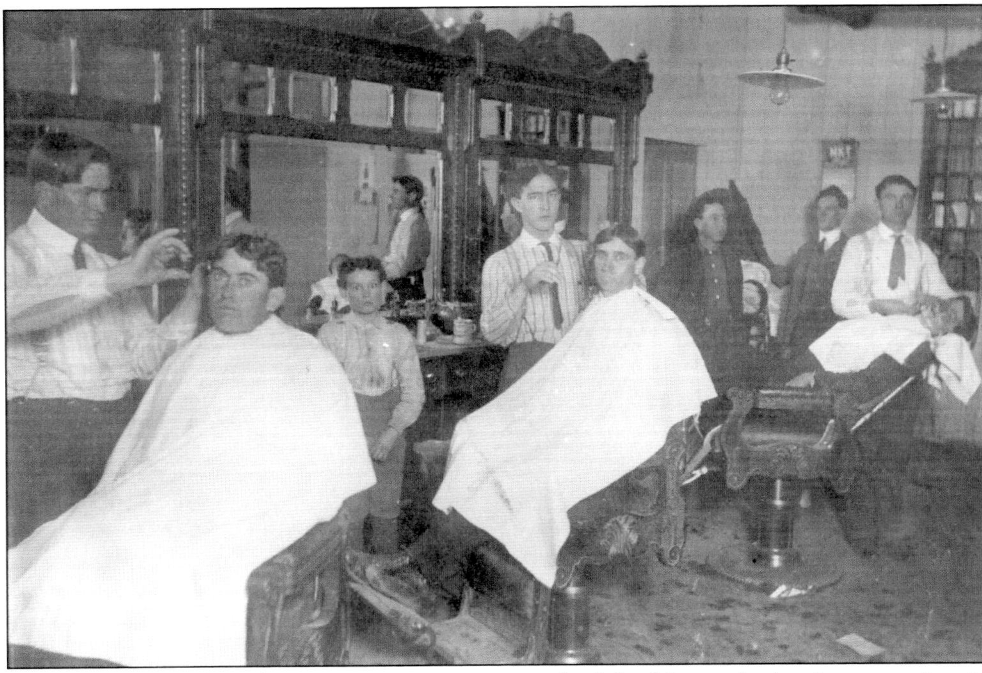

The chairs were full and customers were waiting in the John Vernon barbershop sometime in February 1916. Perhaps it was a first Monday Stray Day, and these men got a shave and haircut while in town to haggle over produce and hay and take advantage of special sales. The shop was elegantly appointed with carved wood-frame and mirrored barber stations. (WPL.)

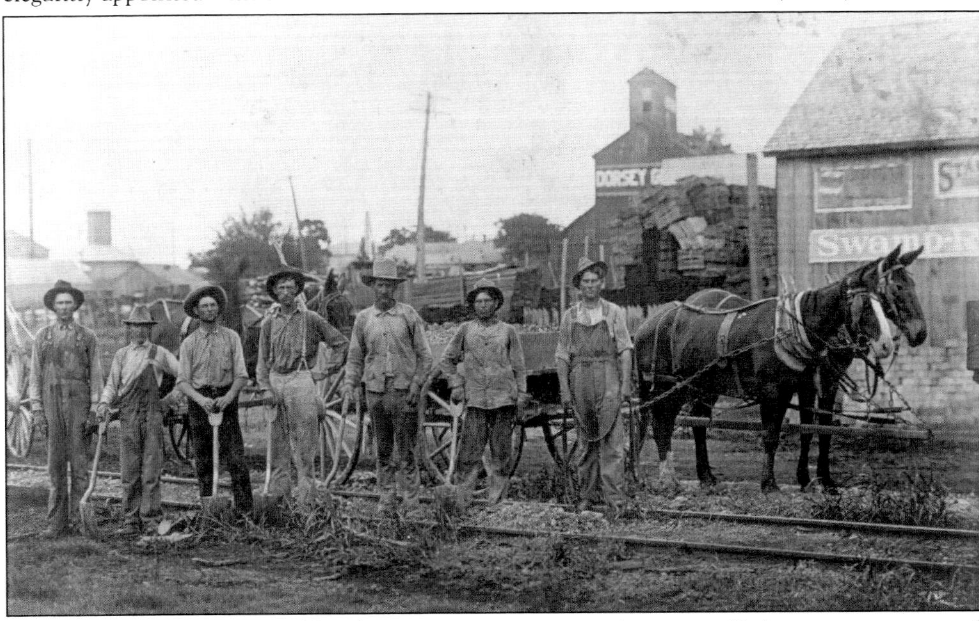

As early as 1894, the city used local manpower to maintain the streets. Ordinances were created, which required able-bodied men 18 to 45 years old to complete 40 hours of street work per year. Some men hired a substitute while others chose to pay a $5 fee directly to the city treasurer. Exemptions were given to active ministers, official militia guards, students, and firemen. This crew worked in 1910. (VC.)

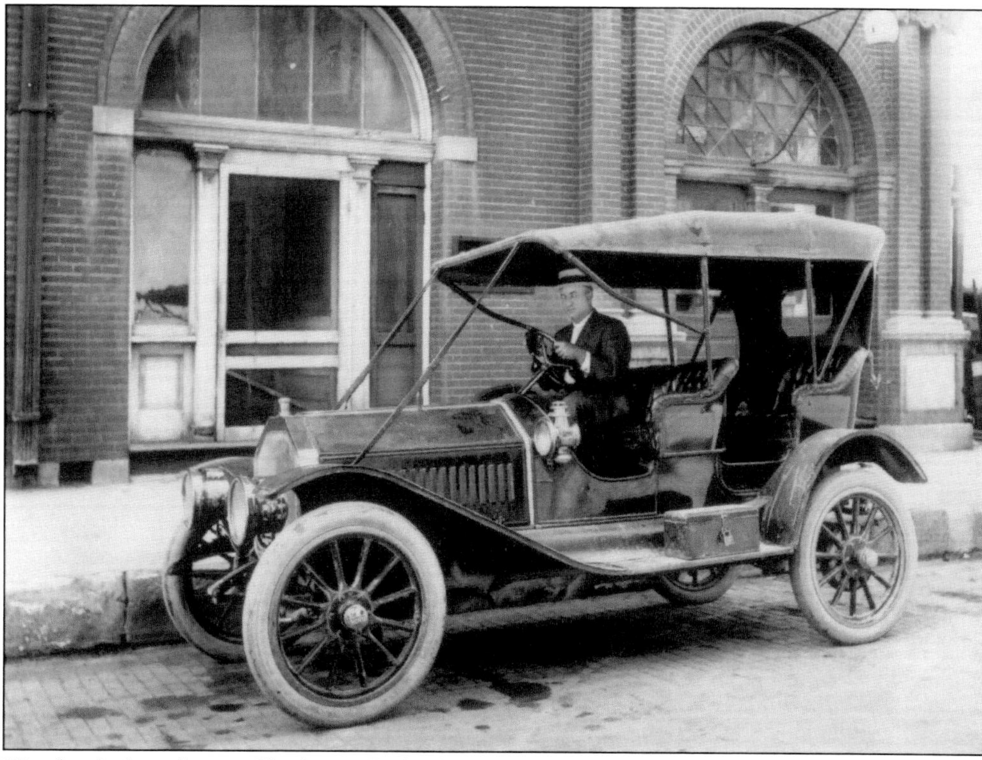

Weatherford cattleman Charles McFarland is pictured in his c. 1910 Buick automobile, probably in Fort Worth. The car has elegant curved fenders, tufted leather seats, and is equipped with a tool kit on the running board. (DHCC, McFarland Family Papers.)

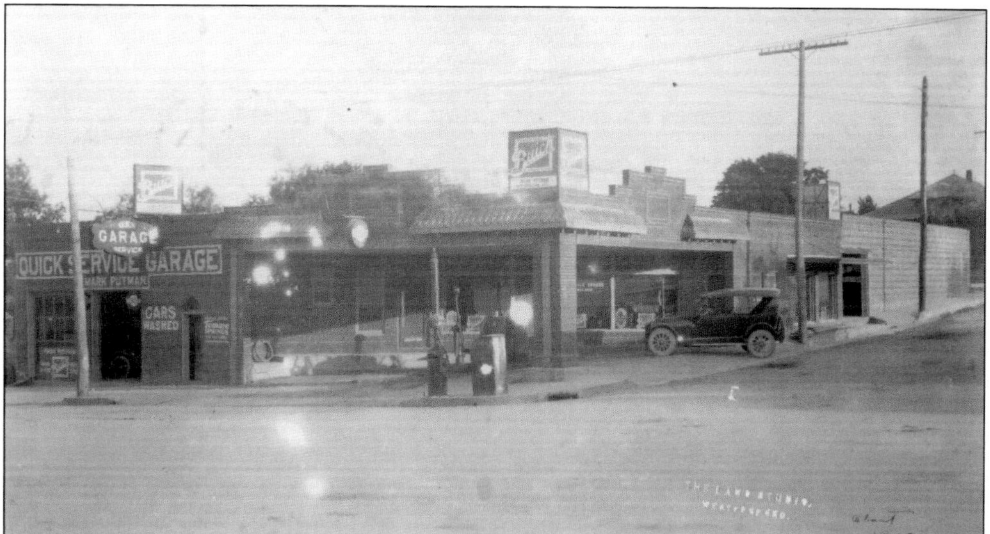

The pre–Civil War building on the southwest corner of the square, which once housed a saloon and a succession of dry goods businesses operated by Munroe Upton, Bell and Miller, and Tucker and Smith, was torn down in 1905. In its place, the Tuckers erected a new building in 1919 that initially housed a filling station and, later, the Mark Putman Buick dealership. (DHCC, McFarland Family Papers.)

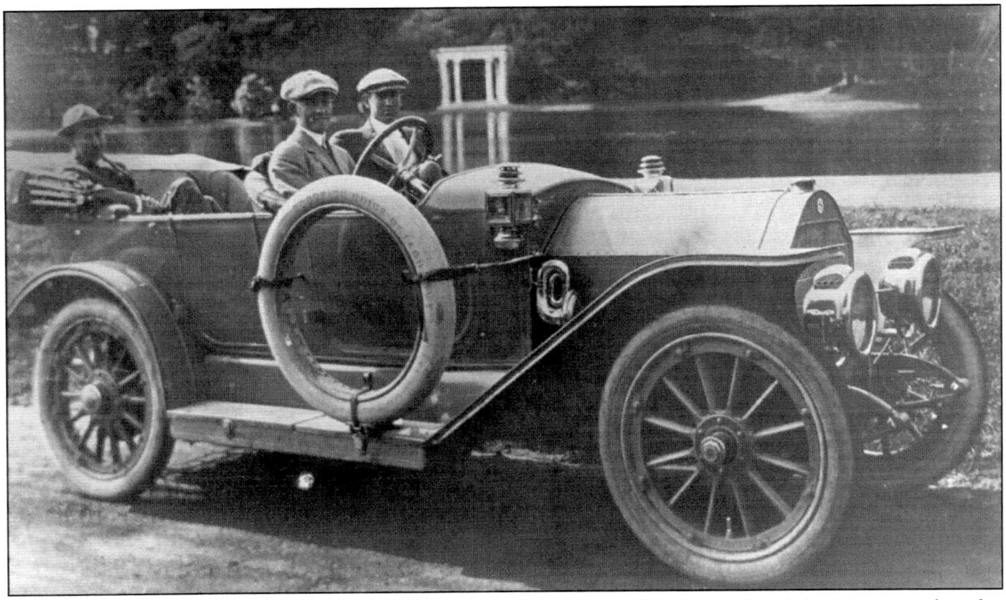

Sam White and Barney Holland of Weatherford and Lem Scarbrough of Austin completed a 6,500-mile automobile journey from Weatherford to San Francisco and back in 1912 that brought national attention. The trio is pictured in San Francisco in their Stoddard-Dayton 48 Saybrook car. Despite poor roads, mechanical failures, and being pulled 30 miles through Mexican sand by a team of horses, the car and passengers returned to Weatherford in "splendid condition." (UTA, Bowie and Holland Family Papers.)

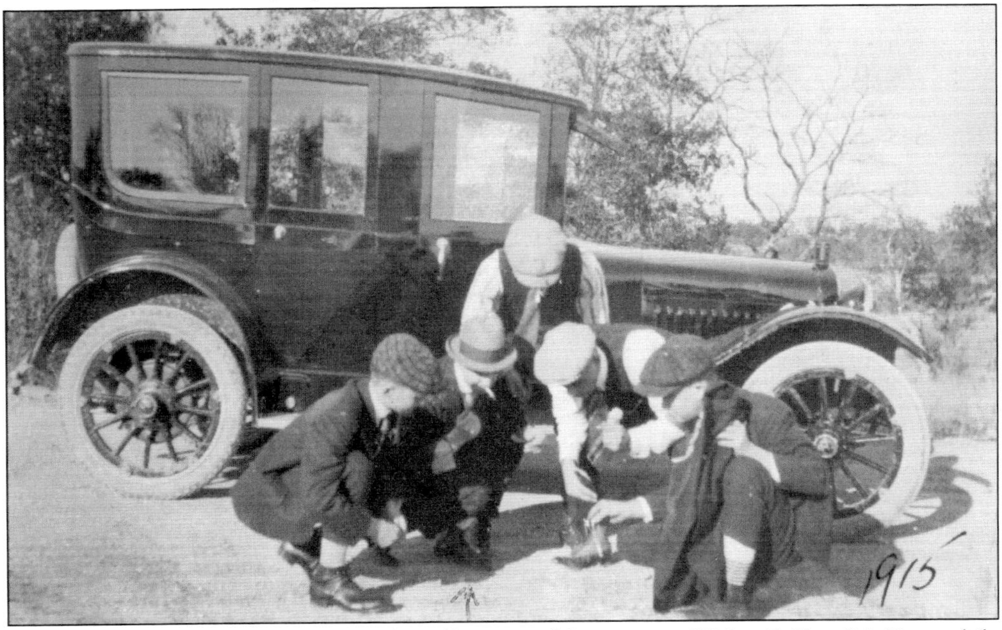

These young men were engaged in a friendly game of dice next to Walter S. Fant Jr.'s Hupmobile in 1915. The arrow points to Fant, the son of the banker of the same name. This Hupmobile featured a removable sedan top that cleverly attached to a touring car body, making it airtight and watertight. A 1915 Hupmobile touring car with removable sedan top was advertised for $1,365. (BF.)

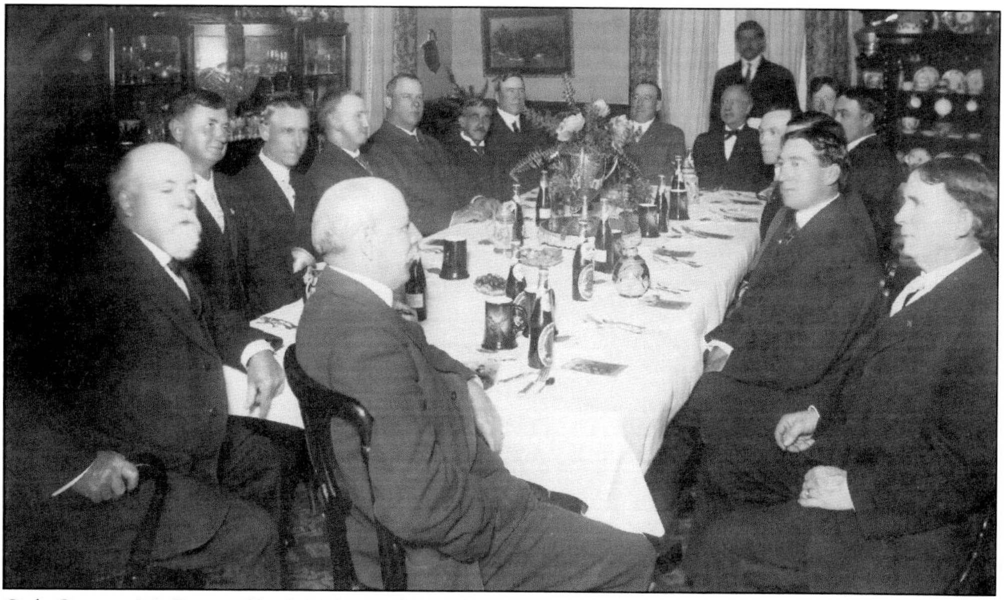

Col. George M. Bowie (far left) hosted a Valentine's Day party at his North Main Street home in 1912. Following a three-course luncheon, the guests played 42. Those attending were, seated from Bowie's left, William Chew, Charles Barthold, Robert Chew, Harry Kuteman, Aaron Gernsbacher, Hugh McGrattan, a Mr. Huey, C.D. Hartnett, Ralph Kindel, Robert Lowe, John Pickard, unidentified, T.S. Carter, Robert Norton, and Asa Grant. (DHCC.)

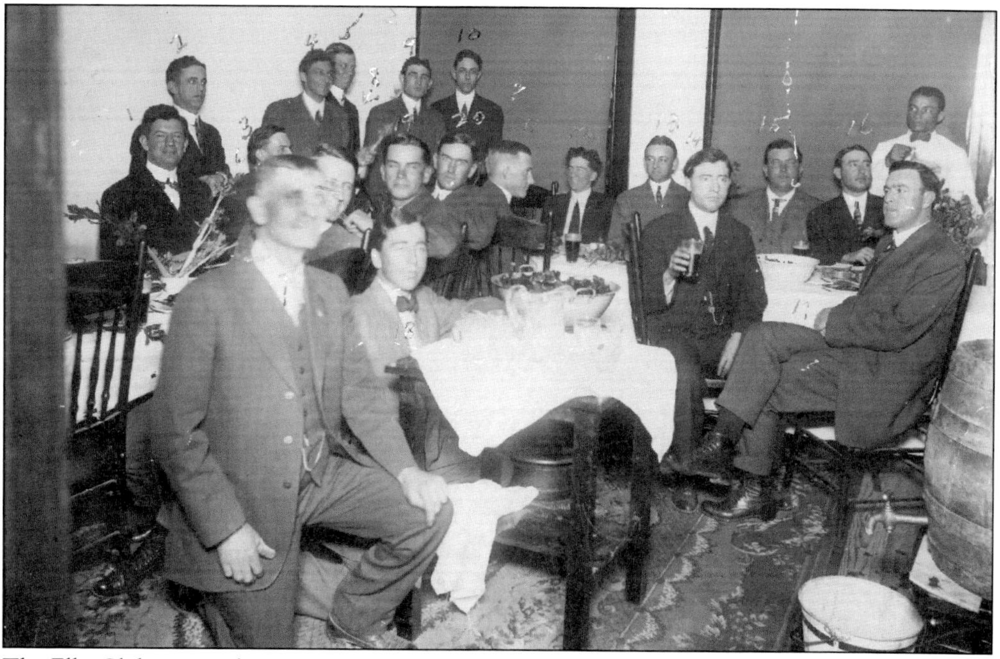

The Elks Club met in the Kuteman Block. Oyster suppers were a favorite pastime of its members. The young businessmen pictured here in the mid-1910s included Elmer Hill, Ed Lee Gannon, Fabian Bell, Isadore Gernsbacher, Charlie Milliken, Oscar Fain, Lucian Bell, Ivy Gardner, Oscar Bellinger, Sam White, Bob Carter, Ed Chew, Joe Davenport, Clarence Hopkins, Charles Fant, George Fant, J.E. Carter, Hugh Christian, and Barney Holland. (WPL.)

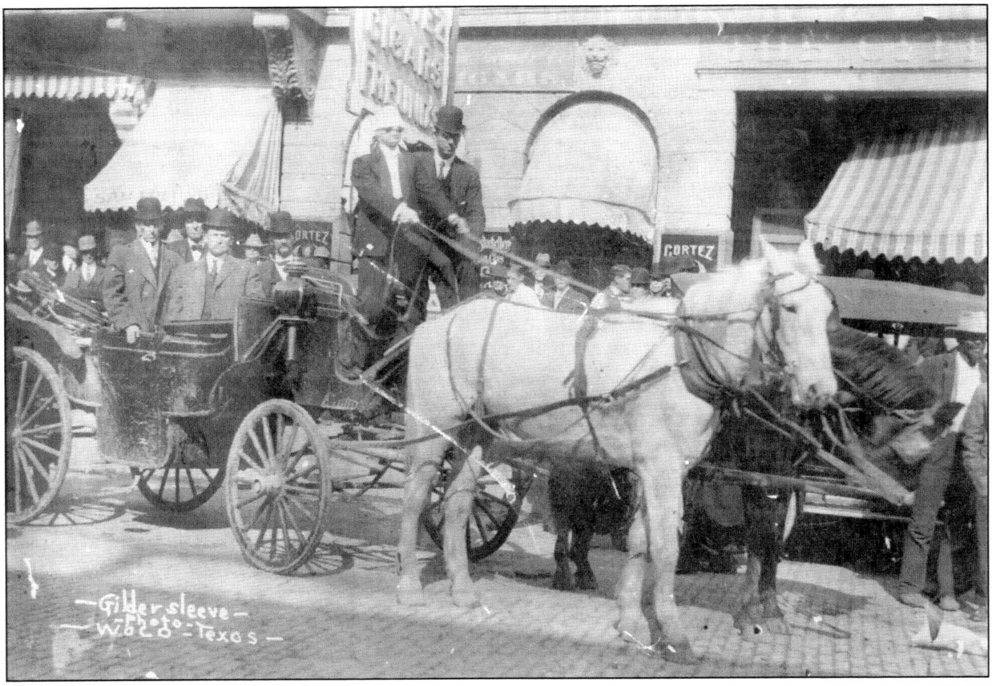

David and Margaret Haynes operated the Haynes Opera House on the northwest corner of the courthouse square. Their son Charles F. Haynes traveled across Texas conducting vaudevillian-style free street tests. Supposedly unable to see while blindfolded, Charley would maneuver a horse-drawn vehicle at breakneck speed through busy streets and public squares. In 1914, he performed his recklessly daring feat for a crowd gathered in downtown Waco. (WPL.)

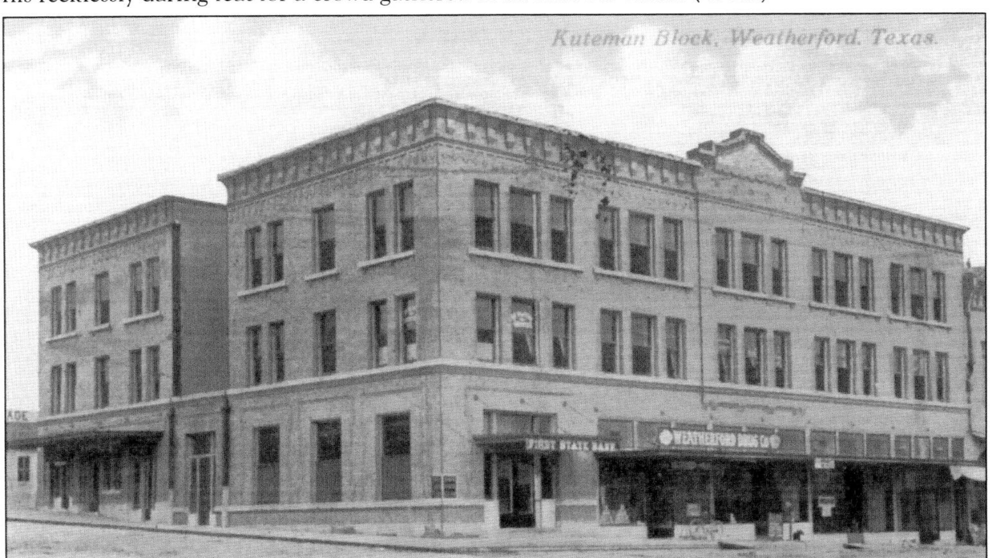

Harry Wentworth Kuteman purchased the Carson & Lewis House and completed this three-story office building on the site by 1911. The Kuteman Block housed First State Bank and other retail interests on the ground floor and professional offices and the Elks Club upstairs. This view dates between 1911 and 1914, as the Haynes Opera House is visible to the right. Later called the Hopkins Building, the structure burned in 1951. (BSM.)

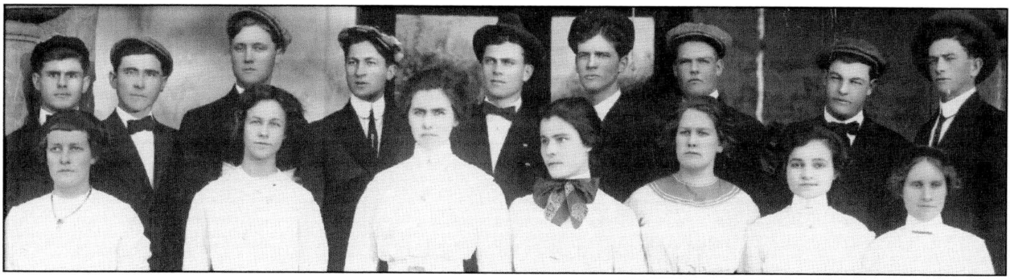

By 1907, Hughey-Turner Training School had become Weatherford College Training School under the tutelage of professors W.T. Roland and J.R. Fisher. Trustees turned the premises over to Polytechnic College in Fort Worth (later, Texas Wesleyan College) as a college preparatory in 1910. The class of 1912 graduated only 16 students, including, from left to right, (first row) Laura Stokes, Anise Doughty, Elizabeth Crosthwaite, Stella Milburn, Margaret Moseley, Charlcie Bond, and Anna Mae Akard; (second row) Edward Rabb, Frank Milburn, Earl Brattan, Walter Carter, Melvin Hutcheson, Carter Moseley, Earl Hobbs, and Robert Crossland. The school closed for three years, reopening on September 13, 1915, again as Weatherford College Training School. The college continued under this format until June 1921, when it was reorganized as a junior college. Members of the 1918–1919 drama club are pictured below in character for a play. (Both, WC.)

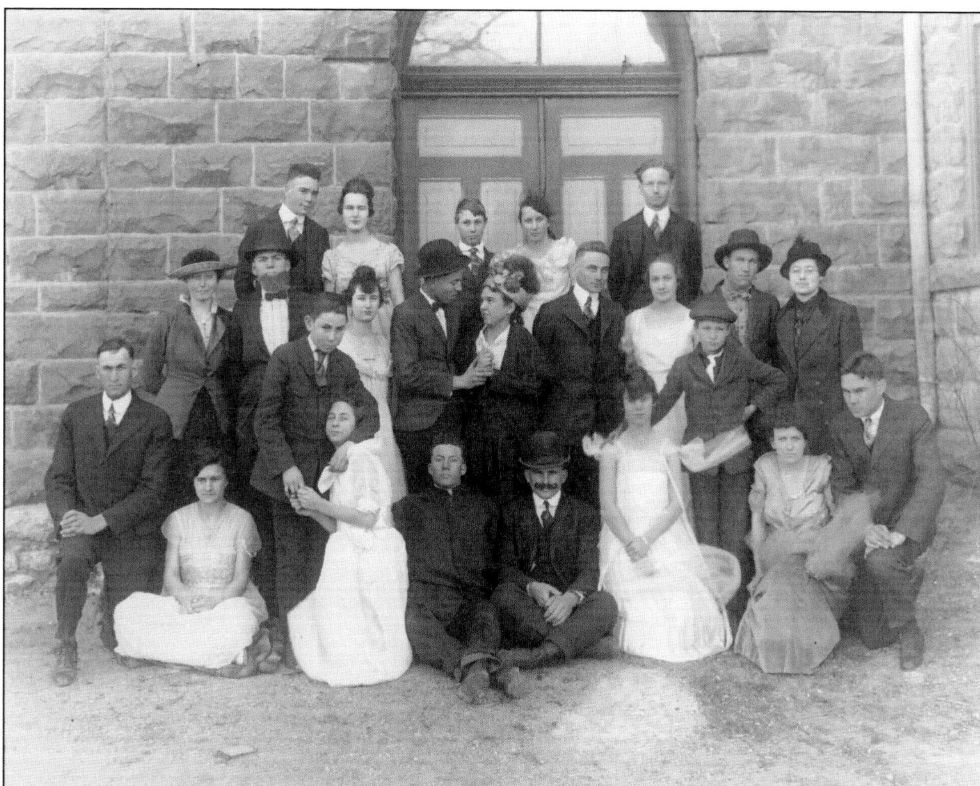

The 1912 Weatherford High School football team line up on the steps of Central High School for this team portrait. Team members included Bob Harris, Farland Collier, Lewis Reynolds, Marcus Chunn, John Scherer, Landon Wythe, Girard Lowe, Garland Raborn, Jack Hart, Bob Campbell, Harrison Morgan, Porter Pickard, and Tom Vincent. The team mascot, "Razor" Harkins donned a leather football helmet with noseguard. (WPL.)

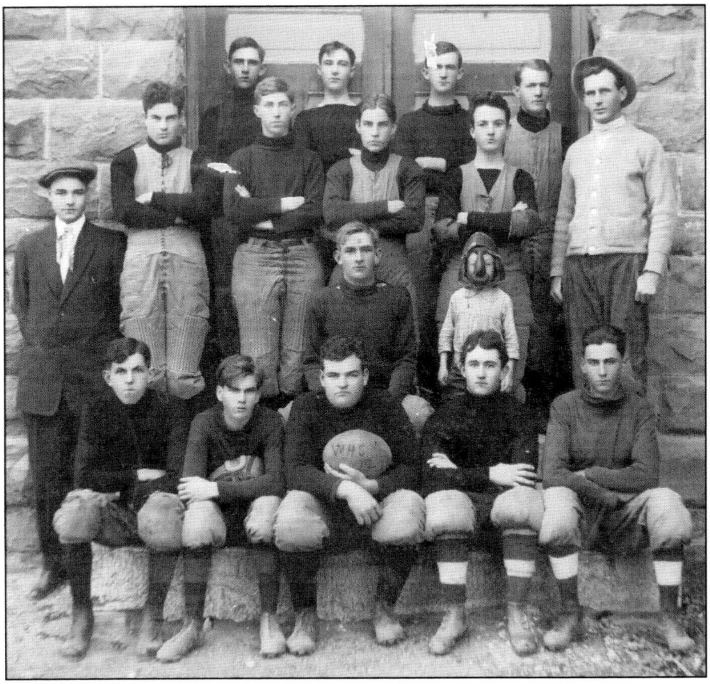

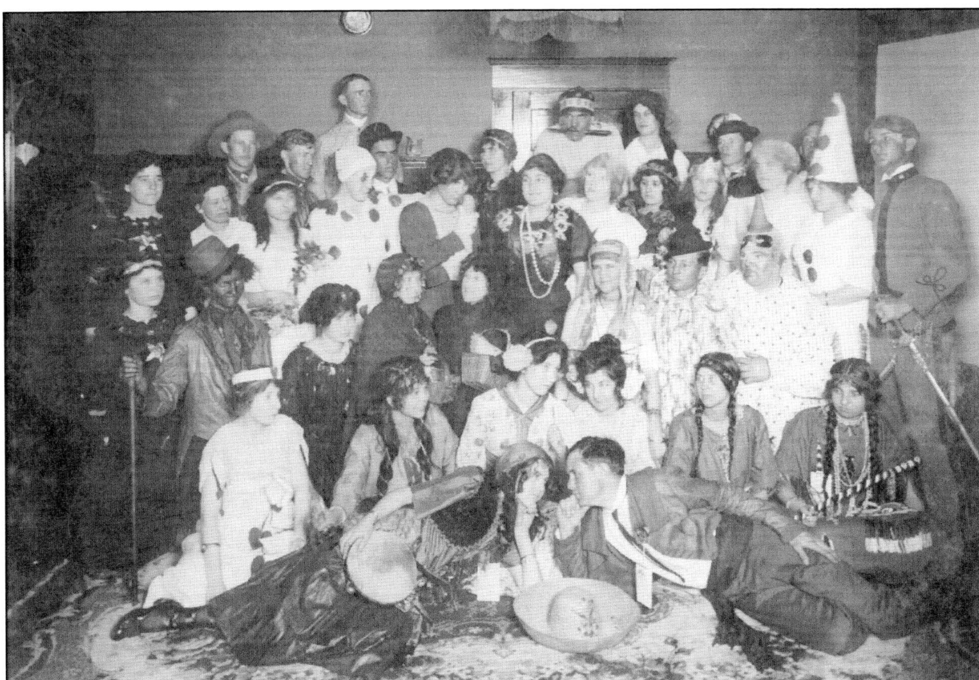

The 1914 Weatherford High School senior class and five of its teachers were honored with a masquerade party hosted by Emma Carter and Rosa Maddox at the Carter home on West Columbia Street. Costumes included the Queen of Hearts, a Roman senator, the goddess of Liberty, and a Texas cowboy. Guests were entertained with games of bunco and 42, songs, and instrumental music, followed by ice cream and cake. (WPL.)

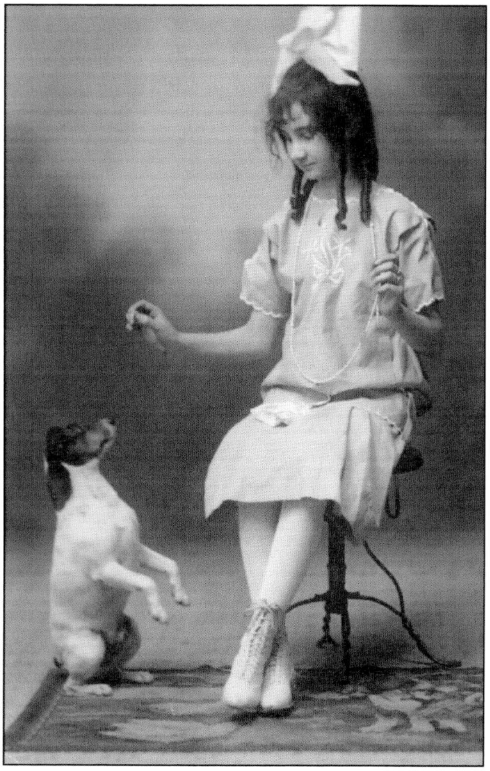

Aleene McFarland, youngest daughter of Charles and Eloise McFarland, rewarded her well-behaved little dog with a treat in this studio portrait taken about 1912. She struck a refined pose in a dropped-waist dress and long necklace that foretold 1920s fashions. Perhaps she is practicing for her future role as a princess (see page 111). This soft dreamy look with romantic ringlet curls and high-top laced boots gave way two years later to more austere fashions dictated by World War I. (CC.)

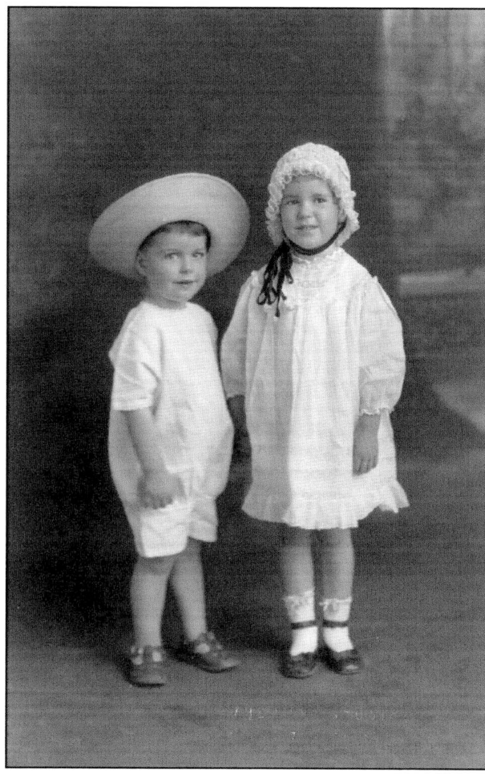

Knox and Marian Fant, children of George and Frances (Pansy) Fant, posed in this September 1918 formal portrait. Attired in a cotton romper, Knox appeared ready to make an escape in his wide-brimmed sun hat. His sister Marian, wearing a lacy smock, embellished cap, and beribboned socks, kept her brother in check. (MW.)

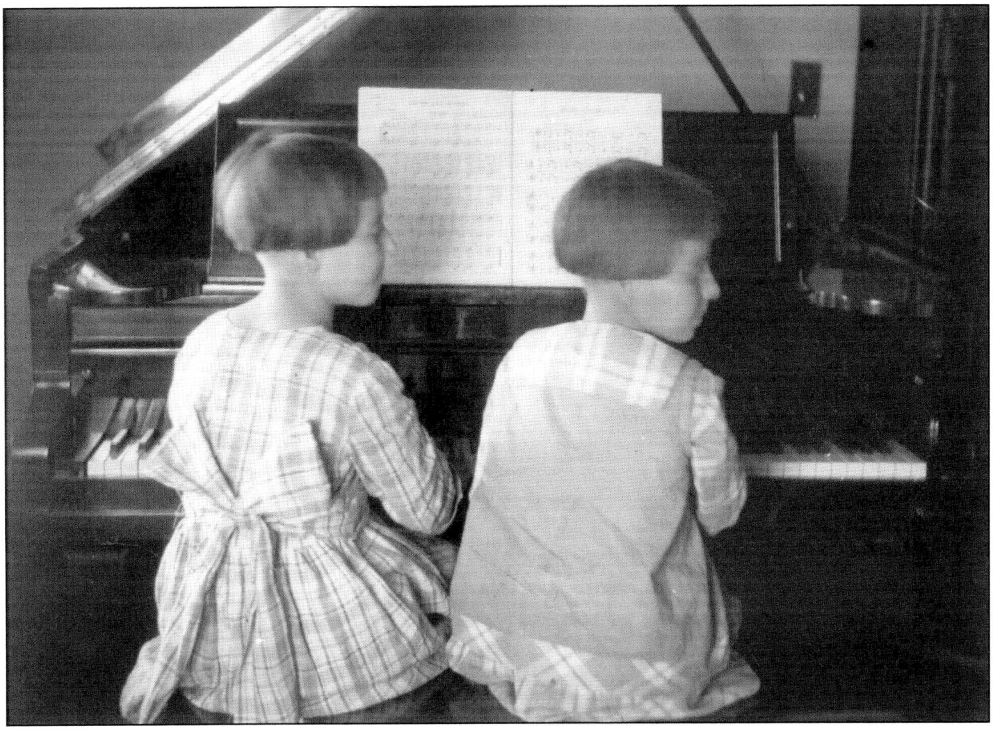

Day-to-day World War I children's fashions were simple and practical. Nellie (left) and Josephine Frantz, attired in cotton plaid dresses, prepared to practice the piano around 1918. The sisters, daughters of Ezra A. and Mary Buckley Frantz, wore easily maintained Buster Brown-style haircuts. The hemlines of their dresses were most likely shorter to conserve fabric during wartime. (MEDA.)

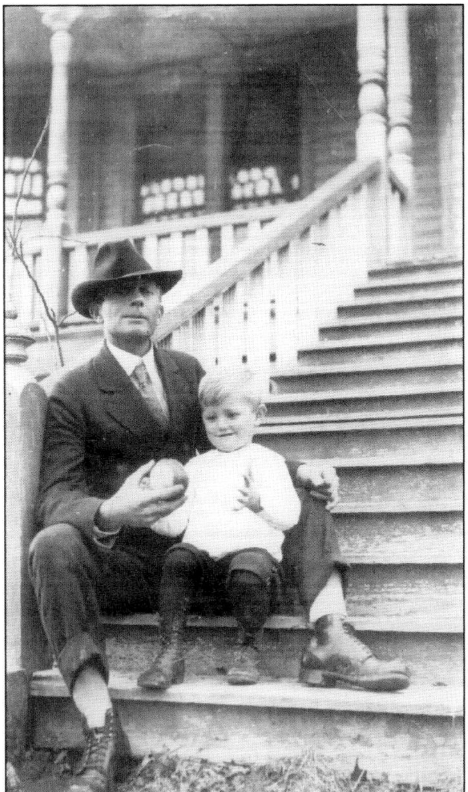

Chester A. Gibbs and his son sat on the front steps of the "old Starr place" around 1919. Chester Jr. gleefully eyed the ball in his father's hand. The boy was dressed to play in high-top laced leather boots, white collared shirt, and dark knickerbockers. The Gibbs were in town to visit the boy's grandparents, William H. and Emma Gibbs. (WPL.)

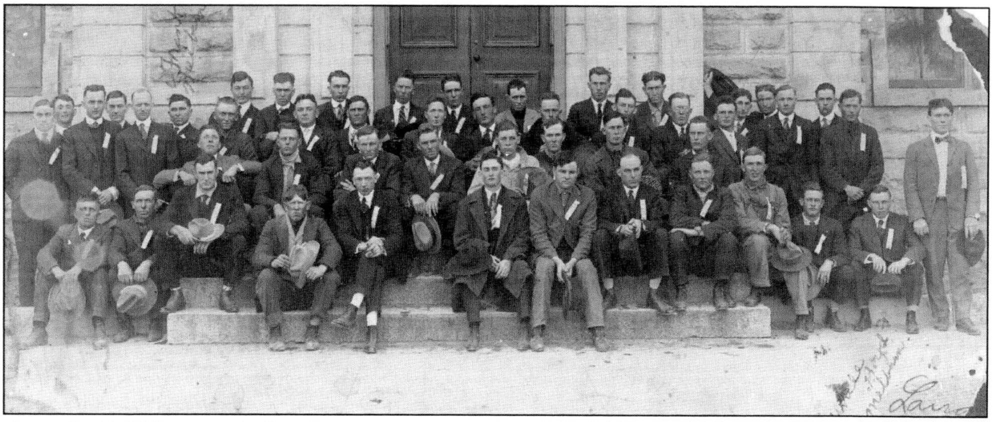

A total of 1,825 young Parker County men completed World War I draft registration cards in June 1917. Among the registrants were four brothers, Albert Edward, James, Frank, and Albert Orville Milburn. Frank and his cousin Boyd Milburn were among this group of inductees photographed outside the courthouse. A variety of activities revolved around the recruits' departure, including farewell speeches, church services, and lunch at cafes around town. (WPL.)

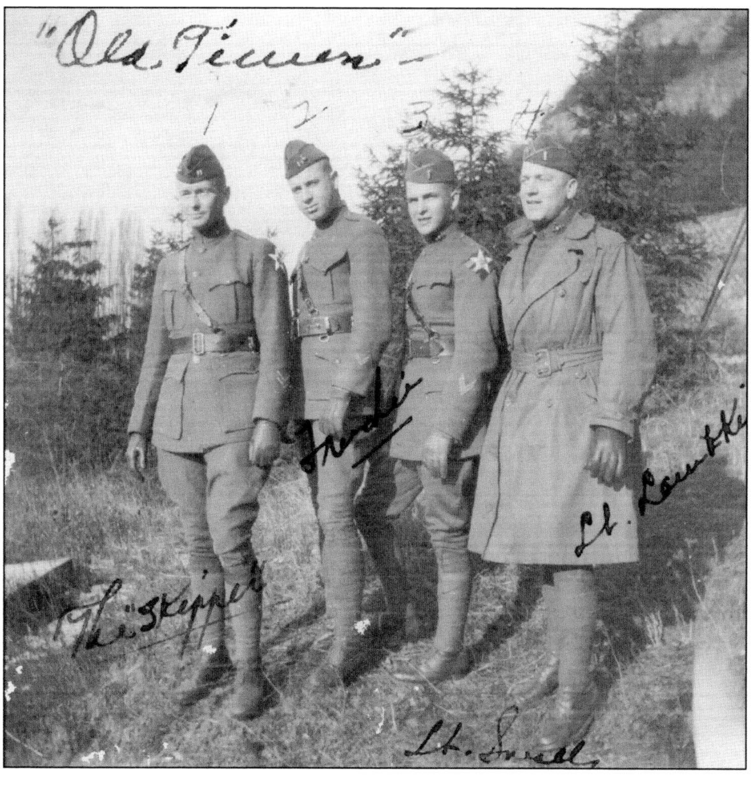

Capt. Walter S. Fant Jr. was awarded two French Croix de Guerre medals for gallantry at Vierzy and St. Etienne, France, in July and October 1918. Fant is pictured among the "Old-Timers" of his 76th Company, 6th Regiment, US Marine Corps. From left to right are "The Skipper," Capt. Fant, Lt. Arthur C. Small, and Lt. Al B. Lambkin on the east bank of the Rhine River, February 11, 1919. (BF.)

Sending a soldier off to war was an experience filled with pride, love, and great trepidation. Each homecoming was a joyful event long remembered by the serviceman and his family. Young Marian and Knox Fant welcomed their uncle Julian McFall home from World War I on October 28, 1918. (MW.)

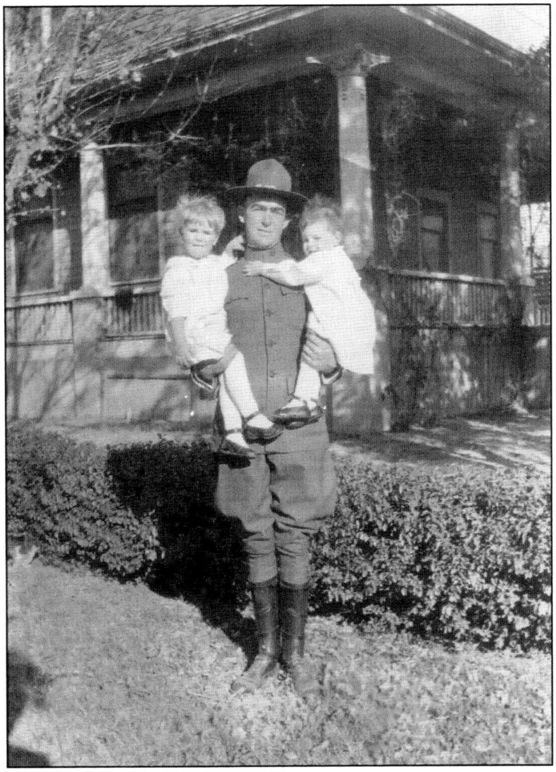

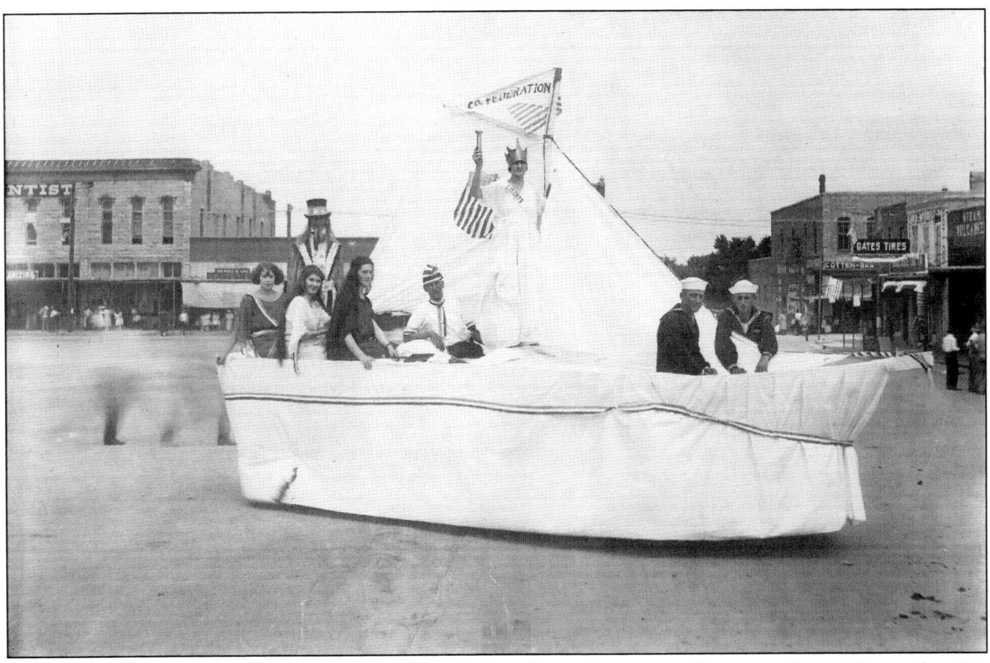

Weatherford celebrated the end of World War I with an Armistice Day parade on November 11, 1918. This naval-themed float featured Maude Campbell as the Statue of Liberty. Cousins Frank and Boyd Milburn, local veterans, are the sailors in the front of the boat. Frank Milburn later became the proprietor of Milburn Hardware. (WPL.)

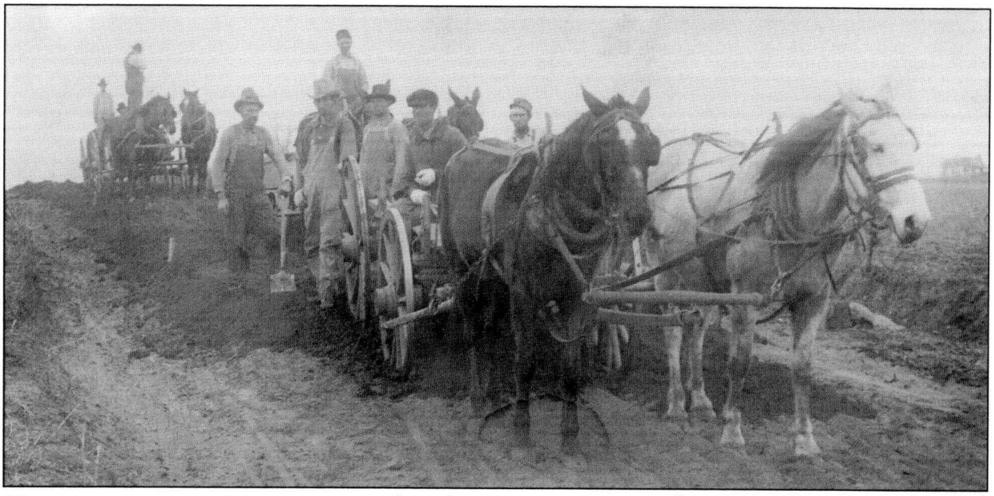

The construction and maintenance of roads was important to vehicular traffic, whether it be a horse and wagon or a new fangled tin lizzie. This horse-powered crew worked east of Weatherford on January 28, 1914. During the late 1910s, the chamber of commerce successfully negotiated the Kuteman Cut-off, which shortened the route to Fort Worth approximately six miles. A contract was also awarded initiating the construction of State Highway No. 1 (Bankhead Highway). Parker County later acquired a new kind of horsepower—these 1923 and 1924 Best Model 60 tractors—for construction purposes. The gasoline-powered crawlers were the most versatile and well-built tractors of their day. Model 60s were made from 1919 by Best and its successor, Caterpillar Tractor, until 1931, when a diesel engine was dropped into the Model 60 chassis, making the first Caterpillar diesel tractor. (Above, BSM; below, WPL.)

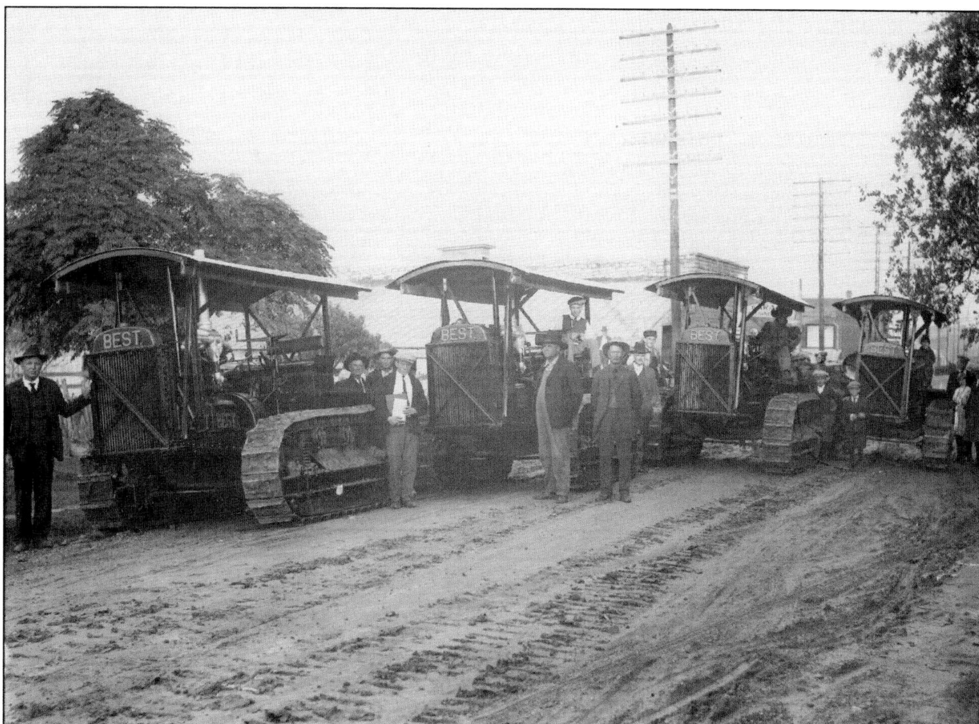

Six

1920–1929

Renewed Hope

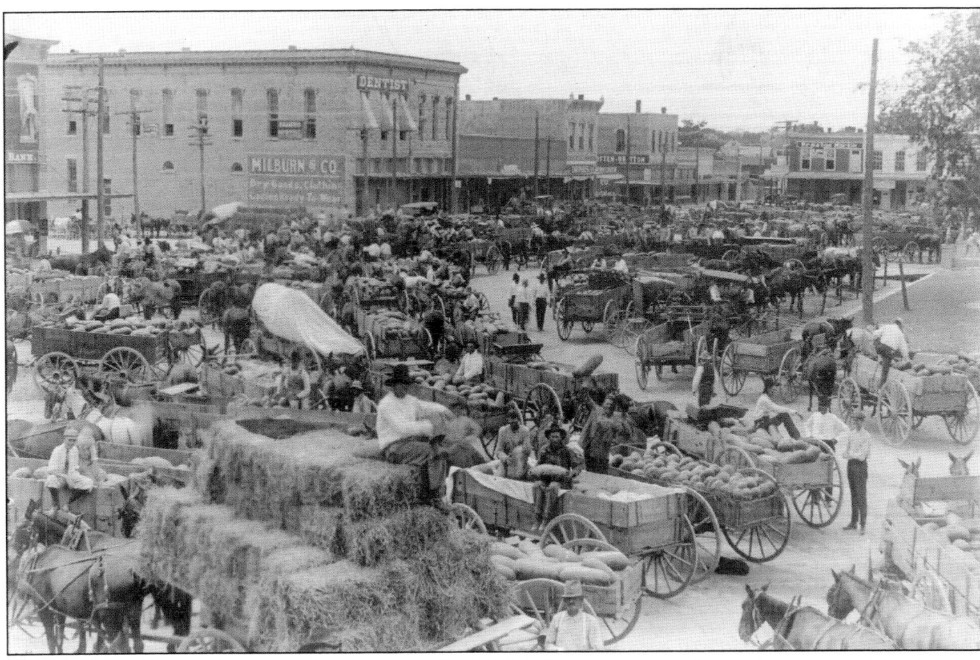

The *St. Louis Dispatch* reported on August 19, 1923, "That county is the native home of the famous Tom Watson melon, accounted the biggest ever, that took first prize at the World's Fair in St. Louis 19 years ago and is producing offspring by the millions." (UTA, Texas Photograph Collection.)

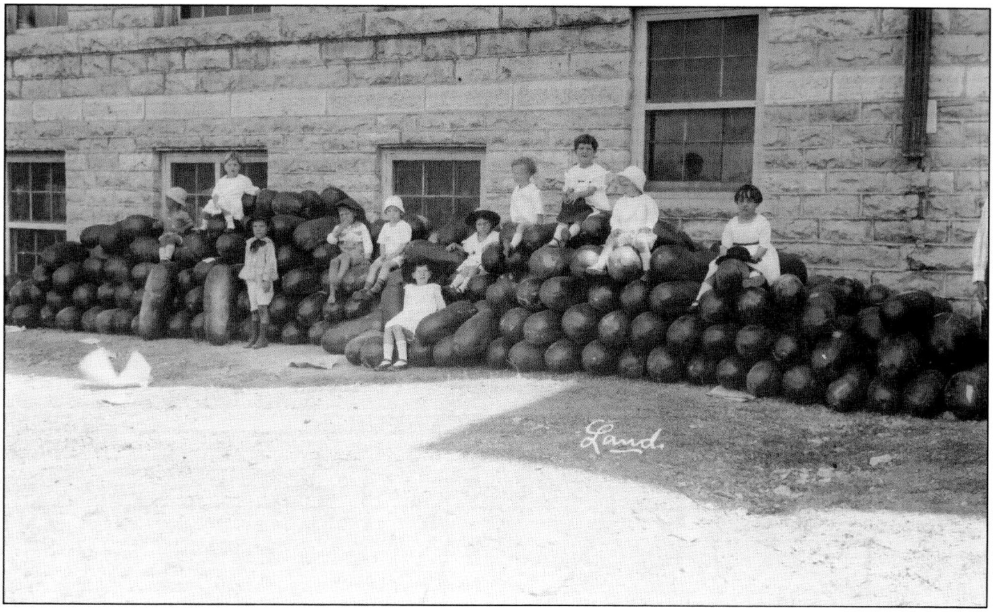

The second-annual Tom Watson Watermelon Slicing was held on August 1, 1921, to celebrate Parker County's growing watermelon produce industry. It took place on the Weatherford High School grounds across Palo Pinto Street from the newly opened Hotel Parker. Children were drawn to the watermelons stacked against the high school building in anticipation of a large attendance (above). The crowd, estimated to include between 5,000 and 10,000 people, traveled by automobile and train to consume between 600 and 1,000 of the long Tom Watson variety melons. The day started when a Fox film crew began shooting a motion picture documenting all stages of watermelon production, from the field to the railcar shipment. The watermelon slicing was also included in the film project negotiated by the Parker County Farm Bureau Melon Growers Association for national distribution. (Above, WPL; below, UTA, Texas Photograph Collection.)

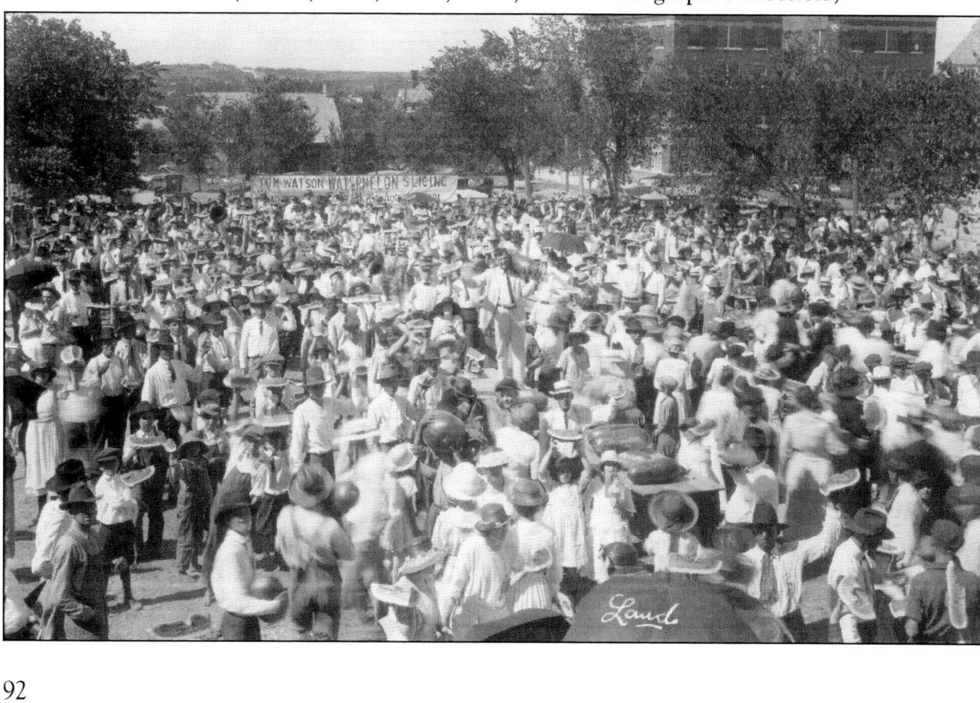

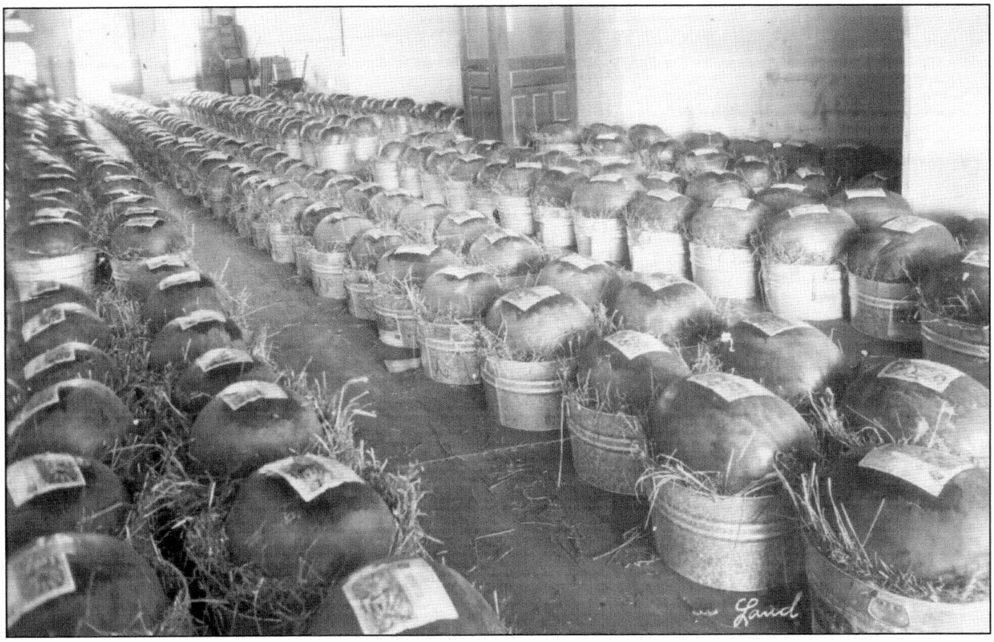

Parker County watermelons were shipped to distant markets via railcar. Triumph (also known as Jumbo) watermelons were individually packed in galvanized washtubs cushioned with hay to assure their safe arrival. This variety was grown especially for its size, which could range from 75 to 100 pounds per melon. (UTA, Fort Worth *Star-Telegram* Collection.)

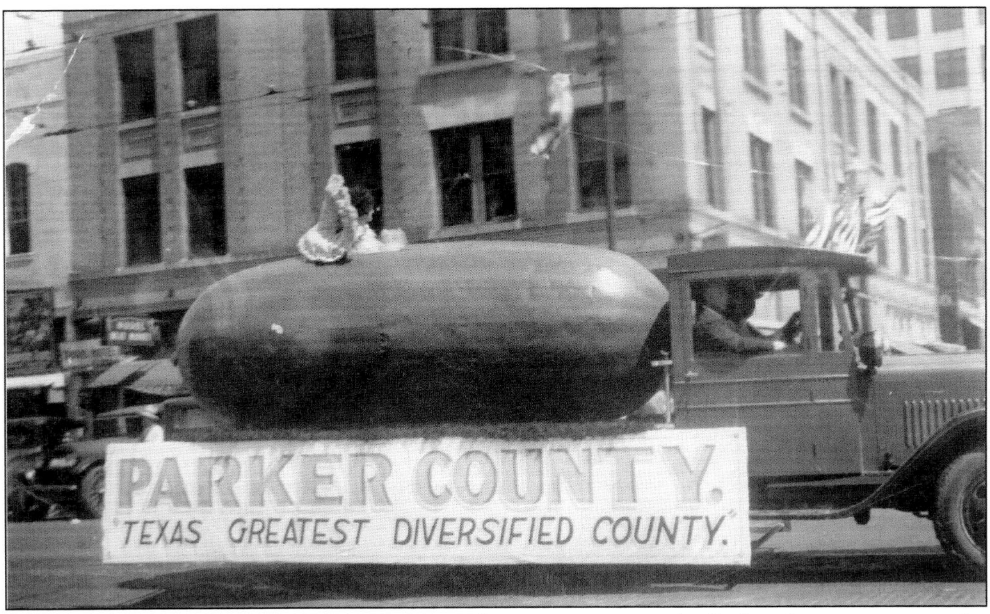

Weatherford's iconic tin watermelon made its first appearance as the Parker County entry in the 1928 West Texas Chamber of Commerce parade in Fort Worth. Helen Massey rode inside the melon and waved to the crowd along the parade route. The tin melon rested on a framed wooden base on the southeast corner of the courthouse for over a decade. (VC.)

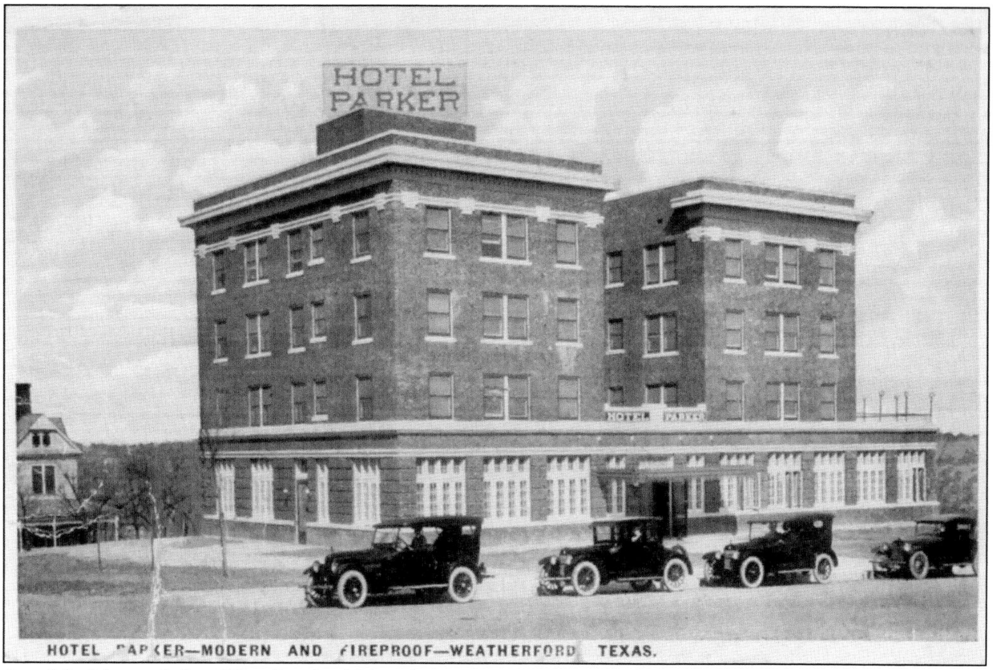

Stockholders of the Weatherford Hotel Company, organized by the chamber of commerce in 1919, contributed $125,000 in capital to construct this modern, fireproof, 52-room hotel on Palo Pinto Street. Completed in 1921 at a cost of $135,000, guest rooms featured steam heat and cold running water. Single rooms rented for $1.50 to $2.50, while double rooms cost $3 to $4. The Hotel Parker accommodated guests for over four decades. (MW.)

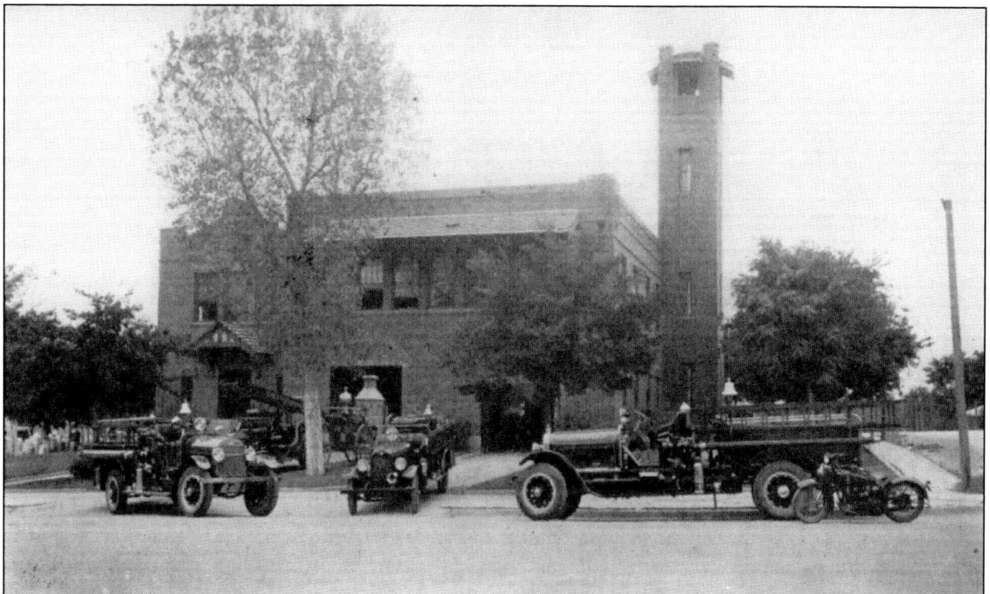

Weatherford's new city hall and fire station opened in December 1911 on the Palo Pinto site used for firehouse purposes since at least 1885. The civic building included a jail, city offices, council chamber, auditorium, and firehouse. This mid-1920s photograph displays firefighting equipment dating from the horse-drawn Silsby steam pumper to the newest fire truck. (BSM.)

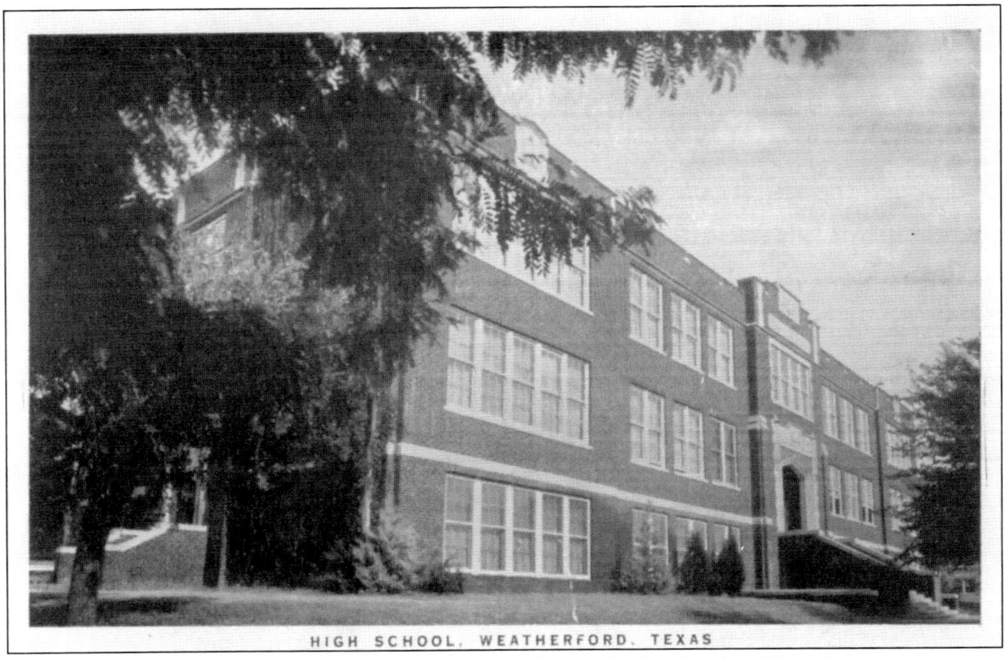

With the student population growing, construction of a new high school building became necessary. In 1921, property behind Central High School was acquired, including the site of the 1876 Episcopal Church, and a three-story redbrick senior high school was constructed for $190,000. The old Central High School with its 1909 addition then became the junior high school. Weatherford City Hall and the central fire station now occupy the adjoining sites of both buildings. (BSM.)

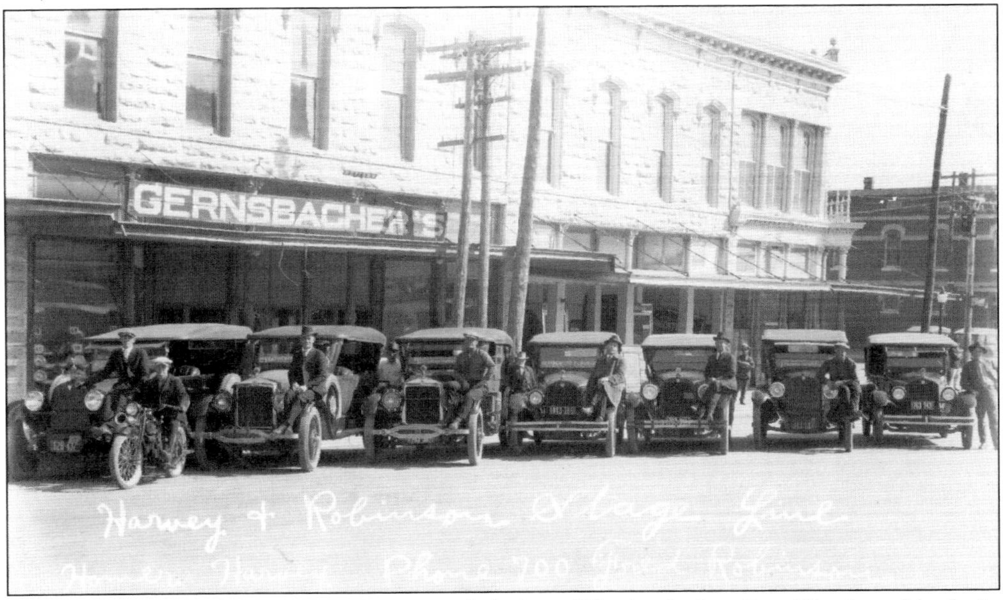

The Harvey and Robinson Stage Line ran daily from Weatherford to Fort Worth and back. In 1924, the fare was $1 each way. Company vehicles are lined up on the northwest corner of the square in front of Gernsbacher Brothers. The Gernsbacher name in Weatherford retailing dates to the mid-1880s. Many Jewish merchant families formerly resided in Weatherford, including Sanger, Neumegen, Haas, and Levy, despite there being no local synagogue for their worship. (WPL.)

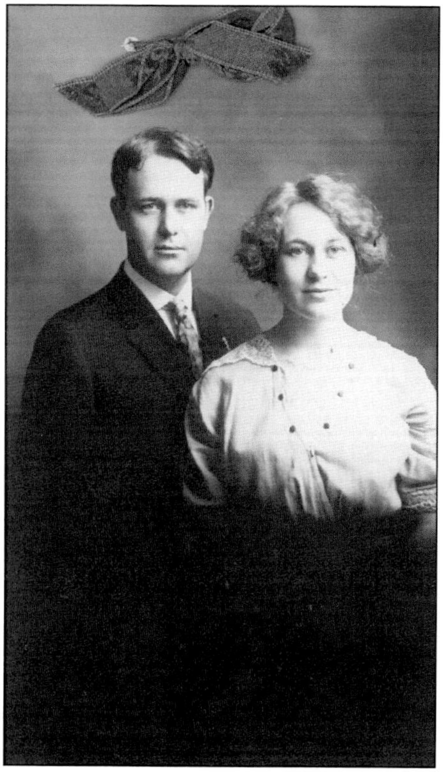

Howard Rea formally opened his drugstore on the corner of South Main Street and the courthouse square on August 15, 1925. Zadie Lee, his wife, dispensed souvenirs and refreshments to visitors while a local orchestra provided music. After Rea's death just 10 days later, Zadie Lee Rea continued to operate the Howard Rea Drug Store, now the locale of the Downtown Cafe, for the next 20 years. (WPL.)

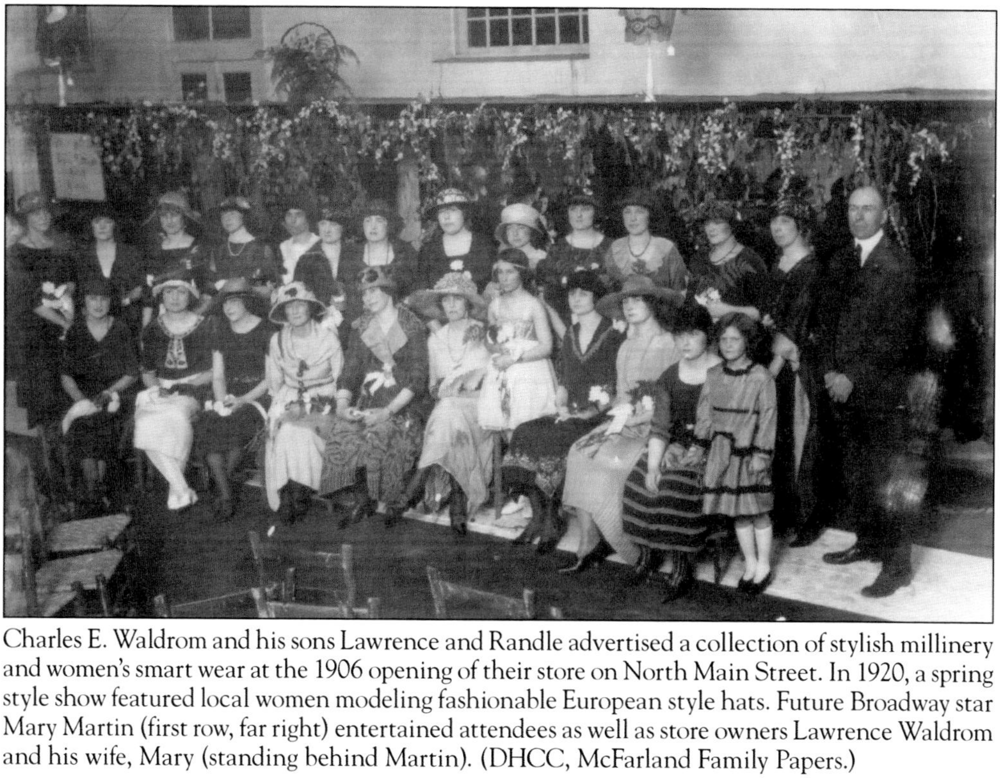

Charles E. Waldrom and his sons Lawrence and Randle advertised a collection of stylish millinery and women's smart wear at the 1906 opening of their store on North Main Street. In 1920, a spring style show featured local women modeling fashionable European style hats. Future Broadway star Mary Martin (first row, far right) entertained attendees as well as store owners Lawrence Waldrom and his wife, Mary (standing behind Martin). (DHCC, McFarland Family Papers.)

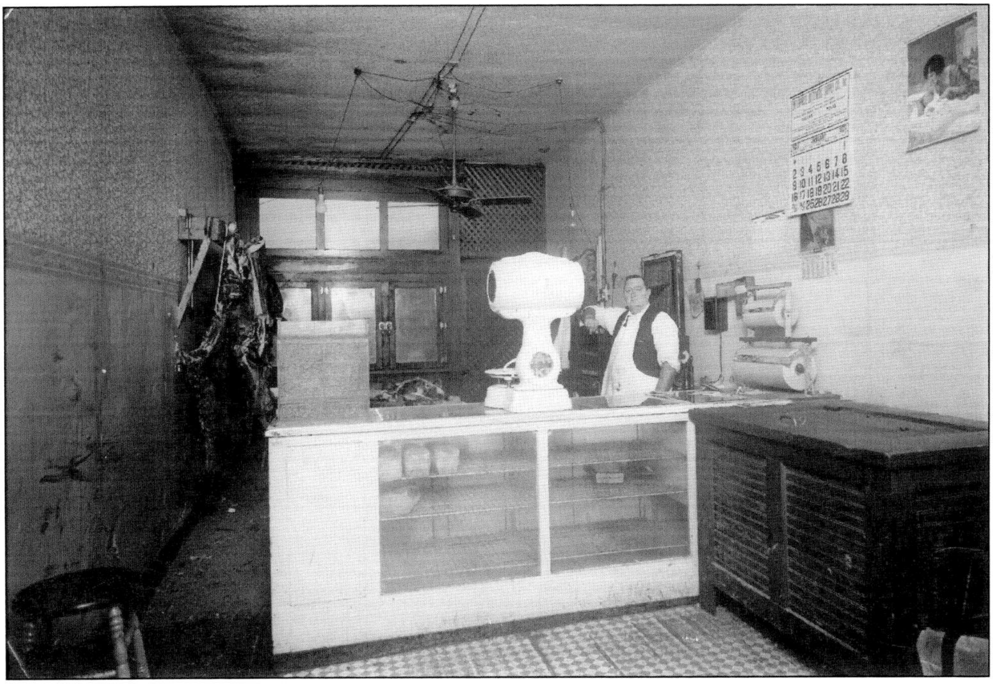

Butcher William Waldock was the proprietor of this meat market located on North Main Street. The wall calendar is turned to January 1927. Contrast the appearance of Waldock's business in 1927 to its 1890s appearance, when he shared it with his brother Harry (see page 47). (WPL.)

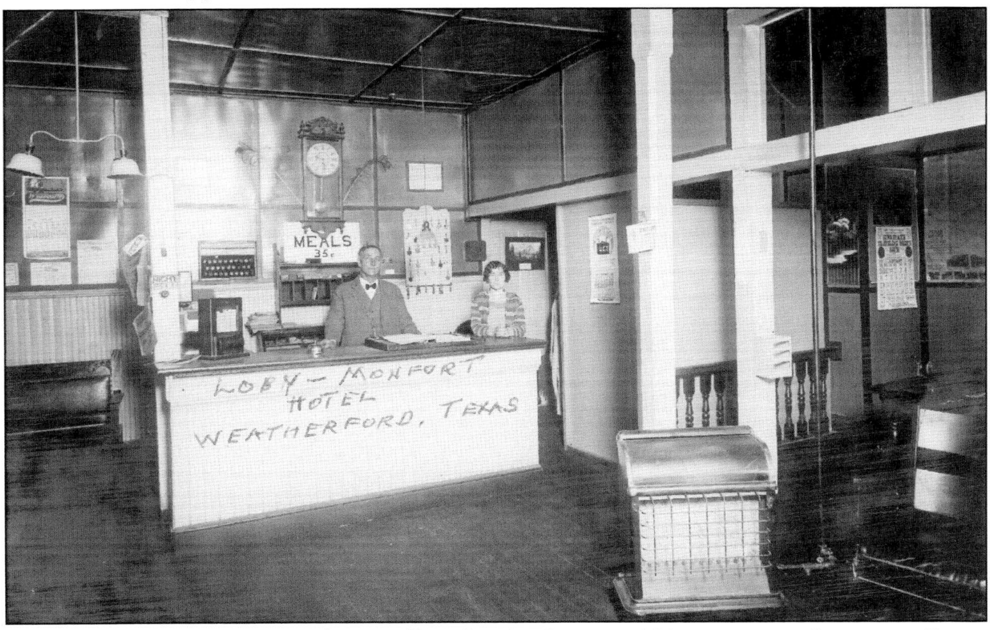

The lobby of the Montfort Hotel was well outfitted in January 1929 to accommodate guests. Room keys were conveniently hung on a board behind the desk. Late arrivals summoned the clerk by pressing the night bell. Meals were available for 35¢. Although J.F. Montfort sold his interest in the hotel on West Church Street in 1907, the inn retained his name until it was destroyed by fire on October 18, 1948. (WPL.)

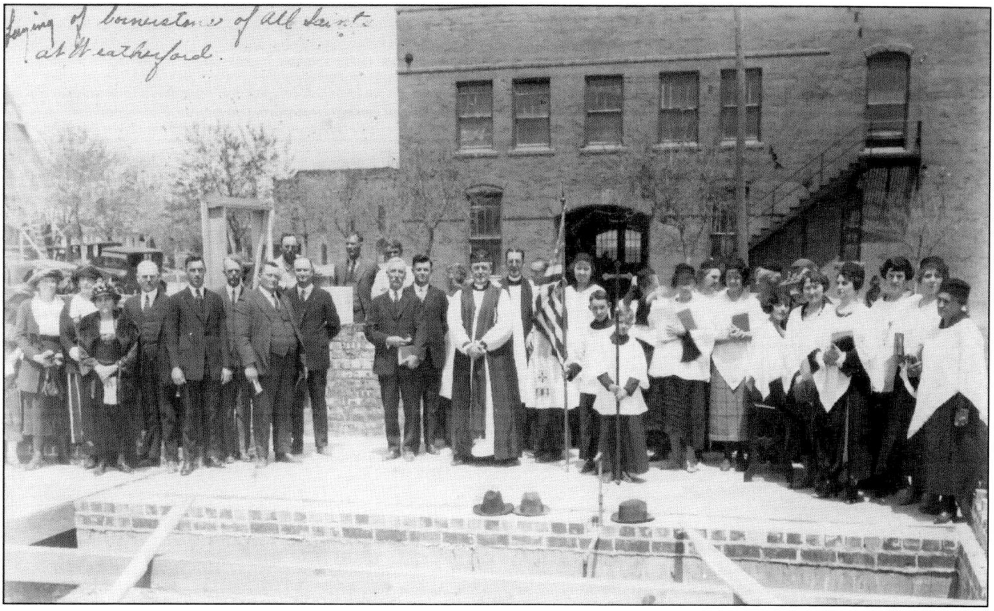

The cornerstone for the old Episcopal church on Wausau (now Davis) Street, north of West Oak Street, was laid on July 4, 1876. The property was sold in 1921 to make way for the new senior high school. To memorialize her daughter, Margaret C. Foat donated the southeast corner of South Waco and West Church Streets for the next church building. The cornerstone for All Saints Episcopal Church was placed in this ceremony on April 18, 1923. Bishop Moore of Dallas (center) and Rector Edward S. Barlow officiated. Behind the congregation, one can see the south side of the city hall and fire station, as well as the front of the county jail. Below, Reverend Barlow stands in the pulpit of the new church, consecrated November 4, 1923. Stained-glass windows illuminate all four sides of the redbrick Gothic structure. (Both, WPL.)

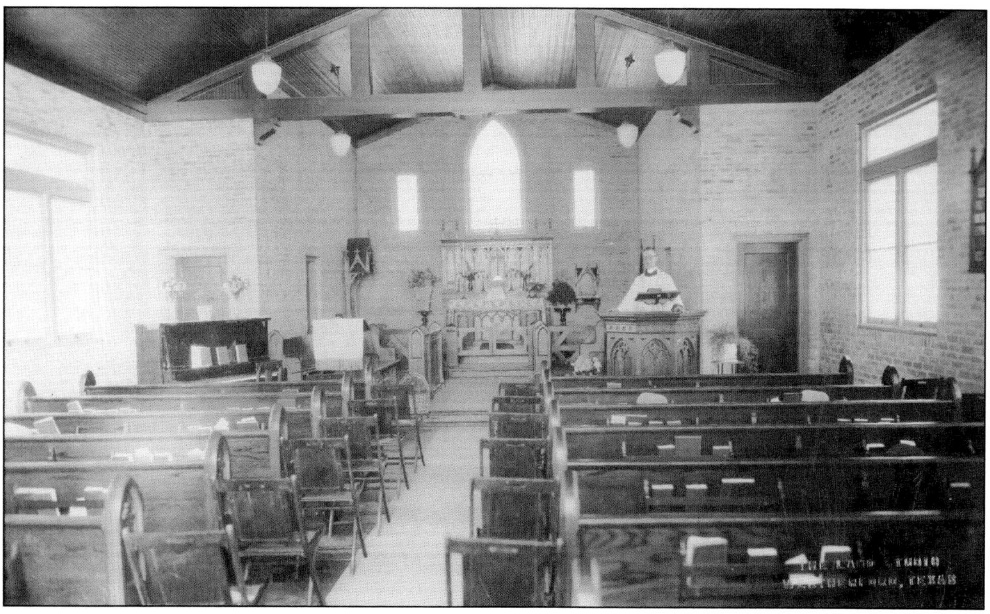

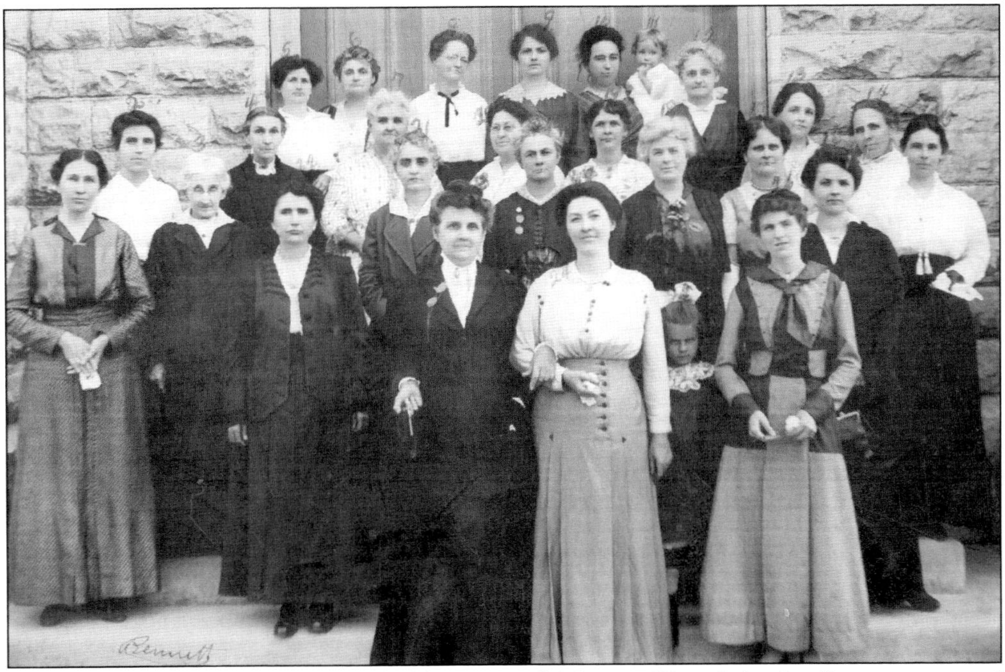

First Methodist Church, a limestone building at South Main and East Columbia Streets, was one of the fastest-growing churches in the city in 1921. The members of the Woman's Missionary Society were charged with the goal of increasing enrollment in the church, as well as the Missionary Society. The group was led by the pastor's wife, Lena Stockton Nelms. (WPL.)

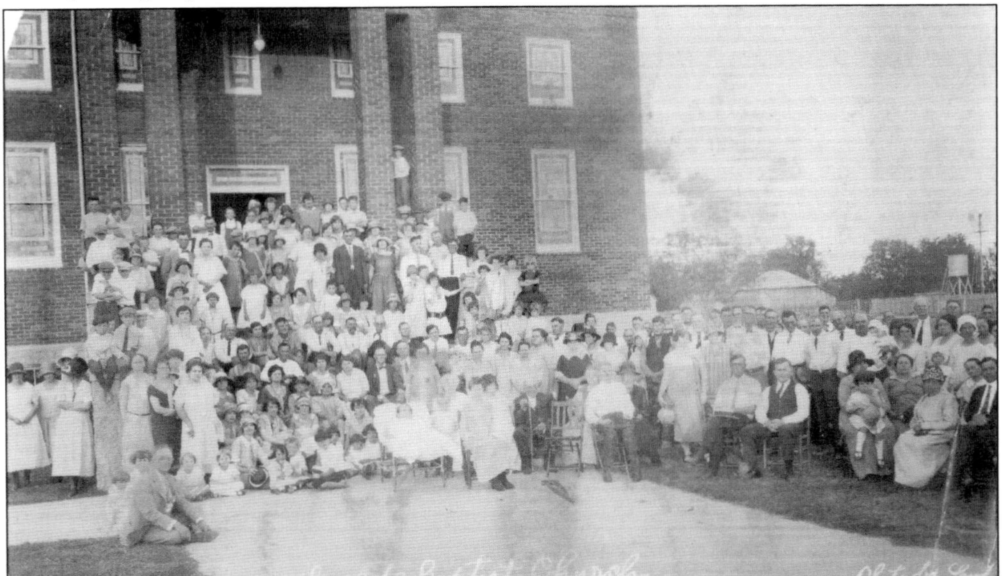

The North Side Baptist Church congregation gathered to break ground on the largest tabernacle in Parker County on June 1, 1925. The 80-by-100-foot concrete structure was built 40 feet south of the church's North Main Street location. Plans called for the tabernacle to be completed by July 15. The open design accommodated approximately 2,000 seated worshippers and allowed physically challenged attendees to enjoy services from their cars. (WPL.)

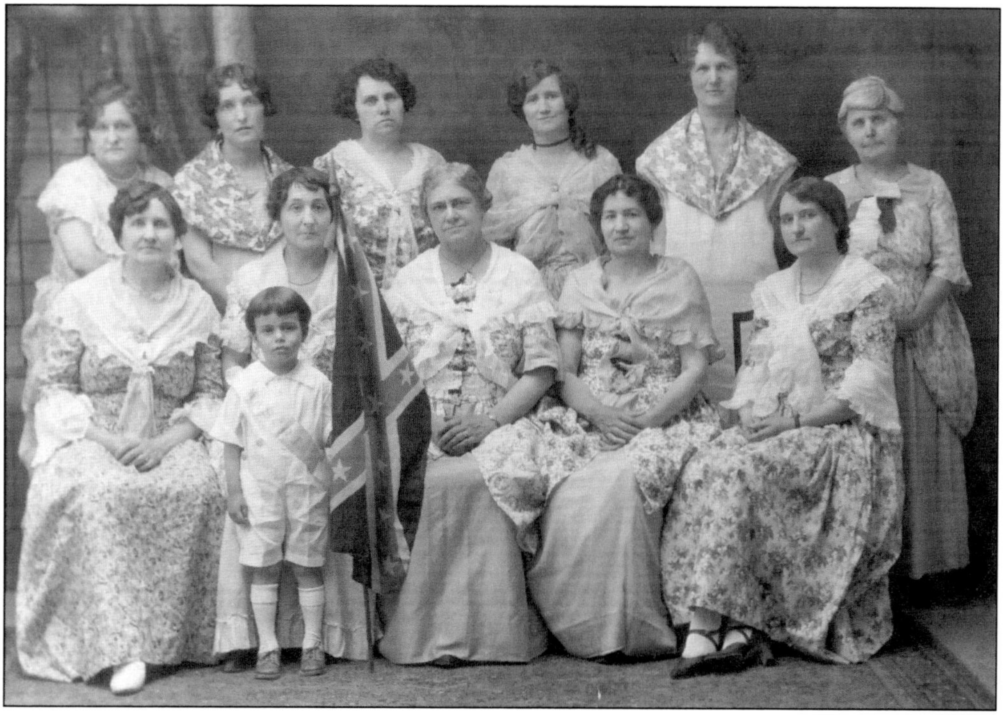

Young Charles Massey holds the Confederate battle flag in this 1925 portrait of the Sam Lanham Chapter No. 733, United Daughters of the Confederacy. His mother, Mollie Massey, is seated behind him. In 1915, the chapter commissioned local stonecutter Alex Rawlins to erect the pedestal for the Confederate monument on the northwest courthouse lawn. The soldier was added in 1929. The memorial was relocated to the southeast corner of the courthouse in 1947. (WPL.)

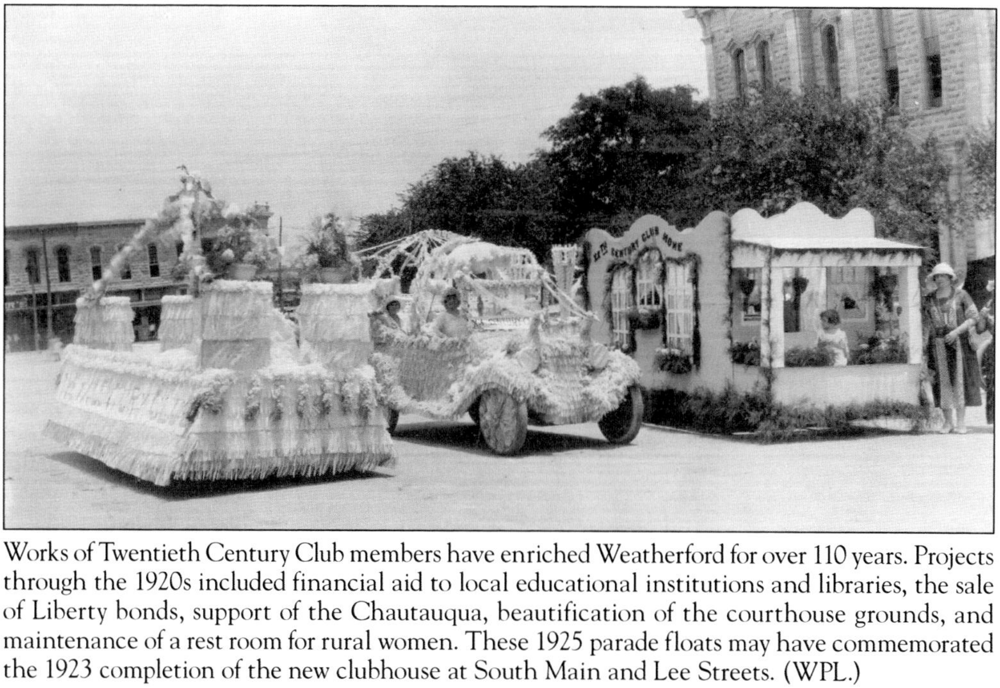

Works of Twentieth Century Club members have enriched Weatherford for over 110 years. Projects through the 1920s included financial aid to local educational institutions and libraries, the sale of Liberty bonds, support of the Chautauqua, beautification of the courthouse grounds, and maintenance of a rest room for rural women. These 1925 parade floats may have commemorated the 1923 completion of the new clubhouse at South Main and Lee Streets. (WPL.)

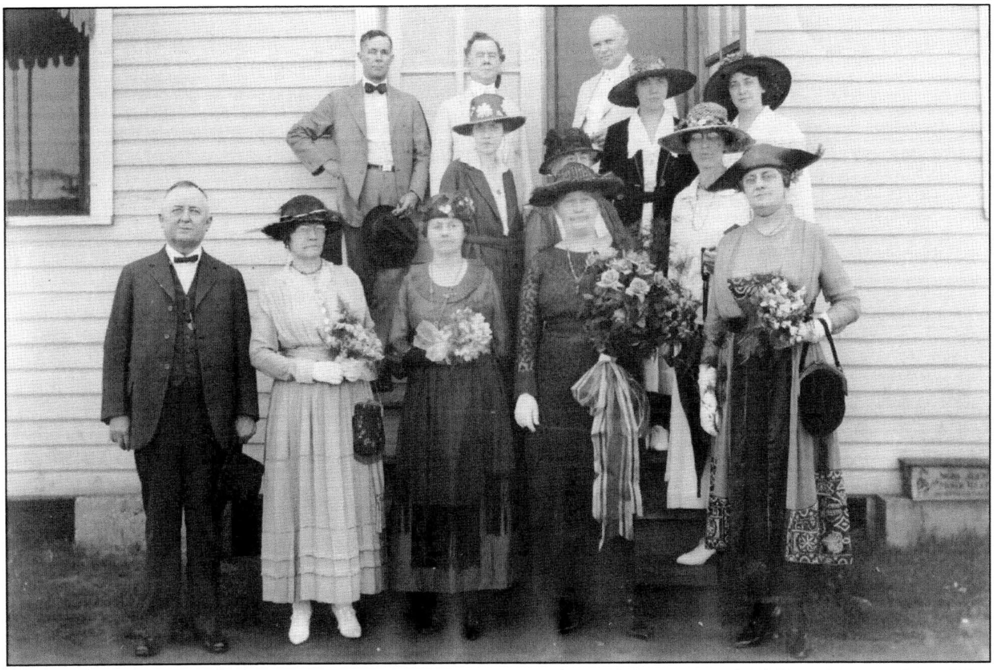

Four World War I Liberty Loan campaigns were conducted from April 1917 to September 1918 to raise money for the Allied cause. A fifth effort, the Victory Liberty Loan campaign, was initiated after the Armistice was signed. Weatherford was one of ten cities in Texas to exceed its subscription quota. The federal government recognized Weatherford's achievement by naming a 9,000-ton ship the SS *City of Weatherford*. A local delegation traveled to Pensacola, Florida, for the launching held on May 22, 1920. Among those attending the ceremony are, from left to right, (first row) Henry Clay Shropshire, chairman of the Weatherford Liberty Loan executive committee, and matrons of honor Margaret Bowie, Magna Dawson, Annie Barthold, and Mary Etta MacKenzie. Annie Barthold, chairperson of the Liberty Loan women's division and sponsor, performed the christening. (WC.)

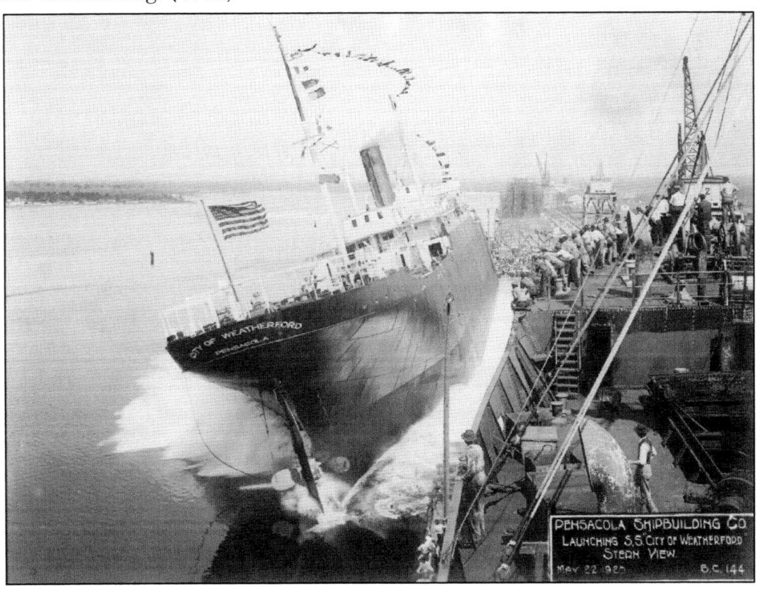

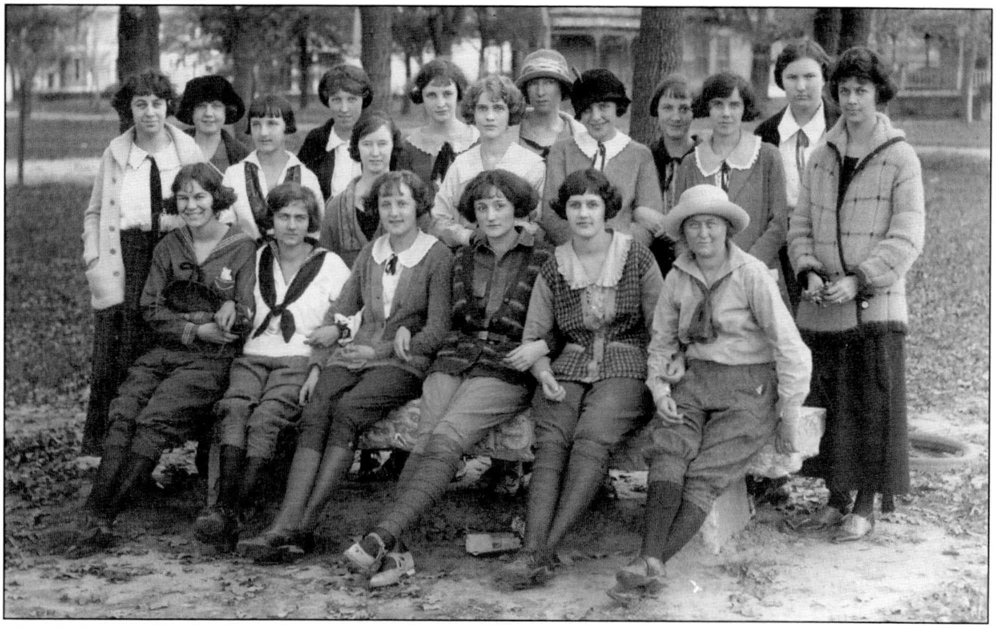

The fashions worn by these Weatherford High School coeds in 1924 demonstrate an awareness of the evolving role of women in society. Hair is short and bobbed to fit under close-fitting cloche hats. Sportswear breeches, sailor blouses, and full skirts allow easy movement. Low-cut shoes are nonrestrictive. This group photograph disproves the opinion prevalent in the 1920s that athletic competition made women less feminine. (DHCC, Kay Fulgham Collection.)

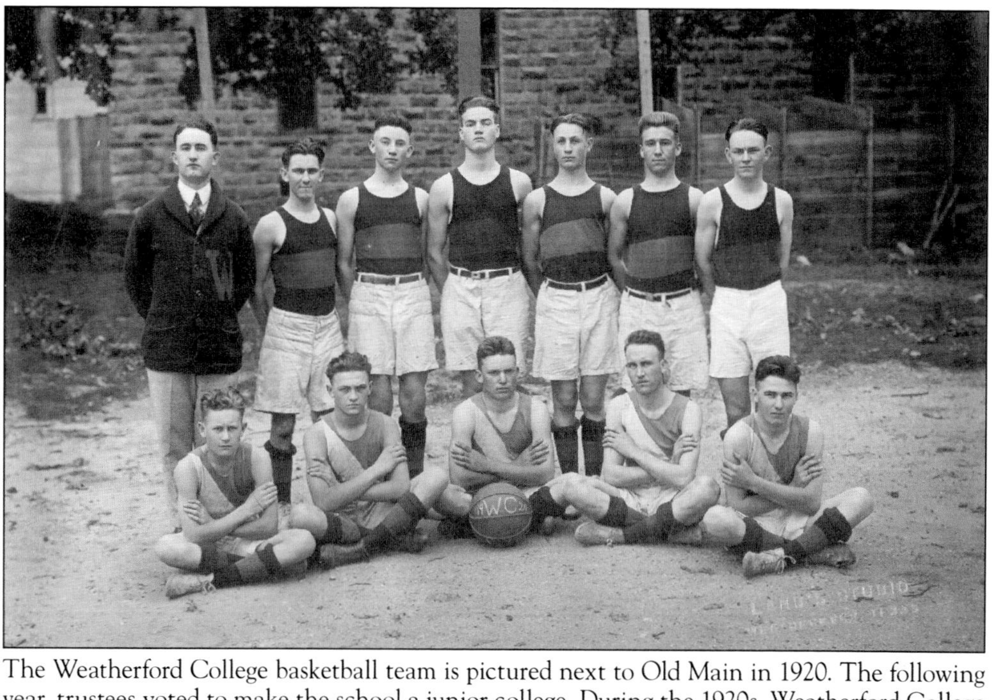

The Weatherford College basketball team is pictured next to Old Main in 1920. The following year, trustees voted to make the school a junior college. During the 1920s, Weatherford College received major endowments from the estates of J.R. Couts (1924) and Edward Disney Farmer (1929), totaling approximately $65,000. (WC.)

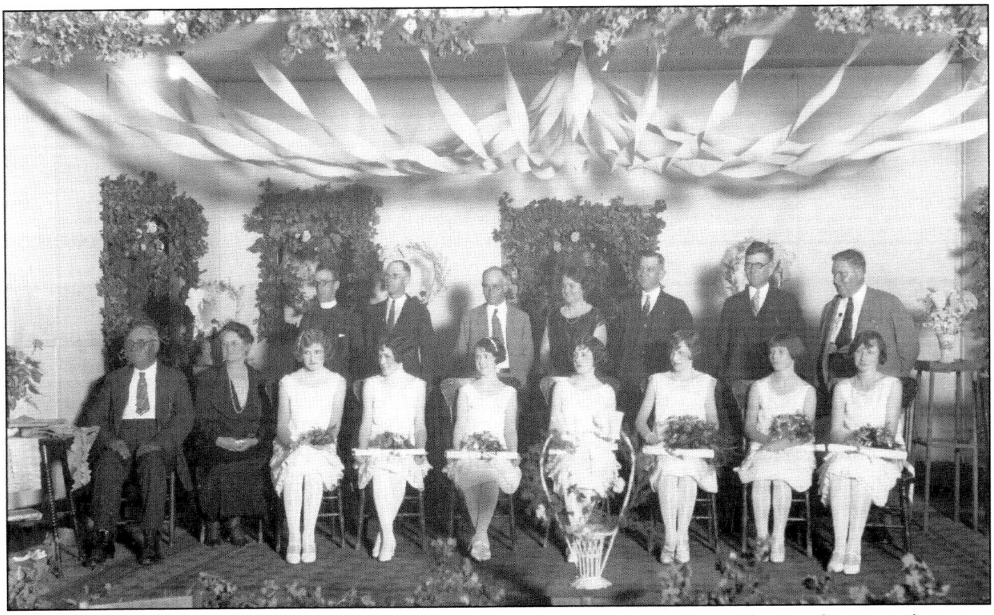

The Texas Pythian Home celebrated its first commencement in 1925. The graduating class was comprised of seven young ladies. Seated are, from left to right, Pythian Home superintendent Fred S. Heffner and his wife, Vera, head matron, and graduates Hertha Synnott, Flora Fowler, Alta Tatom, Agnes Ragsdale, Gladys Norris, Adele Joynes, and Teresa Steele. Local pastors and Pythian dignitaries stand behind the honorees. (TPH.)

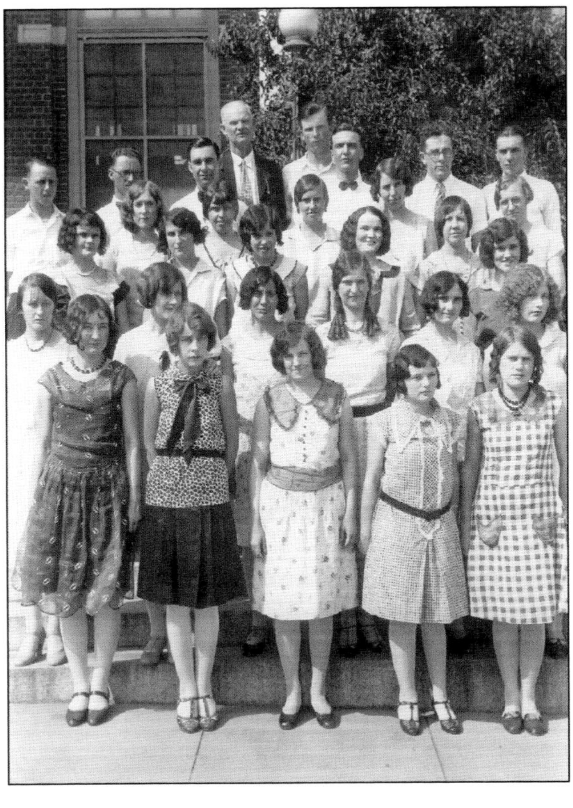

Texas Business College was established in 1919 by T.H. Gatlin. Classes were held above the Duke and Ayres store on the east side of the square. For 40 years, it produced graduates who were sought by businesses statewide for employment as stenographers, bookkeepers, and office assistants. The school newspaper was called the *Gatlin Gun*. T.H. Gatlin (sixth row, left) stands with members of a summer class in 1927 or 1928. (WC.)

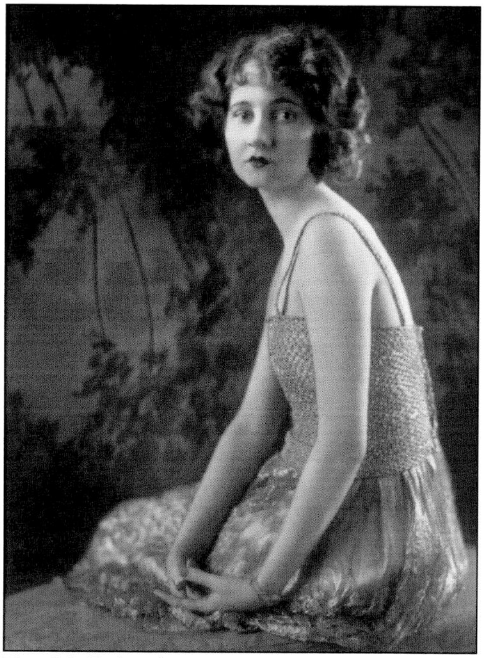

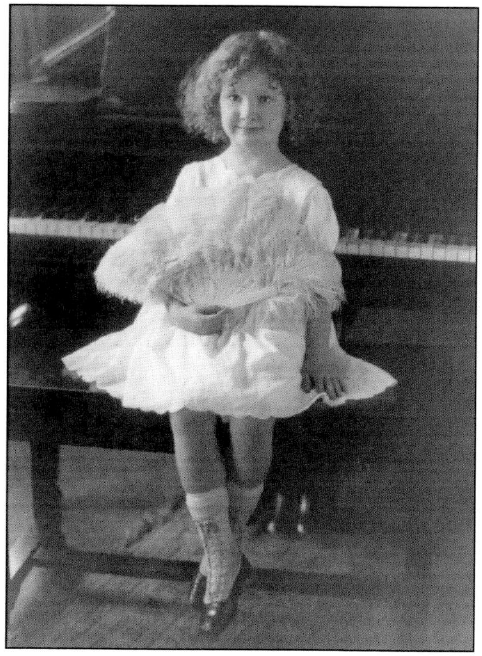

Two McFarland generations posed for portraits around 1921. Aleene McFarland is pictured about the time she was invited by the Waco Chamber of Commerce to represent Weatherford as a duchess at the Queen's Ball during the 1921 Texas Cotton Palace Exposition. Her niece, Louise McFarland, sat on the piano bench in her grandparents' home. Louise became a patron of the arts and introduced many local youths to opera. (Both, DHCC, McFarland Family Papers.)

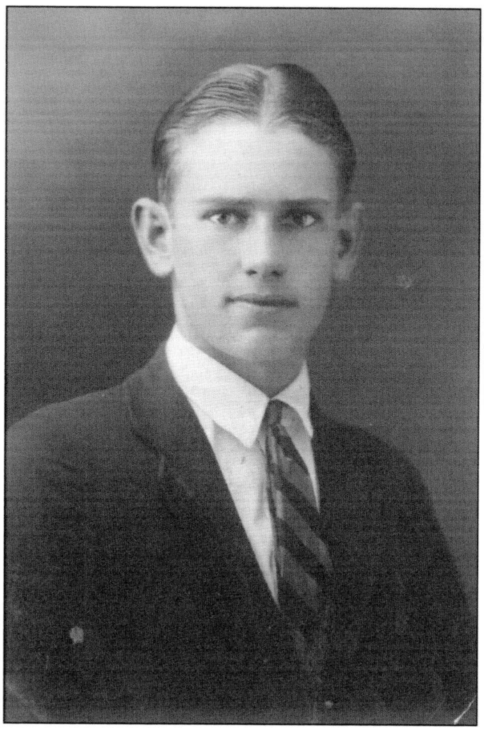

Jack Borden graduated from Weatherford College and the University of Texas Law School. He was twice elected district attorney, was an FBI agent during World War II, and served two terms as mayor. Borden was named America's Outstanding Older Worker on his 101st birthday in 2009. Upon his passing at 102 years young, Borden was the oldest former FBI agent and oldest member of the State Bar of Texas. (BW.)

William B. Buckley was a horse and mule trader who lived in the Dean community with his wife, Mary. She was the daughter of J.B. Pigg, who signed the petition requesting the organization of Parker County in 1855. The couple is pictured in 1925 after retiring and moving to the residence on South Main Street formerly occupied by their daughter and son-in-law, Ezra A. and Mary Frantz. (MEDA.)

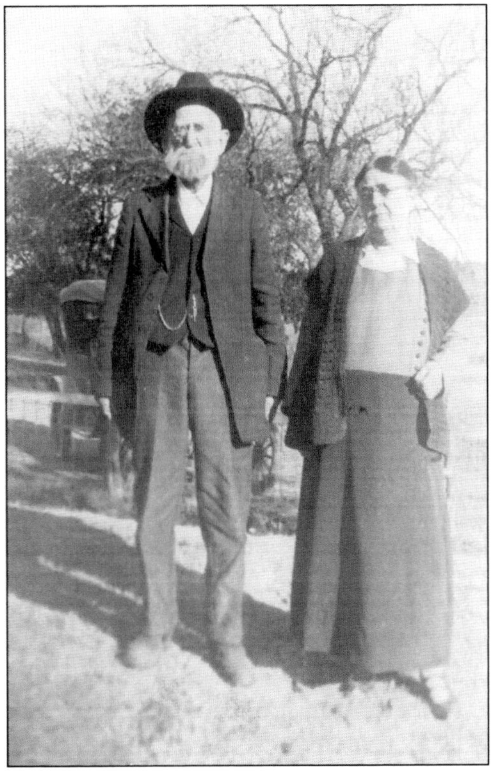

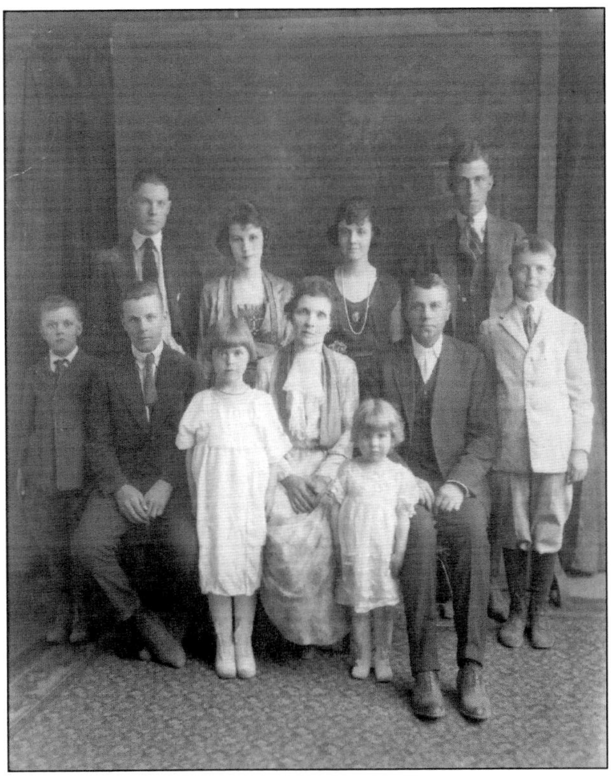

Barney Barker was Weatherford police chief from 1919 to 1922. He, his wife Marie, and their nine children sat for this family portrait around 1920. Barker began his law enforcement career as deputy sheriff in 1903 and served as a peace officer in Weatherford and Parker County for some 30 years, including two terms as sheriff. His uncle was Joshua Barker, elected first sheriff of Parker County in 1856. (WPL.)

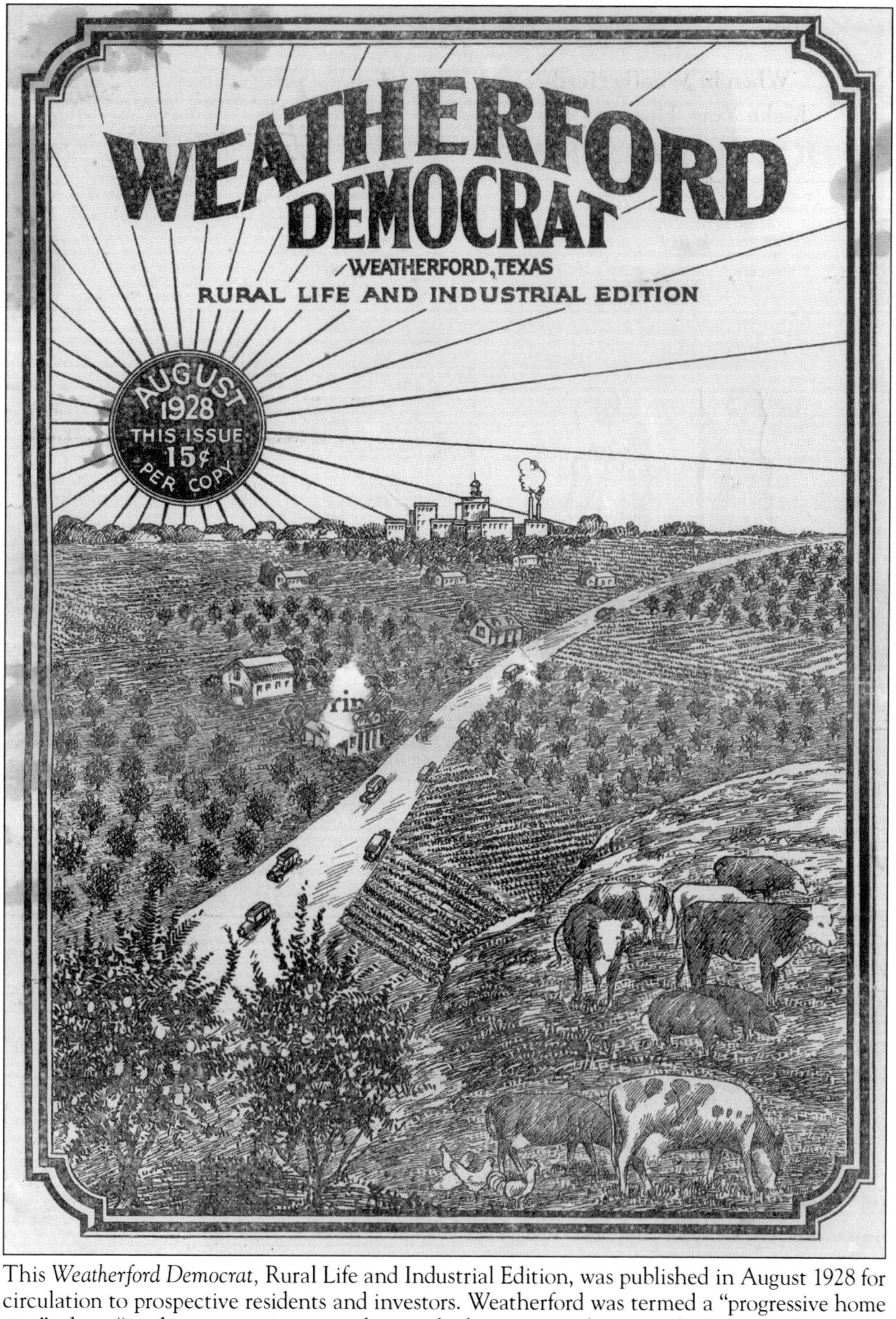

This *Weatherford Democrat,* Rural Life and Industrial Edition, was published in August 1928 for circulation to prospective residents and investors. Weatherford was termed a "progressive home city," where "modern conveniences and natural advantages make it an ideal place to live." The Water and Light Company was cited as a major factor in the city's growth, as was excellent access to local and national markets via highway and rail. (UTA, Moses P. Lamar Papers.)

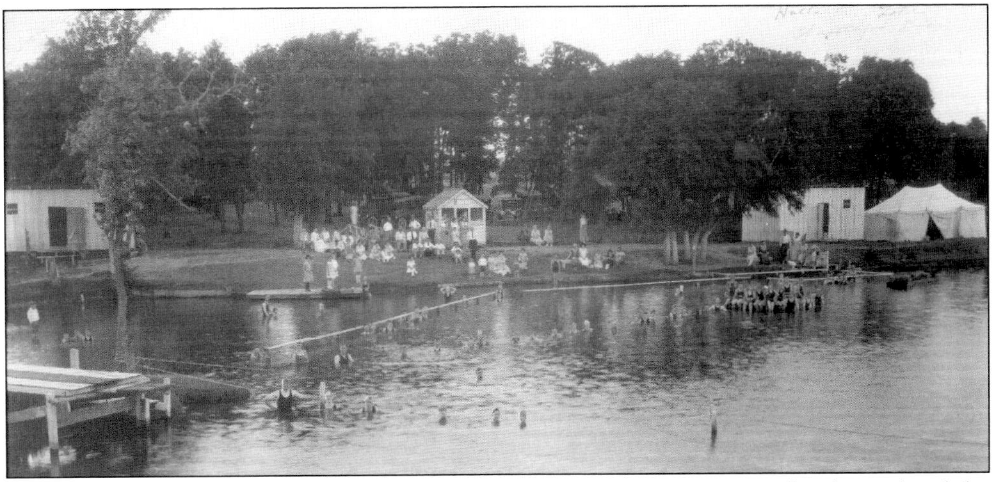

In January 1905, Weatherford banker and political and civic leader G.A. Holland completed the acquisition of the 23-acre Bonham survey, which included a small lake. Lee Coffman soon built the dam, creating Holland's Lake. With additional improvements, the area became widely used for fishing, swimming, and as a public park. In 1928, Holland purchased the historic McCleskey log cabin and moved it to Holland's Lake to become a museum and office for the Old Settlers Association, which held its annual meetings on the grounds each August. Holland deeded the property to the city of Weatherford in 1935. Children of all ages enjoyed this day at Holland's Lake sometime in the 1920s. Holland demonstrated the operation of a spinning wheel outside the log cabin in December 1929. He was known to spin and weave the fabric for his suits. (Above, UTA, Bowie and Holland Family Papers; below, UTA, Fort Worth *Star-Telegram* Collection.)

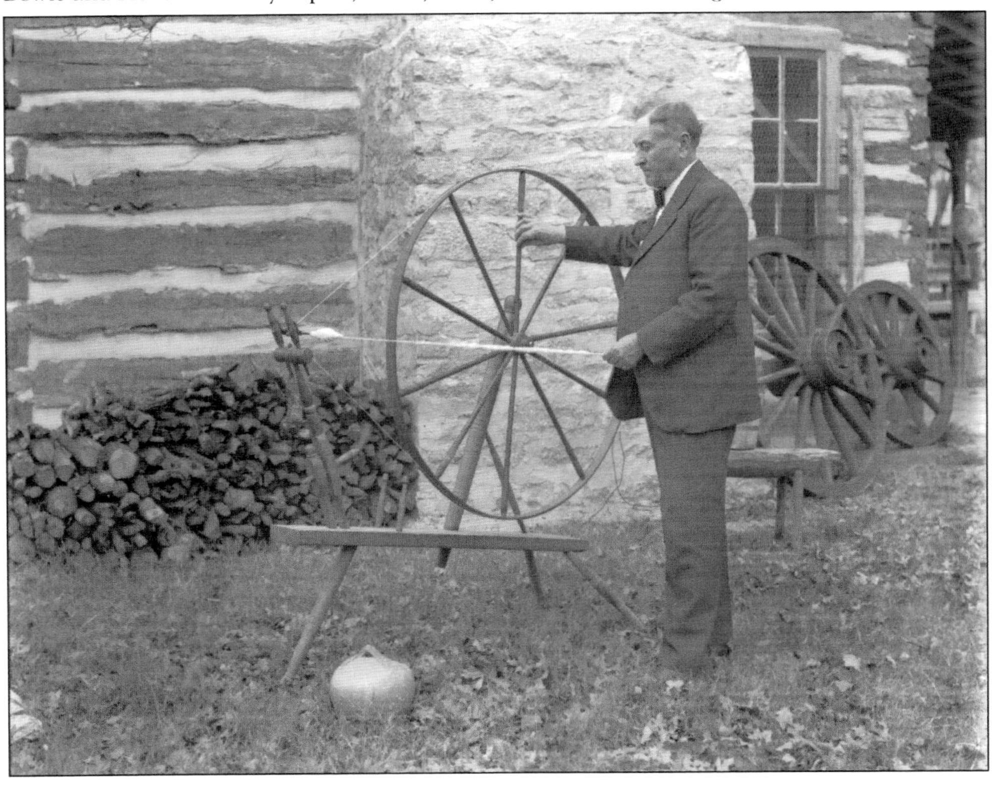

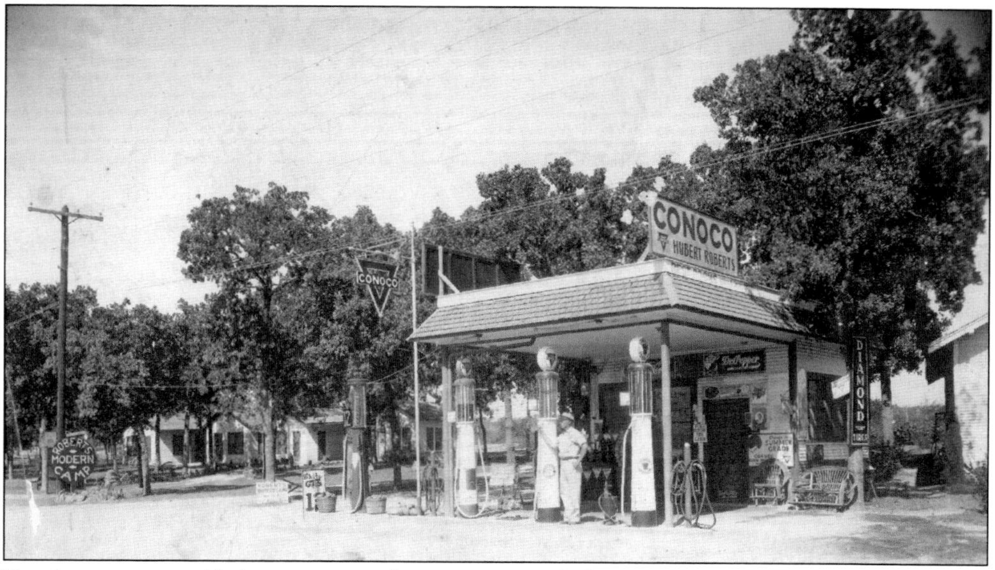

Tourist courts provided motorists with an economical alternative to expensive hotels, offering pleasant surroundings and convenient access to one's automobile. Frequently affiliated with a filling station, tourist courts became popular stopovers for the motoring public. The J. Lee Roberts family settled in the Greenwood community of Parker County in 1885 and moved to a farm in the Dicey area in 1899. Hubert Roberts operated this Conoco gasoline station and adjacent motor court on Fort Worth Street along the Bankhead Highway. The station later offered Texaco petroleum products. (Both, UTA, Roberts Family Photographs.)

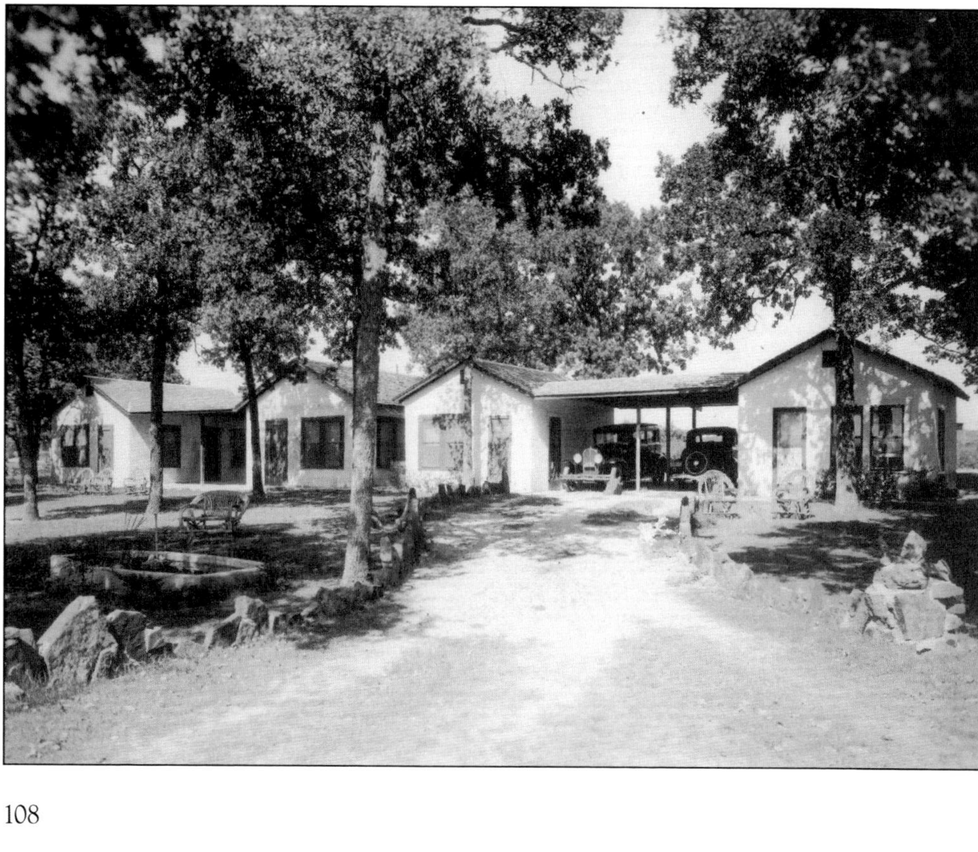

Seven

1930–1939

Weathering the 1930s

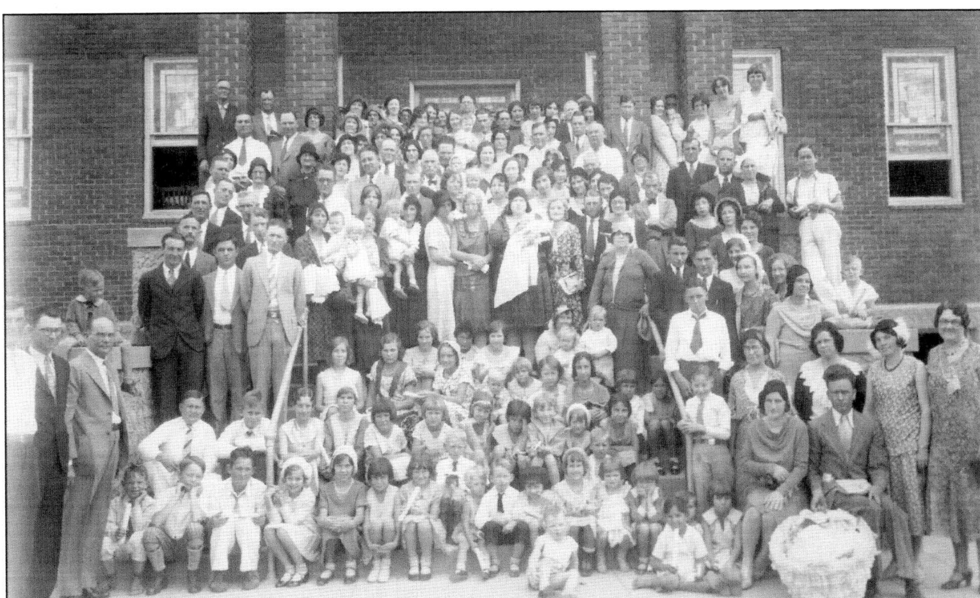

Organized in 1897, Second Baptist Church services were held in a frame building on the southwest corner of First and North Main Streets. Second Baptist changed its name to North Side Baptist Church in 1908. The congregation built a three-story brick building on the east side of North Main Street in 1917. This congregational photograph is dated September 27, 1931. (WPL.)

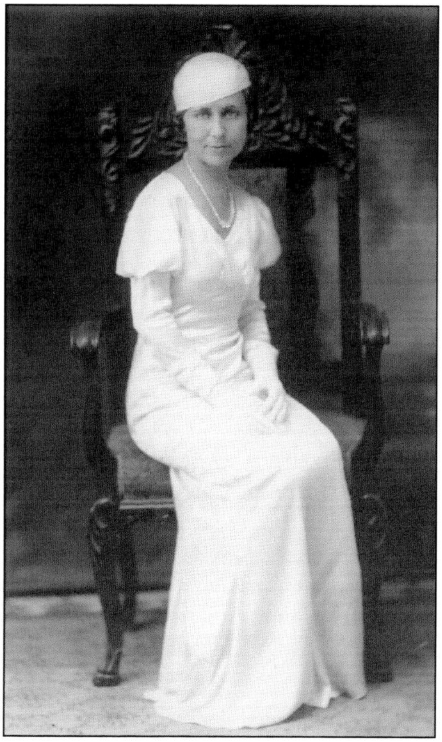

Nellie Frantz married Escal Duke in a twilight ceremony in the home of her parents, Ezra A. and Mary Buckley Frantz, at 312 Bridge Street, on September 3, 1933. An elaborate wedding cake centered on the elegantly appointed dining room table awaited reception guests. Mary Martin Hagman and her mother, Juanita Presley Martin, honored Nellie with a bridal shower prior to the ceremony. (Both, MEDA.)

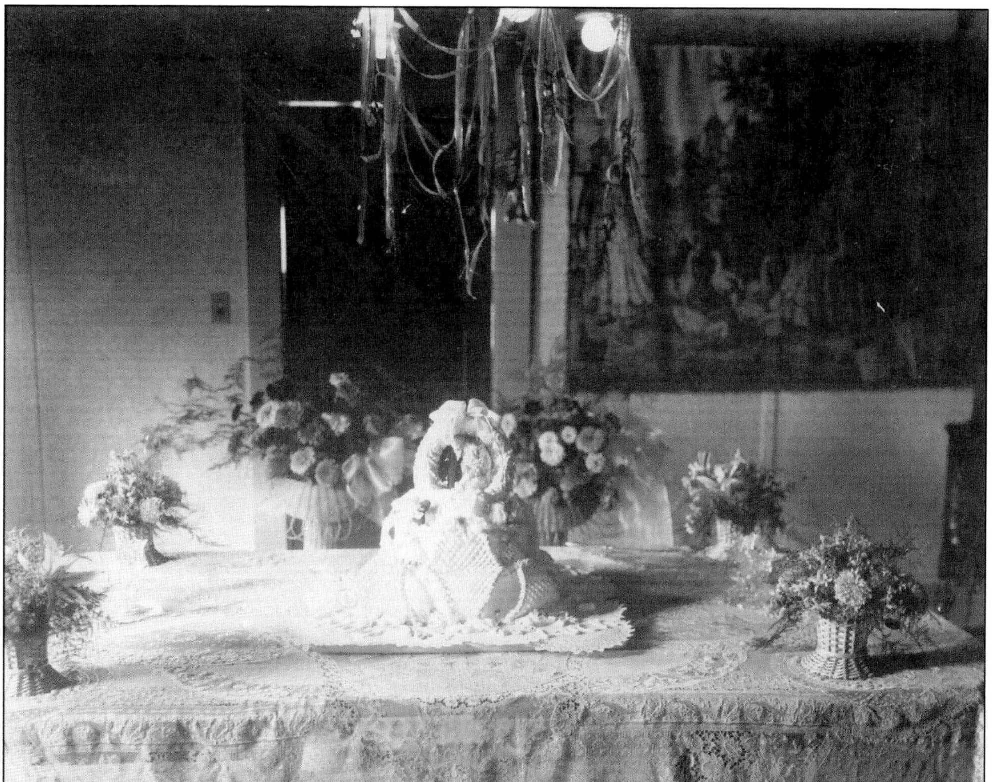

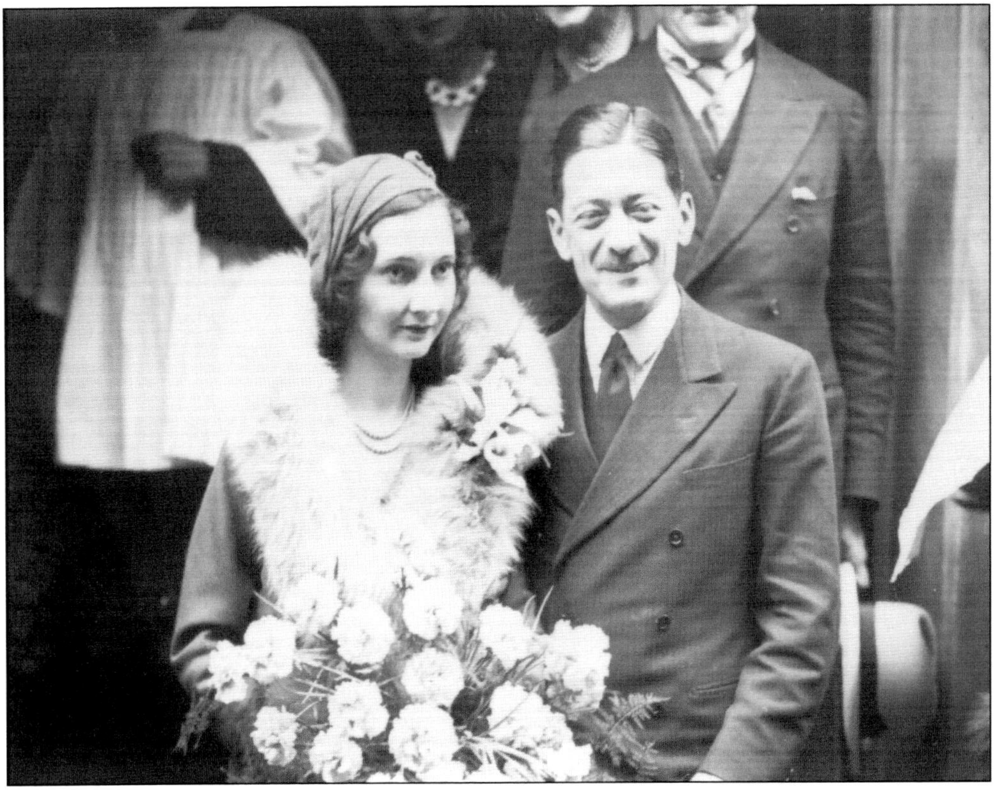

Following the death of Charles McFarland in 1926, his wife, Eloise, and their youngest daughter, Aleene, lived in Europe for several years. Aleene fashioned herself a dancer and met Prince Johannes of Liechtenstein following her performance in Paris in 1926. Weatherford gained its very own princess when she married Prince Johannes at the Church of Our Lady of the Assumption in London, England, on July 29, 1931. (DHCC, McFarland Family Papers.)

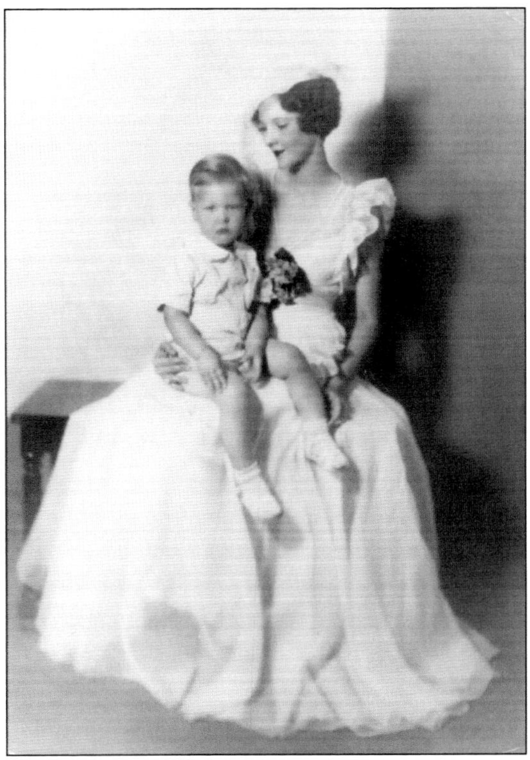

Mary Martin exhibited a flair for entertaining at the age of five when she sang for audiences gathered at the bandstand on the courthouse square. She posed for this portrait with her son, Larry Hagman, around 1933, wearing her high school graduation dress. Martin won Tony Awards for *Peter Pan* and *The Sound of Music* performances. Hagman, who was raised in Weatherford, played J.R. Ewing in the television series *Dallas*. (DHCC, Mary Martin Papers.)

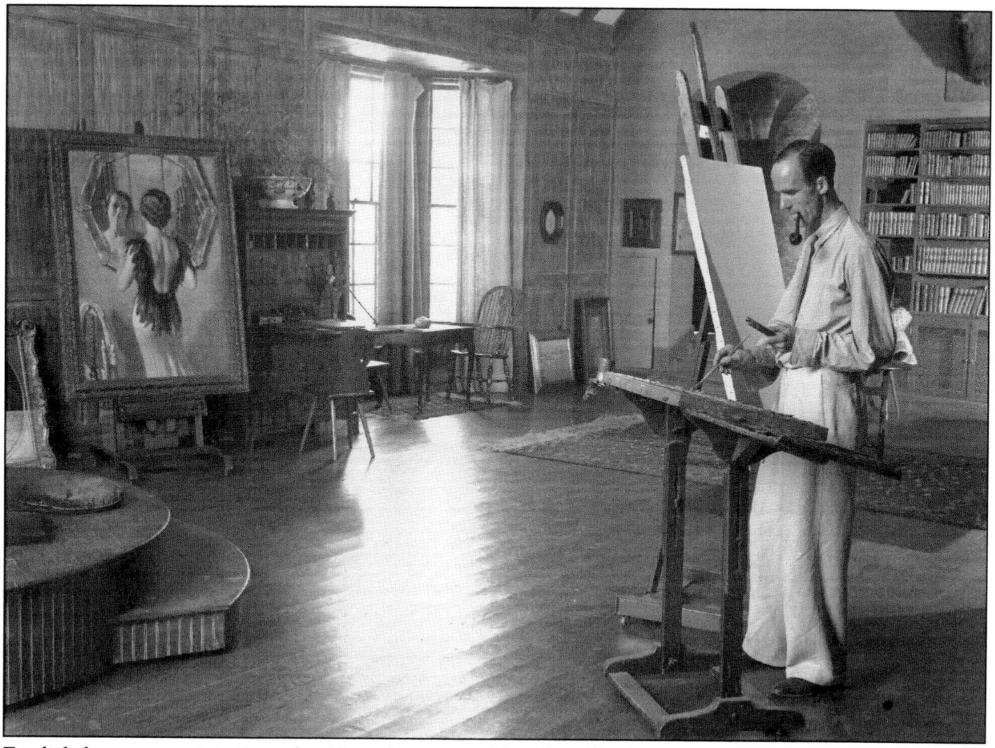

English-born portraitist Douglas Chandor married local girl Ina Kuteman in 1934. His many portrait subjects included Queen Elizabeth II, Winston Churchill, and Franklin and Eleanor Roosevelt. Fort Worth architect Joseph Pelich designed their home, including Chandor's studio, on a seven-acre parcel on Simmons Street, adjacent to the home of her parents. Chandor transformed the caliche soil into a widely acclaimed English garden with fountains, ponds, and Chinese statuary. After her husband died in 1953, Ina Chandor changed the name of their home garden from White Shadows to Chandor Gardens and opened the outdoor paradise to the public. The city of Weatherford now owns this enchanting property. Chandor is pictured in 1939, painting in his studio alongside the completed portrait of Ina and working in the bowling green of his garden, which is now a favorite spot for wedding ceremonies. (Both, UTA, Fort Worth *Star-Telegram* Collection.)

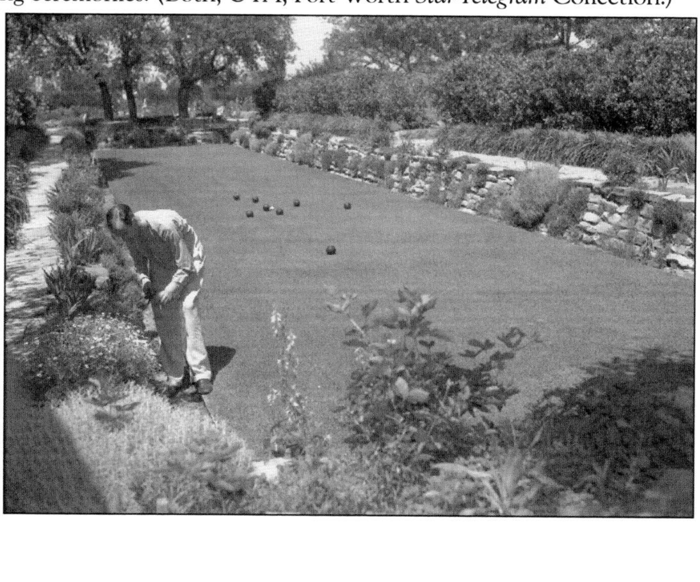

First National Bank president Walter S. Fant Sr. and family paused for a portrait in the backyard garden of the Fant home at 401 Palo Pinto Street. Three generations of the family are represented in this 1931 photograph. From left to right are (seated) Walter S. Fant Sr., Melvin Worthington, Walter Worthington, and Fannie Fant; (standing) Charles Fant, Frances Fant Worthington, and Louise Knox. Note the carriage house in the background. (BF.)

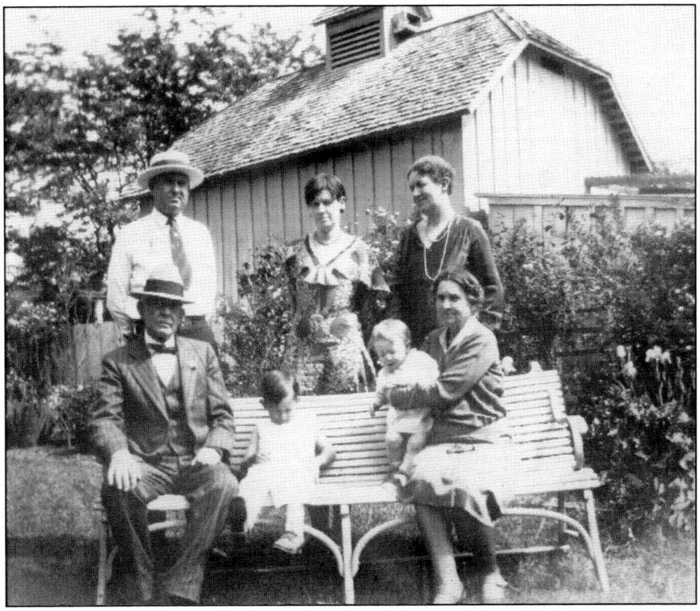

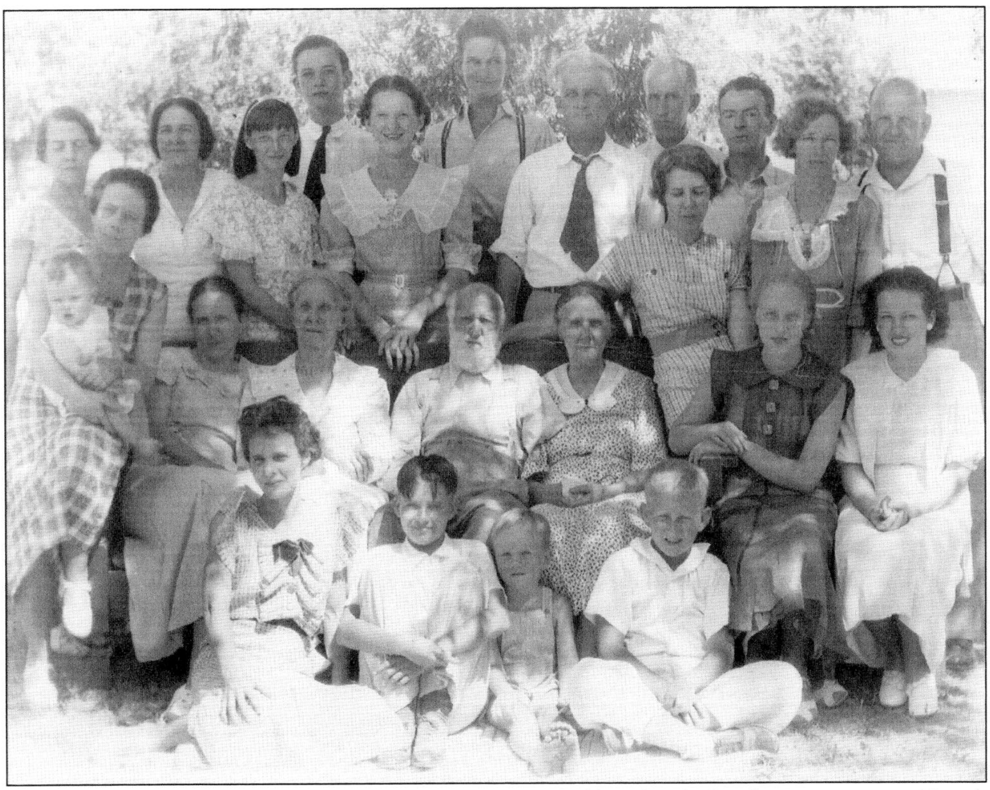

Judge John James Stoker (center, second row) assembled his family for this portrait in 1934. A former Confederate soldier, Stoker served as district clerk of Hill County, county judge in Foard County, and district clerk in Parker County from 1912 to 1918. Stoker was among the longest-living Confederate veterans in Parker County and attended the reunion of Civil War veterans at Gettysburg in 1938. (JM.)

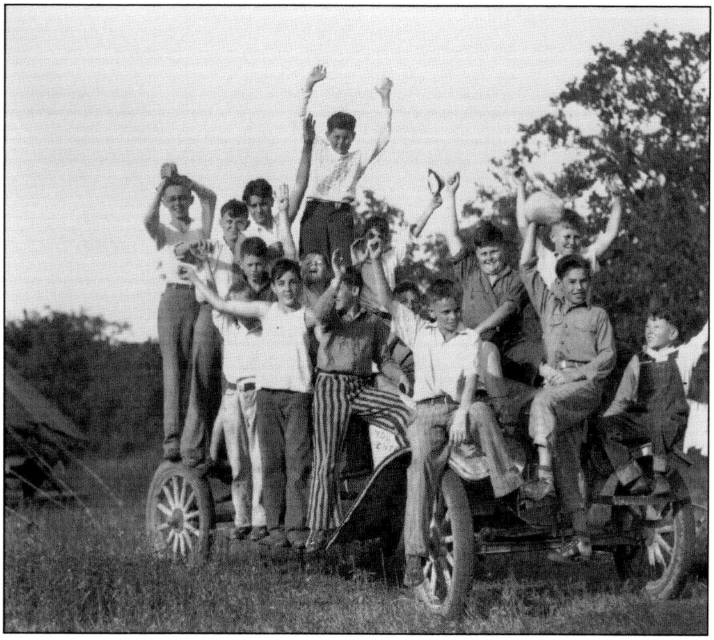

The Fort Worth YMCA conducted summer camp sessions at Camp Holland, located just east of Holland's Lake. Campers could engage in a variety of activities, such as swimming, baseball, archery, nature studies, and leather crafts. This group of happy campers waved from an automobile in 1931. (UTA, Fort Worth *Star-Telegram* Collection.)

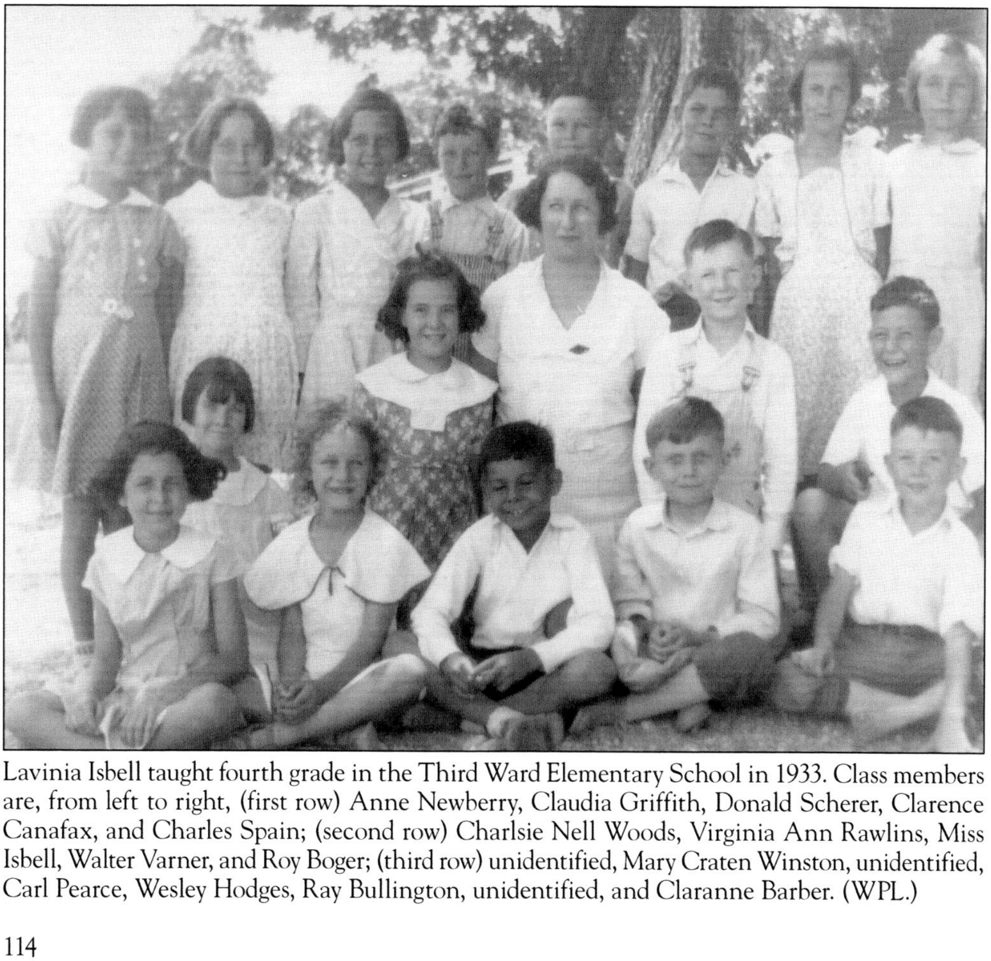

Lavinia Isbell taught fourth grade in the Third Ward Elementary School in 1933. Class members are, from left to right, (first row) Anne Newberry, Claudia Griffith, Donald Scherer, Clarence Canafax, and Charles Spain; (second row) Charlsie Nell Woods, Virginia Ann Rawlins, Miss Isbell, Walter Varner, and Roy Boger; (third row) unidentified, Mary Craten Winston, unidentified, Carl Pearce, Wesley Hodges, Ray Bullington, unidentified, and Claranne Barber. (WPL.)

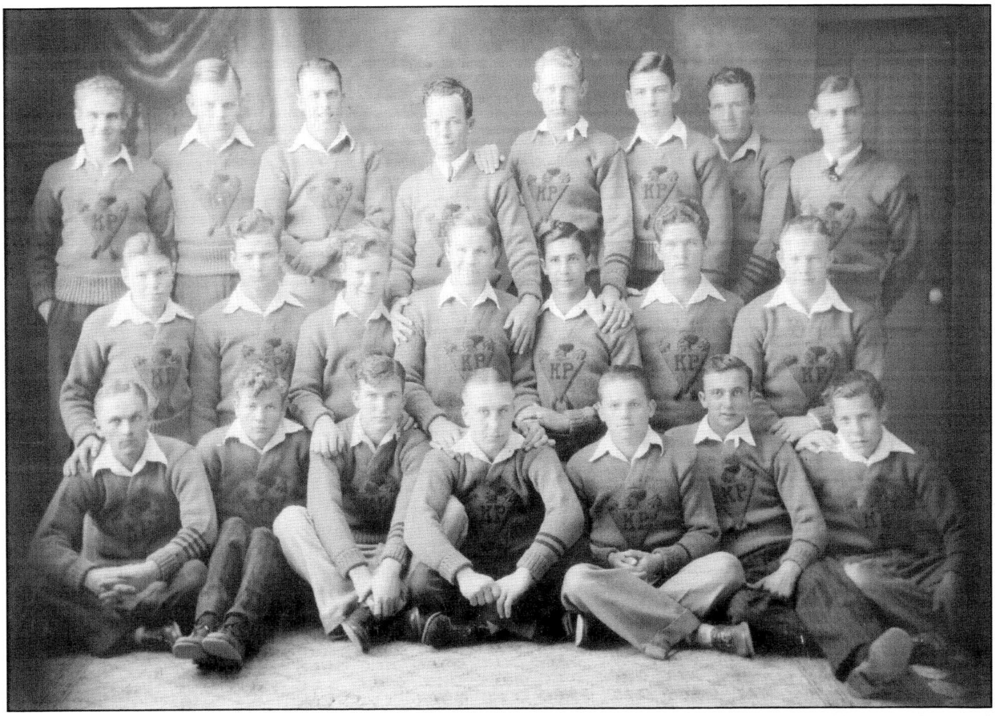

The 1929–1930 Texas Pythian Home football team included, from left to right, (first row) Cecil Walden, Radford Melton, Audie Morrison, Bobby Rea, Albert Brandt, Adam Joseph, and Edwin Ozment; (second row) Emil Lovelady, Myrl Wiley, Ford Defee, August Bergman, Julio Joseph, Clarence Faubain, and Norman Letts; (third row) Bill Bolton, Marcel "Max" Shannon, Ralph Wittington, coach W.W. "Jack" Hill, Curtis Waldrop, Mike Parrent, Lloyd Grimes, and team manager Earl Maisel. (TPH.)

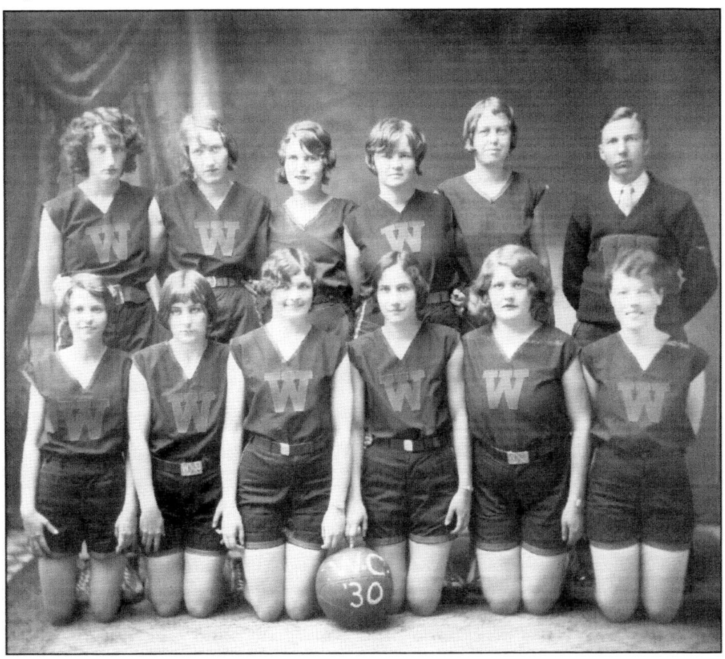

Enrollment at Weatherford College increased from 296 in 1929 to nearly 500 in the 1930–1931 academic year. The college sported basketball teams for both men and women. The 1930 women's team is featured here. Coached by W.C. Beard, the team won three of its four games, losing only to Millsap by two points. W.B. McDaniel coached the men's basketball team to a state championship in 1930. (WC.)

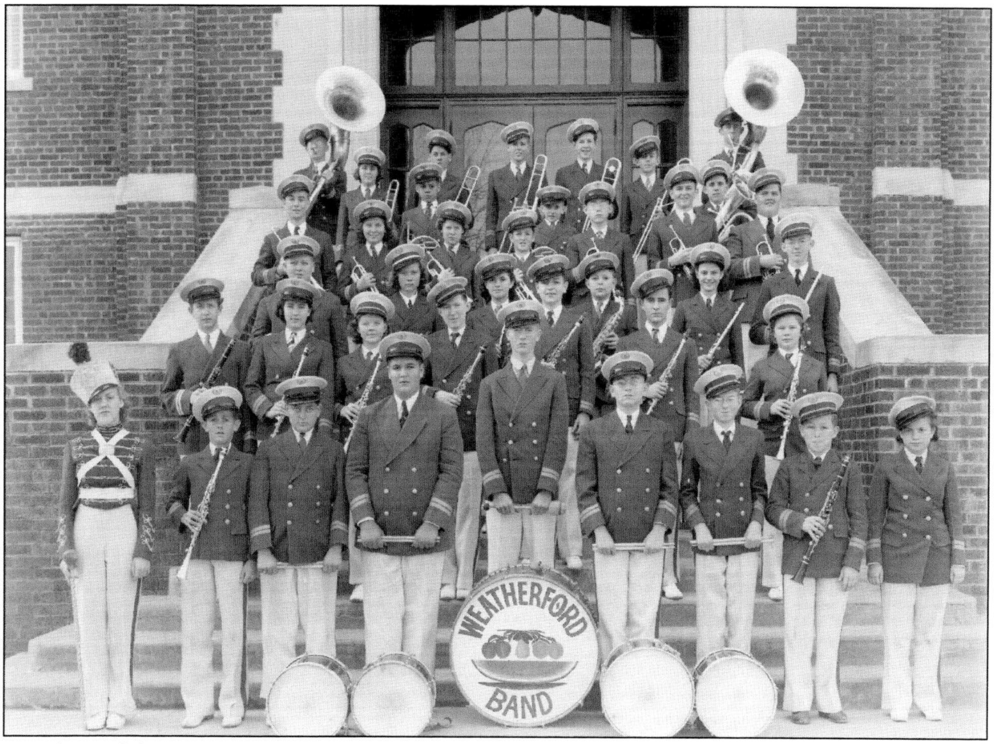

Members of the Weatherford High School Band traveled to Waco on March 31, 1939, to compete against 32 other high schools in regional marching and musical competitions. They brought home 11 medals, including first place, given to Kelfra Bowden for a cornet solo. Band members were pictured on the steps of the senior high school located on Alamo and Oak Streets prior to their departure. (WPL; UTA, Fort Worth *Star-Telegram* Collection.)

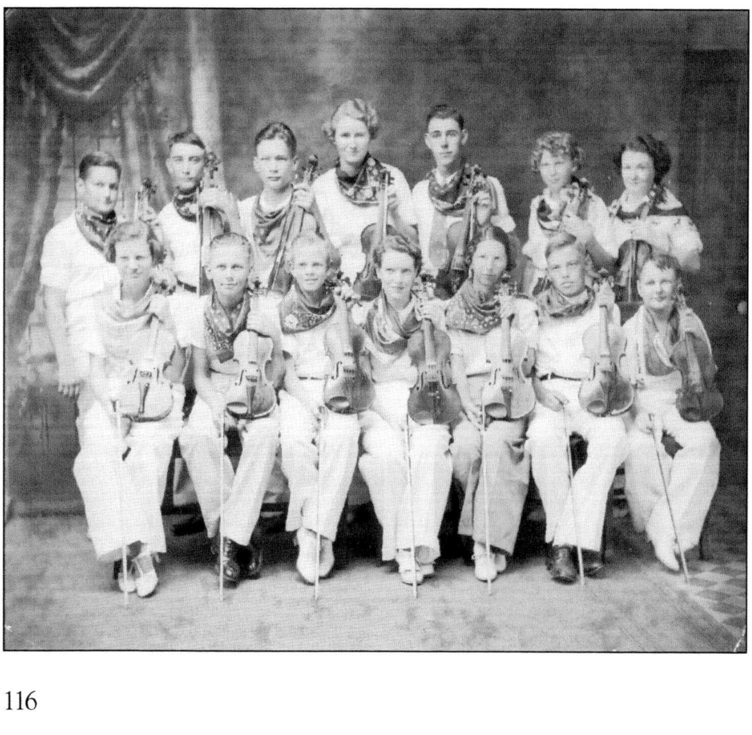

Mary D., Bessie S., and Lucy A. Baker were refined, well-educated sisters who instructed hundreds of students in violin, voice, and piano in their family home studios on Spring Street. Mary proudly advertised that she taught her students First National Institute of Violin techniques. The musicians of the Baker Sisters Orchestra were crowd pleasers wherever they performed. (WPL.)

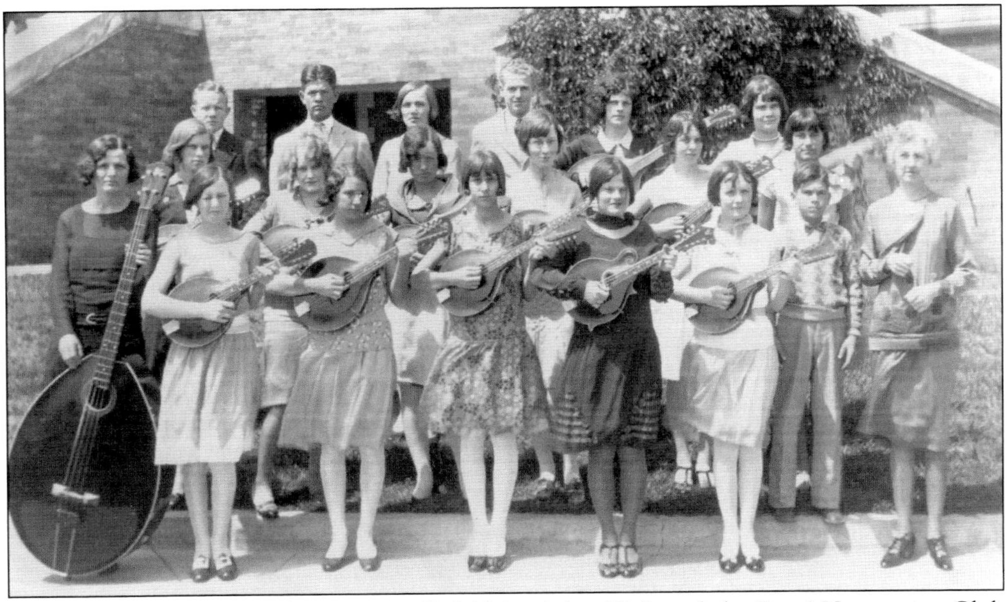

Members of the 1931 Pythian Home Girls' Mandolin Club and the Boys' Harmonica Club included, from left to right, (first row) Delphia Fowler, Evelyn Oakley, Kathryn Hayes, Cordelia Neville, Lorraine Butler, Clara DeFee, Sam Graves, and director Julia Struve; (second row) Lillian Grimes, Mary Farrow, Maureen Roberts, Elizabeth Neville, Phyllis Phillips, and Lydia Hayes; (third row) Norman Letts, Clarence Faubion, Arah Fowler, Bill Bolton, Bea Patton, and Pollyanna Nersworthy. (TPH.)

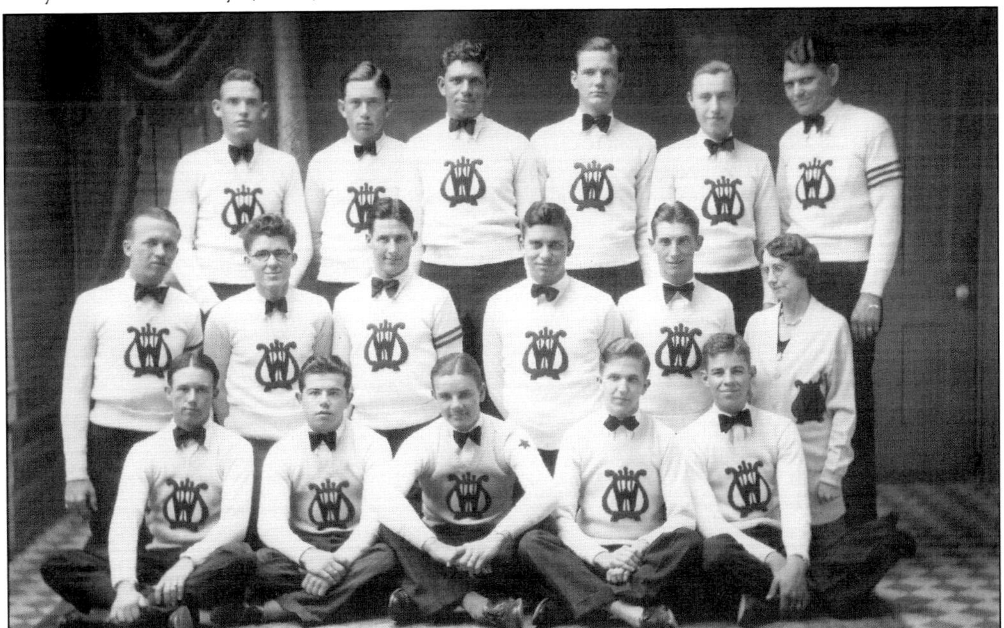

The Weatherford College Glee Club was designated just for young men. Its activities included annual tours, concerts, and various programs. Members of the 1930 Glee Club were led by Franklin Grafa, president (first row, center); Nona Akard, pianist (second row, far right); and Frederick P. Giles, director (third row, far right). (WC.)

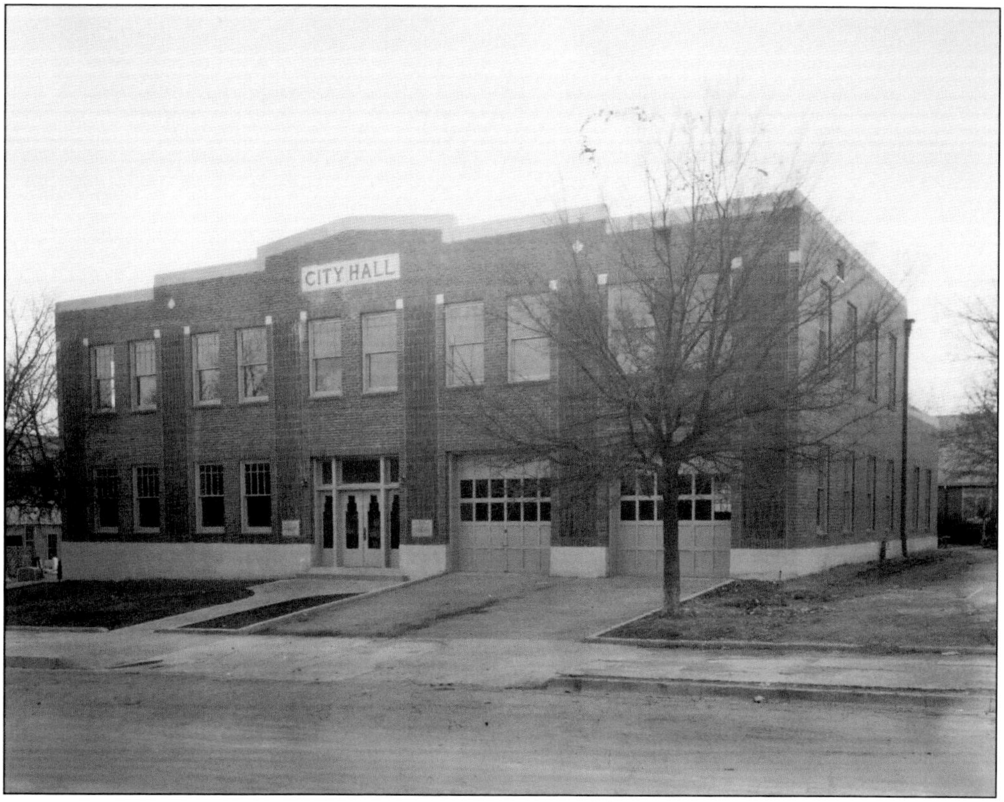

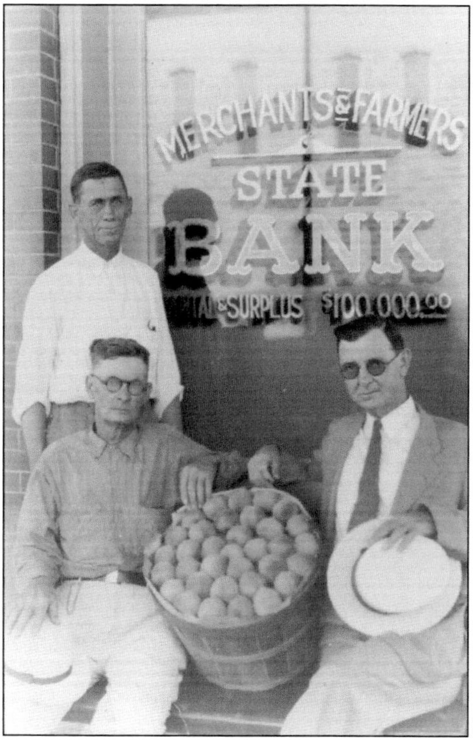

Financed by a 1933 bond election, the construction of the new city hall and fire department building at 119 Palo Pinto Street provided needed jobs for Weatherford's unemployed during the Great Depression. Dedicated on January 16, 1934, the new building replaced a similar smaller municipal building constructed in 1911. Sanborn maps indicate a fire engine house had been located on the site since at least 1885. (UTA, Fort Worth *Star-Telegram* Collection.)

Peaches have grown in Parker County orchards since the 1870s. R.B. Alexander abandoned cotton cultivation to begin the commercial peach industry here in the early 1900s. Charlie Wooldridge (standing) and Charlie Ames (seated, left) met with Merchants & Farmers State Bank vice president W. Virgil Shadle during the bank's 1934 peach exhibit. The 1939 Peach Blossom Pilgrimage, precursor to today's Peach Festival, mapped driving tours through the orchards. (DHCC, James Doss Collection.)

F.U. McCutcheon, secretary of the Weatherford Chamber of Commerce, and mayor G.A. Holland headed the Weatherford delegation visiting the Frontier Fiesta, a year-long Fort Worth celebration of the Texas centennial, in June 1937. Seen admiring an old wooden-spoked wheel, Holland was noted as having one of the finest collections of early relics in Texas housed at his log cabin museum at Holland's Lake. (UTA, Fort Worth *Star-Telegram* Collection.)

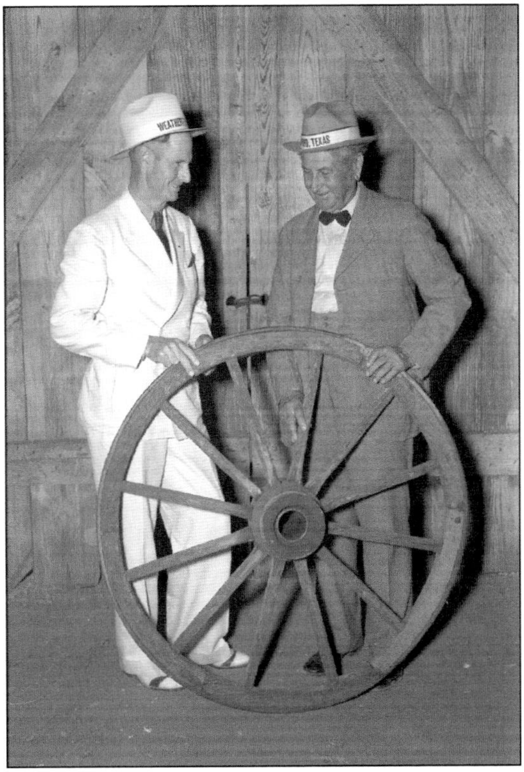

Large crowds packed the oversized tent and exhibition buildings during the June 1937 Parker County Fair. Attendees visited textile, floral, culinary, agricultural, and farm stock competitions. New activities included a beef cattle exhibit, spelling bee, as well as fiddler and square-dancing contests. Winning exhibits were forwarded to the Texas State Fair to promote Parker County resources. Floyd Tinsley Jr. of Weatherford is pictured with his grand champion baby beef. (UTA, Fort Worth *Star-Telegram* Collection.)

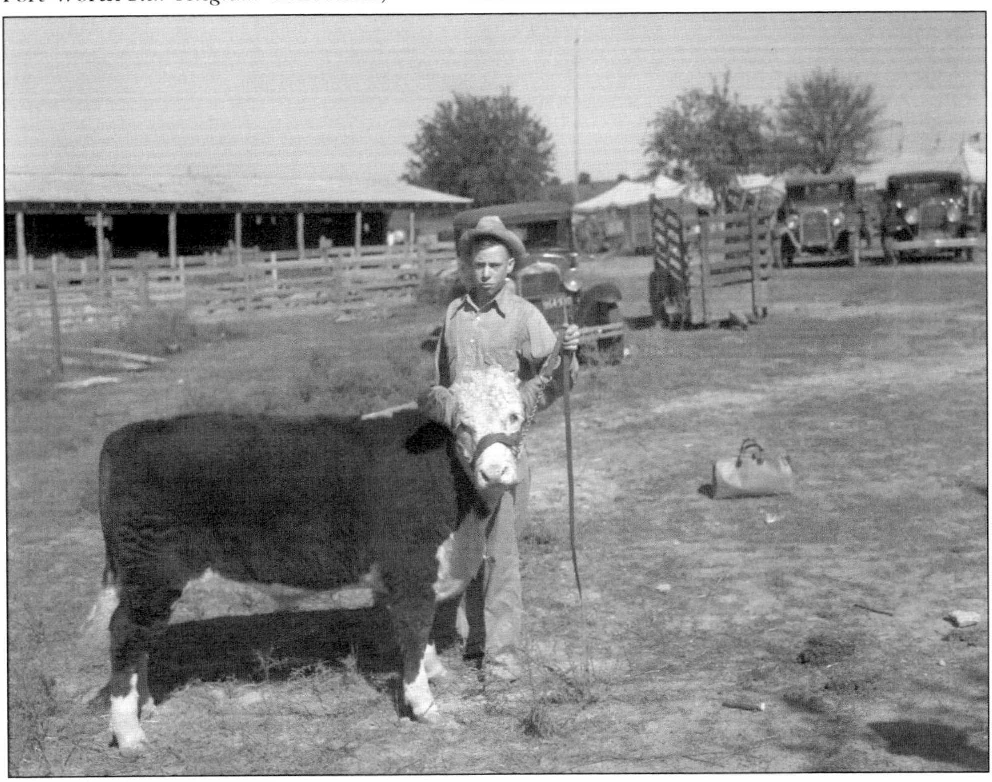

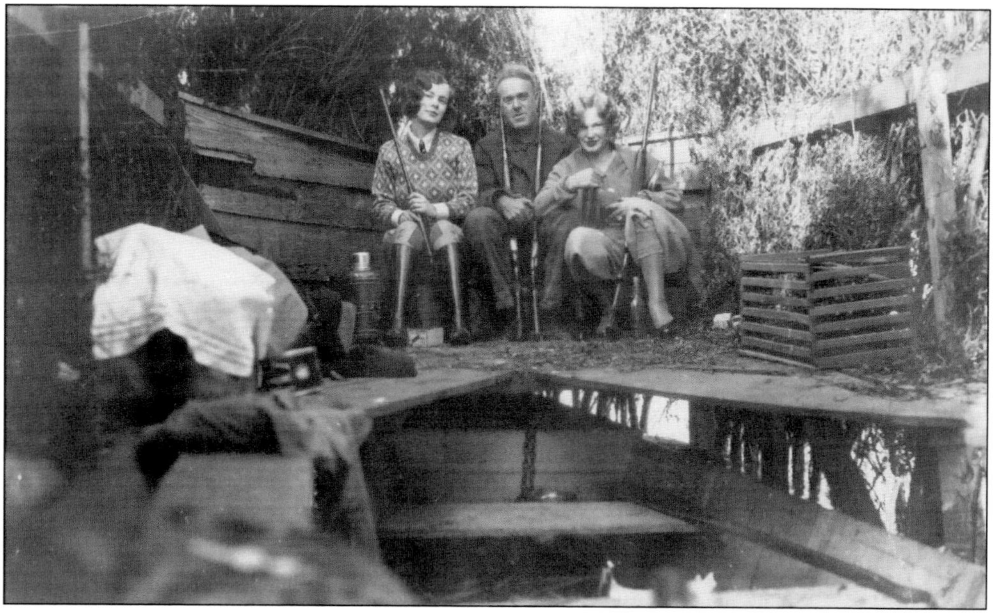

According to Bill Fant, his uncle George Fant had an agreement for years with the Texas & Pacific Railway granting him and his family and friends exclusive use of Sunshine Lake, now in Cartwright Park, in return for keeping the lake in good, clean condition. Fant put a lock on the gate. Bill Billman, Fant's fishing and hunting buddy, jokingly referred to it as the "public lock," since many had the key. Fant built a fine rock clubhouse wrapped in a screen porch. A fireplace warmed the poster-decorated interior when the weather turned chilly. Guests could swim, boat, fish, or hunt from the cabin. George Fant is pictured above in the duck blind with friends. The clubhouse was destroyed by fire many years ago. (Above, BF; below, MW.)

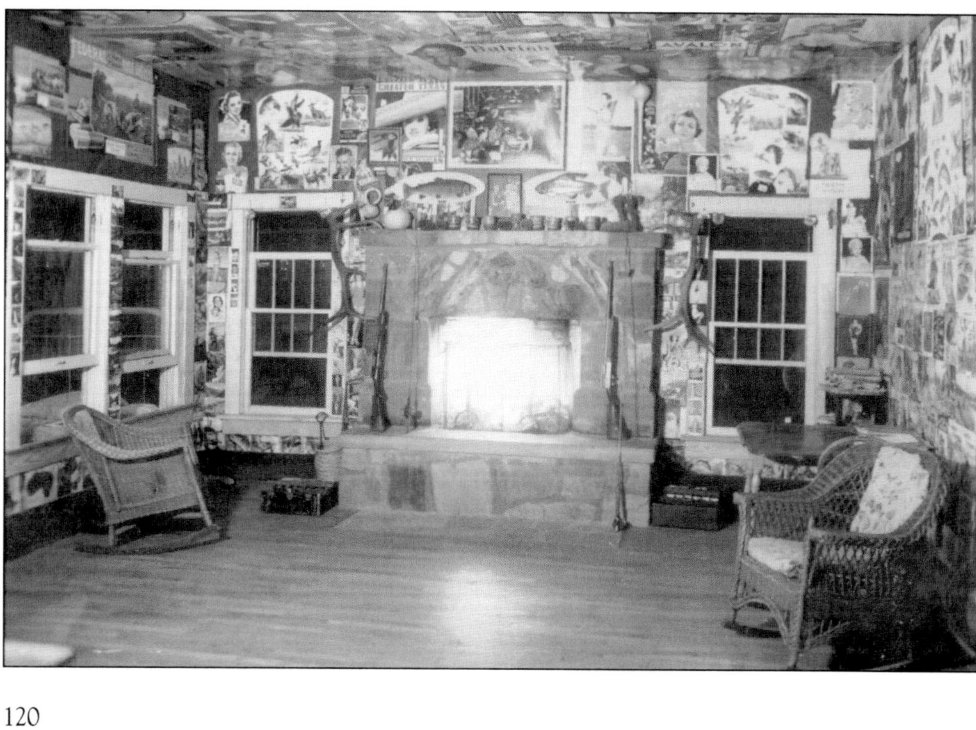

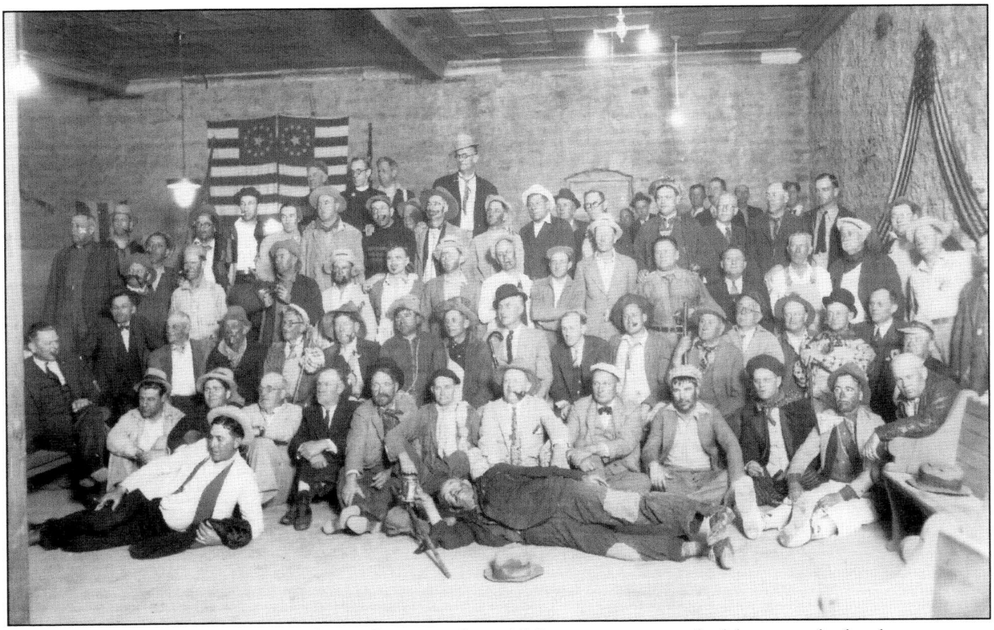

The Weatherford Rotary Club, in honor of its 15th anniversary, held a stag hobo banquet at the American Legion Hall on March 6, 1936. Toastmaster George Fant awarded prizes to Ezra A. Frantz, Dr. T.L. Bloom, Frank Milburn, and Dr. Hubert Leach for their authentic-looking costumes. Congratulatory telegrams—purportedly from President Roosevelt, Adolph Hitler, and Mae West—prompted outbursts of applause and laughter. (WPL.)

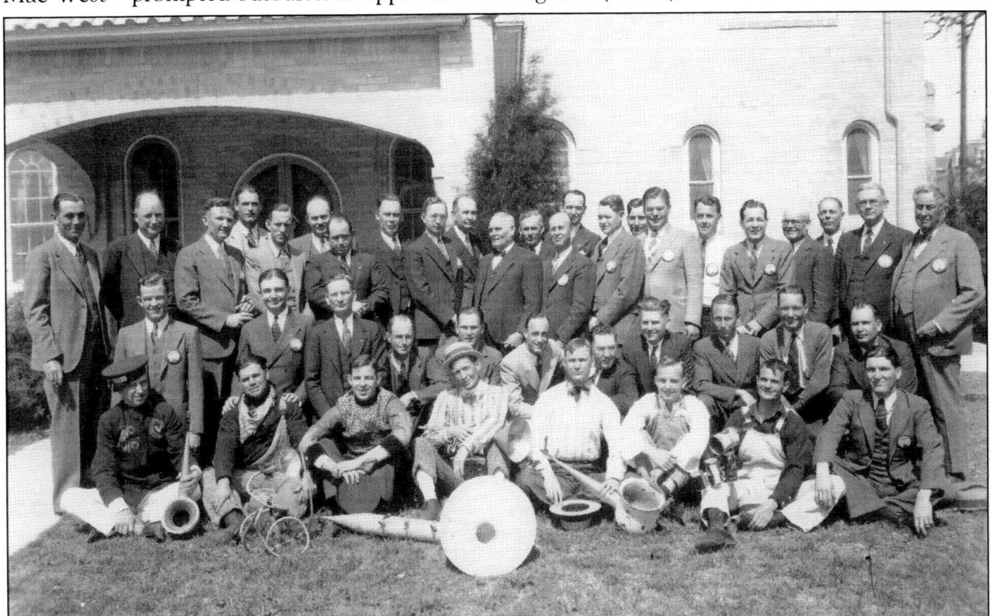

The Weatherford Lions Club and its Bazooka Band gathered in front of White's Funeral Home on Houston Street on March 18, 1936. Costumed Bazooka Band members seated in the first row include, from left to right, Joe Witherspoon, Arthur Cato, Harry Akard, Worth Barnett, Ed Bowden, DeVere Bowden, and Ford White. DeVere Bowden composed the music to the Weatherford High School song, "Blue and White." (WPL.)

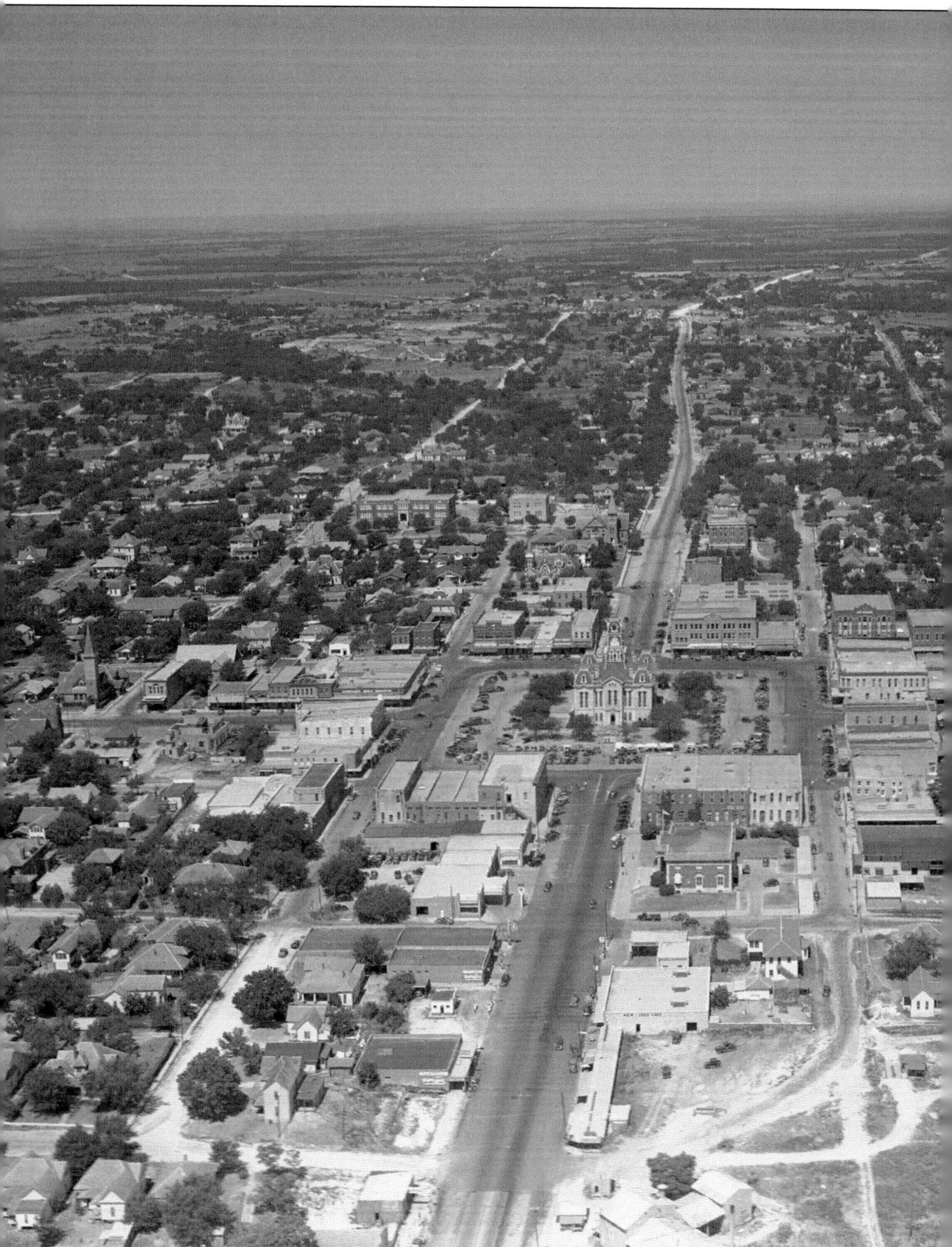

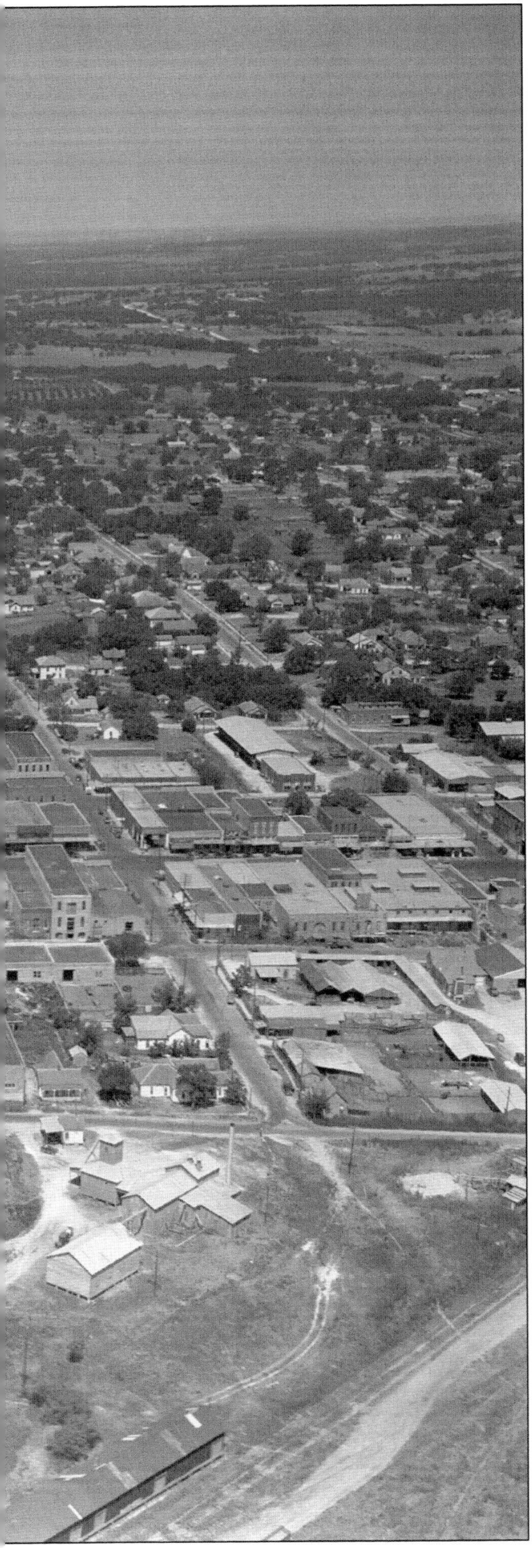

Two aerial views of Weatherford ran in the August 12, 1938 issue of the Fort Worth *Star-Telegram* as part of a series of aerial photographs of Texas cities. This vista, taken from the east, is reminiscent of that used in the 1877 bird's-eye-view map featured in an earlier chapter. Weatherford was noted as the fruit and melon center of Texas, boasting a population of 6,000 people. (UTA, Fort Worth *Star-Telegram* Collection.)

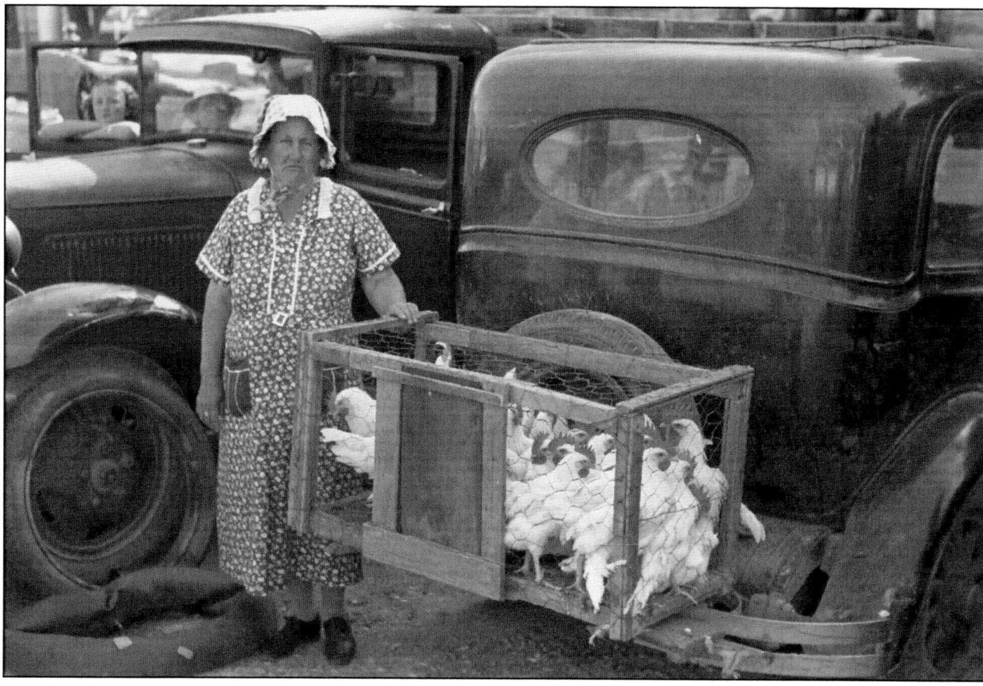

The Farm Security Administration (FSA) employed photographers to document the plight of farmers during the New Deal years of the Great Depression. Russell Lee joined the FSA photography team in 1936 and created some of the agency's most iconic images, particularly those of San Augustine, Texas, and Pietown, New Mexico. He visited Weatherford on First Monday Trade Day in May 1939, snapping a series of 16 photographs. (Both, LC.)

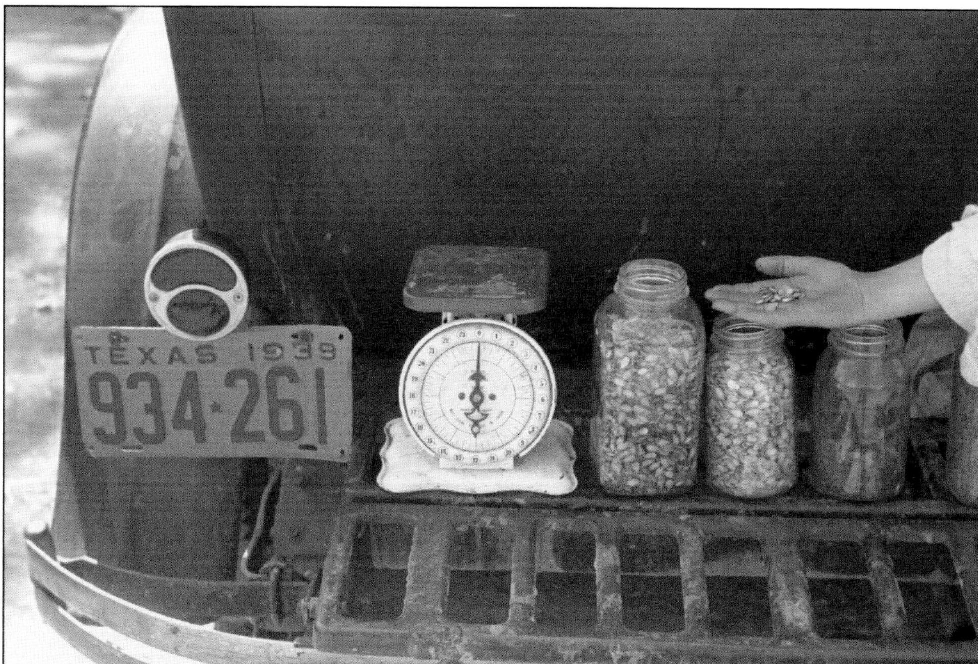

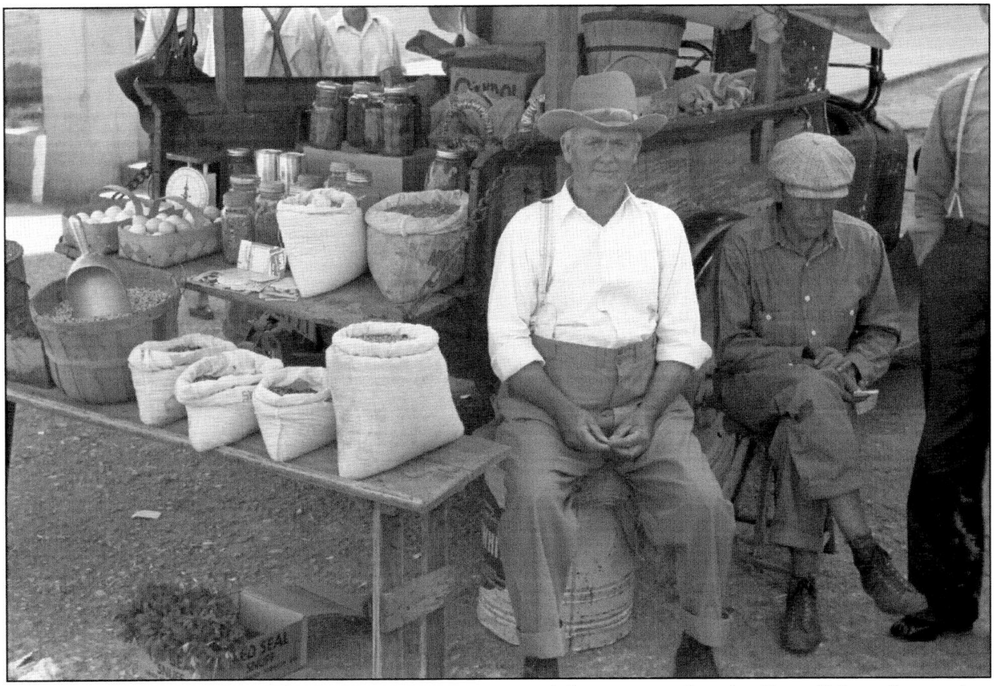

The four photographs on these two pages are part of the series taken by Russell Lee during his First Monday visit to Weatherford in May 1939. Lee's camera lens captured the heart and character of the local farmers and townsfolk who ventured to Weatherford's courthouse square bringing animals, seeds, and produce for sale and catching up on all the current news. (Both, LC.)

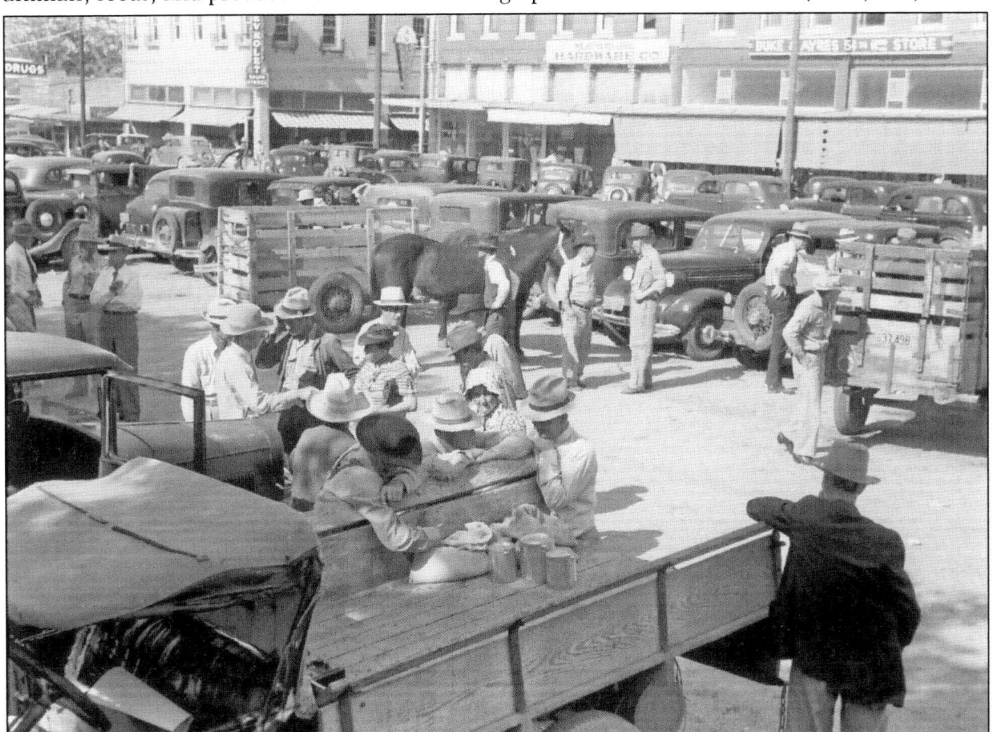

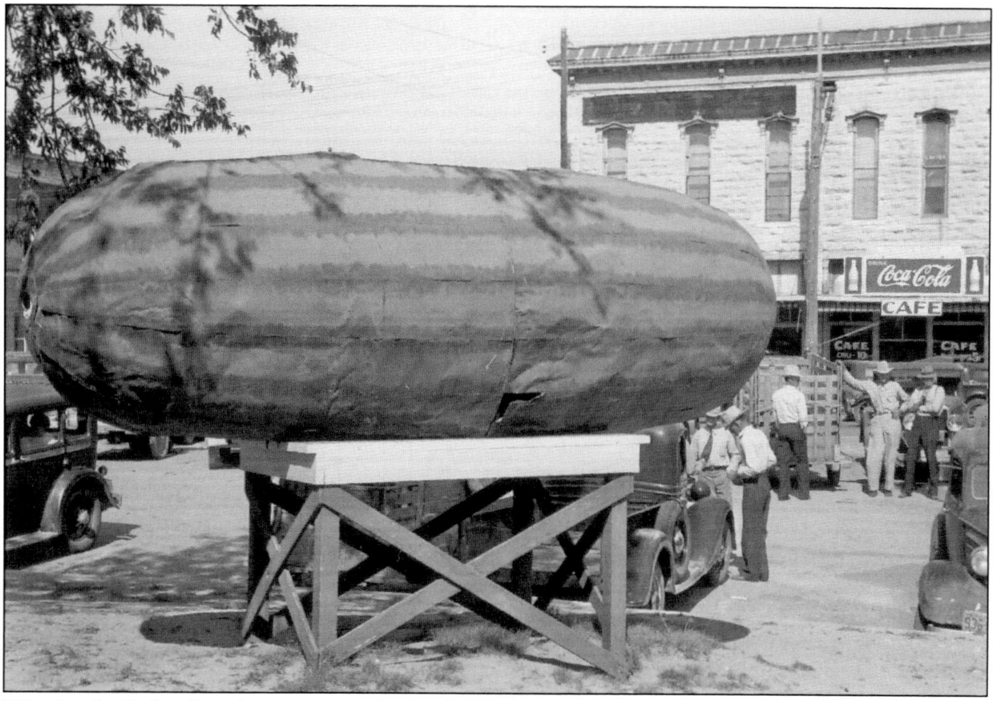

Weatherford's landmark tin watermelon and its picturesque Parker County Courthouse were also part of Russell Lee's series of FSA photographs snapped at First Monday in May 1939. A favorite subject of local lore, the tin melon resided on the southeast corner of the square for years. Although the exact dates of its creation and demise are unknown, it was entered in a 1928 Fort Worth parade. Many old-timers claim the tin melon was dismantled and donated to a World War II scrap metal drive. Two additional landmarks funded by Rotary and Lions Club community campaigns were added to the east and west sides of the courthouse in 1937. Arched neon signs proclaimed Weatherford to be the "Texas Fruit and Melon Center." Note the pedestal-mounted signal light, which controlled traffic flow around the courthouse square. (Both, LC.)

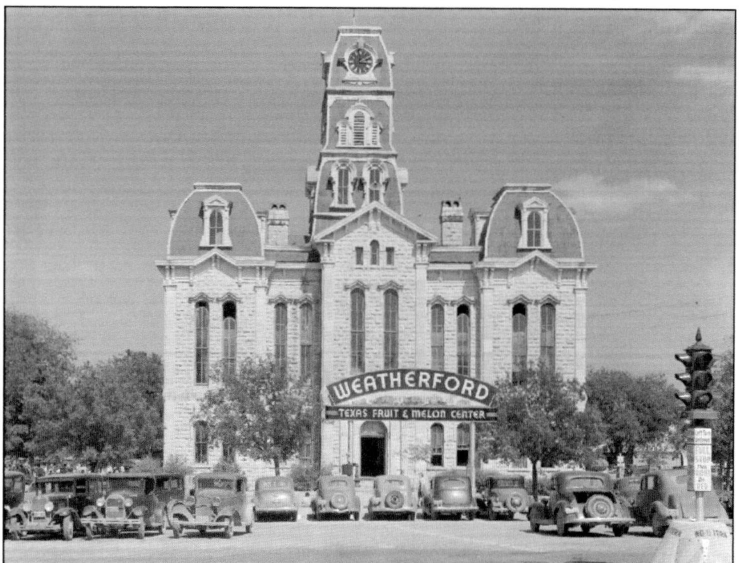

Bibliography

Aiken, David W., and Barbara Y. Newberry. *Weatherford, Texas.* Charleston, SC: Arcadia Publishing, 1999.

Bartoli, Jonelle Ryan, and Brenda S. McClurkin. *Weatherford, Texas, Historic Downtown Walking Tour.* Rev. ed. Weatherford, TX: Weatherford Chamber of Commerce, 2012.

———. *Weatherford, Texas, Historic Residential Driving Tour.* Weatherford, TX: Weatherford Chamber of Commerce, 2009.

Doss, James. *Once a Country Bank: A History of the Merchants & Farmers National Bank, now Texas Bank, 1889–1989.* Weatherford, TX: self-published, 1988.

Grace, John S., and R.B. Jones. *A New History of Parker County,* 1906. Reprint, Weatherford, TX: Parker County Historical Commission, 1987.

History of Parker County. Weatherford, TX: Parker County Historical Commission, 1980.

Holland, Ellen Bowie. *Gay as a Grig: Memories of a North Texas Girlhood.* Austin, TX: University of Texas Press, 1963.

Holland, G.A. *History of Parker County and the Double Log Cabin.* Weatherford, TX: Herald Publishing Company, 1937.

Marshall, Doyle. *A Cry Unheard: The Story of Indian Attacks In and Around Parker County, Texas, 1858–1872.* Aledo, TX: Annetta Valley Farm Press, 1990.

McClung, Bill and Martha McClung. *First Baptist Church, Weatherford, Texas: The First 140 Years.* San Antonio, TX: Walsworth Publishing Company, 1997.

Pictorial History of Parker County. Weatherford, TX: Parker County Historical Commission, 1985.

Sammons, Dexter. *Phoenix Lodge: The First Twenty-Five Years, 1864–1889.* Weatherford, TX: Phoenix Lodge Number 275, 1987.

Smythe, H. *Historical Sketch of Parker County and Weatherford, Texas.* St. Louis, MO: Louis C. Lavat, 1877. Facsimile reprint, Waco, TX: W.M. Morrison, 1973.

Taylor, Virginia H. *The Franco-Texan Land Company.* Austin, TX: University of Texas Press, 1969.

Vandagriff, Jon R. *The Story of Parker County, Texas, 1852–1956.* Virginia Beach, VA: Donning Company Publishers, 2010.

Witherspoon, Joe B. *Seventy Five Years of Benevolent Service: A History of the Texas Pythian Home, 1909–1984.* Fort Worth, TX: Miran Publishers, 1983.

Discover Thousands of Local History Books Featuring Millions of Vintage Images

Arcadia Publishing, the leading local history publisher in the United States, is committed to making history accessible and meaningful through publishing books that celebrate and preserve the heritage of America's people and places.

Find more books like this at
www.arcadiapublishing.com

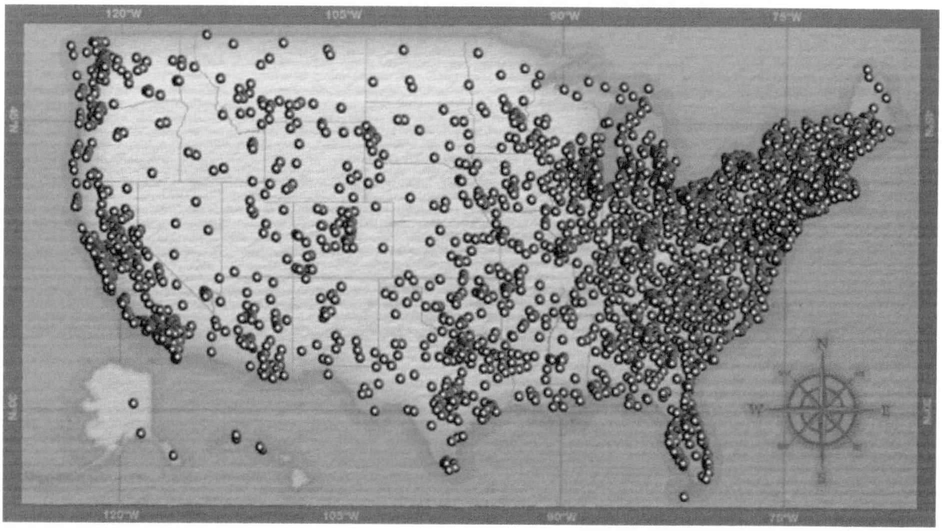

Search for your hometown history, your old stomping grounds, and even your favorite sports team.

Consistent with our mission to preserve history on a local level, this book was printed in South Carolina on American-made paper and manufactured entirely in the United States. Products carrying the accredited Forest Stewardship Council (FSC) label are printed on 100 percent FSC-certified paper.

MADE IN THE USA